The War that Wasn't

The War that Wasn't

Religious Conflict and Compromise in the Common Schools of New York State, 1865–1900

Benjamin Justice

State University of New York Press

Published by
State University of New York Press, Albany

Printed in the United States of America

For information, contact State University of New York Press, Albany, NY
www.sunypress.edu

Production by Michael Haggett
Marketing by Michael Campochiaro

Library of Congress Cataloging in Publication Data

Justice, Benjamin, 1971–
The war that wasn't : religious conflict and compromise in the common schools of New York, 1865–1900 / Benjamin Justice
p. cm.
Includes bibliographical references and index.
ISBN 978-0-7914-6211-9 (hardcover : alk. paper)
ISBN 978-0-7914-6212-6 (pbk. : alk. paper)
1. Religion in the public schools—New York (State)—History—19th century. 2. Church and education—New York (State)—History—19th century. 3. Church and state—New York (State)—History—19th century. I. Title.
LC112.N7J87 2004
379.2′8′097471—dc22

2004013799

For Jennifer

Contents

Tables and Figures

Acknowledgments

On the western edge of the Stanford campus lie the Santa Cruz Mountains, a verdant tumble of hills stretching from South San Francisco to San Jose. Those hills hold back the Pacific fog, giving Stanford a world-class climate and a picturesque setting. It is also in those hills that my friend and mentor, David Tyack, can often be found, leading a troop of students on some tangled trail though the old-growth redwoods, grassy fields, or sandy Pacific dunes. David conducts these outings with the same democratic ethic that characterizes his scholarship—the conversation, like the walk, is open to all.

On a hot day in 1998, I had the pleasure to hike with David to a place called Windy Hill, a bald, sun-baked hump overlooking the sprawl of Silicon Valley. As I struggled to follow what he calls his "geriatric pace," I happened to notice that my footprints fell rhythmically into his, so that, quite literally, I was walking in his footsteps. My mind quickly jumped from the humor of the obvious metaphor to a rebellious panic: wasn't I my own scholar? I shifted my stride in a fairly ridiculous—and fruitless—attempt to avoid each of his footprints completely. (My wife, who walked behind me, asked if everything was okay.)

Finally, regaining my senses, I realized that it did not matter where I stepped, as long as I kept pace and walked comfortably. First with mild trepidation and then with confidence, I began walking naturally again and found that my feet fell sometimes in synch with David's and sometimes not. Lesson learned, I smiled secretly and tramped onward.

This book wends through much of the scholarship that David Tyack has written in the last forty years. Through the process of my writing it, he has been generous with his time, energy, and ideas. Much of this book revisits ground he has covered, sometimes in stride with him and sometimes not. (It would be difficult for any historian of education not to tread ground visited by David Tyack.) I wholeheartedly thank him for sharing his expertise and for being my guide. At the same time, I accept sole responsibility for any wrong turns, as this book chronicles my own journey into the tangled trails of history.

I also wish to thank the following people and organizations:

The Graduate School of Education at Rutgers University for giving me a research semester in the fall of 2002 to prepare this manuscript;

The Charlotte W. Newcomb Dissertation Fellowship Program, for its yearlong support of my writing;

The New York State Archive and Trust for its support through the Larry J. Hackman Research Residency Fellowship Program, Jim Folts for his unfailing support and advice, and the staff of the New York State Archive for their ideas and efforts;

The Spencer Foundation and the Graduate School of Education at Stanford University for research and travel grants;

Kelly Roll, Barbara Celone, Ann Latta, and the staff of Cubberley Education Library, Stanford University, for their expert help with historical sources;

David Ment, Bette Weneck, and especially Althea Bernheim of the Special Collections Department, Milbank Memorial Library, Teacher's College, Columbia University;

The staff of the local history departments of the Buffalo, Rochester, Lockport, and Albany Public Libraries, Sister Mary Christine Taylor of Ogdensburg, Alvina Tyropolis of the Board of Education of Yonkers; the Board of Education of Lockport; the staff of the Saratoga County Archives; Martha Stonequist and the Saratoga City Archives;

Lynda Justice (my mother and sometime research assistant) for her first-rate work and generosity; Neil and Lucie Crocker for their hospitality, and Michael and Cathy Katz for their generous help with child herding;

Professors David Kennedy, Larry Cuban, Eamon Callan, and John Meyer, and my (at the time) fellow students Amy Hightower, Angela Schmiede, Dana Mitra, and Sam Bersola for reading various drafts of the project and offering careful criticisms and praise;

The many people, students, neighbors, and colleagues who shared thoughtful conversations with me about the topic;

And, finally, Jennifer Ann Katz for her intellectual and emotional support, child-watching time, editing, and the title.

Chapter 1

Explaining the History of Religion in Public Schools

> For, above all things, we wish to stamp deep upon the inmost minds of all readers of the signs of the times, that the solution of this practical question will and shall come, not from the general government, nor for many a year even from the official action of the States in severalty, but from the peaceable adjustments of communities and neighborhoods.
>
> —Bishop Thomas Jefferson Jenkins, "Education: To Whom Does It Belong?" (1892).

In the mid-nineteenth century, Americans in the northern United States created an unrivaled system of mass education: publicly funded, democratically controlled, and largely secular "common schools." This movement rested on the twin suppositions that neighborhood schools could offer an ideologically common education, and that democratic control afforded the best means for organizing and maintaining such schools. It should be no surprise that the common school flourished before the Civil War in the North and Midwest, where the district meeting and decentralized government formed pillars of a mostly rural, mostly Protestant society, and when the Age of Jackson brought universal white male suffrage.

What is surprising—and important—is that the common school system should have expanded in the decades *after* the Civil War, when non-Protestant voters flexed new muscle at the polls, and when American society grew more diverse, more urban, and more stratified than ever before. Religious diversity in particular proved challenging to the common (increasingly called "public") system, as leaders from powerful minority religions, especially Catholicism, challenged the very assumption that one education could be common to all. They also questioned the idea that the voters, as opposed to the Church, were best suited to run the schools. Religious conflict shot through American political and social life, yet the public school enjoyed an impressive period of growth and consolidation. By 1900, public schools looked much like those that exist today: they commanded nearly all public educational expenditures and garnered more than 90 percent of the enrollment of school-age children.

The expansion of public schooling after the Civil War happened in the context of another remarkable transformation: the flowering of popular participation in the democratic process. From 1876 to 1900, over 80 percent of the non-Southern electorate voted in presidential-year elections. And these voters came from all walks of life, with no appreciable differences among them regarding education or social status.[1] Active, aggressive, and sometimes corrupt political parties nurtured these remarkably high turnouts through parades, voluntary organizations, stump speeches, and outright payments.[2] Whatever their motivations for voting—concern over the issues, party loyalty, or profit—voters flexed considerable political muscle and practiced skills that they could bring into other political domains, including local school elections.[3]

These two factors, intense religious diversity and an entrenched system of local democracy, directly affected public school policy and played key roles in the expansion of public schooling. But what was the relationship between the two?

The Warfare Thesis

To explain the historical development of religious policy in public schools, most histories of the *post-bellum* era have looked to the words and actions of religious and political leaders, and to changes in state law. The period is a political historian's trove. From the end of the Civil War until 1900, the issue of religion in public schools cycled twice through national politics, and both times engendered bitter rhetorical battles in leading periodicals, at the pulpit and atop campaign stumps.

Before the Civil War, ethnoreligious differences among Americans played a significant role in how political parties wooed voters and, in turn, how the electorate voted.[4] Tension between different groups sometimes flared violently in cities across the nation; anti-Irish and anti-Protestant mobs drew blood in New York City in 1835 and in Brooklyn in 1854.[5] During the virulently nativist 1850s, Catholic and Protestant antipathy spilled over into public school policy debates in major Northern cities where Catholics settled.[6] To some degree, however, the Civil War changed the way that Americans regarded religious diversity. Ethnoreligious conflict returned—an 1871 Orange Day riot between Catholics and Protestants in New York City killed over 100 people—but not with the same support or effect that it had enjoyed before.[7]

The media frenzy over religious diversity subsided during the war, but the lull did not last. By 1869, events in Ohio gave Protestant axe grinders nationwide a chance to open old wounds. In Cincinnati, Catholic Church officials and the city board of education had reached a tentative compromise agreement to move parochial schools under the weekday control of the board of education in exchange for the cessation of Protestant religious exercises. When an anti-Catholic newspaper published a withering exposé, the Church retreated, and the deal collapsed. The board of education continued with its half of the bargain, however, and banned Bible reading and hymn singing from city schools. Protestant activists quickly challenged the decision on legal grounds, and "Cincinnati Bible War" made its way through the courts of Ohio and newspapers nationwide. (The Ohio Supreme Court eventually sided with the school board in 1873.)[8] Meanwhile, in New York State, another controversy erupted involving the state legislature's secret approval of a bill giving public funds to parochial schools in New York City.[9]

By the early 1870s, the Republican Party officially adopted religion in public schools as a pet project. Party leaders waved the Catholic menace like a bloody shirt, and nativist organizations linked Americanism to staunch Protestantism. The party promised to protect public schools from the Catholic threat and the Bible from removal. Both reflected a wide effort to scare up Protestant votes as Reconstruction faltered.[10] After a disastrous Republican Party defeat in 1874, President Grant played to anti-Catholic sentiment in an 1875 speech warning that if the nation should again go to war, the new Mason-Dixon line would be drawn at the common schoolhouse door, and sectarian (Catholic) influence would be the new enemy.[11] Radical Republicans in Congress sponsored a constitutional amendment banning public money to church-controlled schools and sectarian instruction in public schools. The amendment rocketed through the House (180 yeas, 7 nays, and 98 abstentions), later falling short in the Senate.[12]

The Republican agenda penetrated New York State politics as well, though with less effect. As the Republican Party's fortunes fell in the mid-1870s—in part in response to its perceived overextension of the powers of government—state party leaders tried to arouse anti-Catholic passions and denigrate the Democratic Party (which rested on strong Catholic support).[13] An 1876 party tract charged that Democratic Governor Tilden intended to "break up our public schools by establishing a system of parochial schools under the management of the Romish priesthood." Another charged that "the Democratic party is false and untrustworthy on every living issue...FALSE ON THE QUESTION OF THE SAFETY OF THE SCHOOLS, FOR THE SOLID DEMOCRATIC VOTE IN THE UNITED STATES SENATE DEFEATED AN ADEQUATE AMENDMENT TO PROTECT THE SCHOOL SYSTEM FROM SECTARIAN ATTACK."[14] The party did not manage to push its goals through the state legislature, however, which failed to act on religion in public school policy. By the end of the 1870s, the party set aside religion in public schools, and the rhetorical crossfire largely subsided in national media throughout the 1880s.[15]

As anti-Catholicism flared again at the end of the 1880s, the question of religion in public schools returned. Nationwide, a number of Republican-controlled states passed or nearly passed compulsory education laws directly targeting parochial schools' ability to hire teachers, set curriculum, and, in a few cases, even to exist. In Massachusetts, religious conflict over public school policy dominated statewide elections in 1888 and 1889. And in 1889, both houses of the New York State Legislature passed a bill requiring state-certified teachers in private schools, which the governor vetoed. As it had in the 1870s, the question of religion in the public schools in the late 1880s and early 1890s captured the imagination of rabid anti-Catholics, who warned of popish plots to take over American schools and who championed nonsectarian Bible reading in public schools and blocked state aid to parochial ones.[16]

The Republican Party did not bear sole responsibility for stirring the bog. Throughout the 1870s and 1890s, major Catholic Church leaders adopted a militant stance toward public education that eschewed compromise and actively encouraged controversy. In the 1870s, Rochester's Bishop Bernard McQuaid emerged as a leading spokesperson for the "Catholic position," charging that public schools gave Catholics "a defective, injurious, poisonous education" and were either offensively Protestant or dangerously infidel. He also railed against "mixed schools," worrying about the negative effects of Catholic children fraternizing with Protestant ones. Making matters worse, McQuaid and other leading bishops in New York State openly threatened Catholic parents and their children with denial of the Sacraments (and thus eternal damnation) for refusing to send their children to parochial schools.[17] Leading Catholic periodicals railed against public schools in pointed editorials.[18] By the 1890s, a few liberal Catholic leaders broke ranks with the militants, suggesting compromise with public schools and reconciliation with Protestant America, but the resulting internal crisis in the American Catholic Church hierarchy led to a decade of infighting and no clear resolution.[19]

Picking up where the antagonists left off, twentieth-century historians largely followed the paradigm set by these paroxysms of politics and polemic.[20] Bitter battles, the argument goes, Catholic versus Protestant, drove public school policy toward religion. "Some things were sorted out in [the] crucible of Nativism," writes David Grimstead, "such as the relationship between religion and the nation's public and parochial school systems."[21] Whether emphasizing conflicting ideas, parties, or religious groups, explanations for the history of religion in public schools in America have centered on warfare.[22]

Though the heroes and villains have changed with the times, this "warfare" thesis has endured for nearly a century. Progressive interpretations of American education in the early twentieth century reflected the agenda of professional leaders of public education—in many cases, men who had participated actively in early-twentieth-century public school policy. Best characterized by the example of Stanford's Elwood P. Cubberley, himself a professional school reformer, these historians celebrated the triumph of the public school in successive "battles" with the divisive elements in American society—penny-pinching aristocrats, ignorant immigrants, and scheming clerics—who promoted "private" schooling.[23] Because Cubberley's implicit task was to justify the present by means of the past, he overemphasized the religious neutrality of public schools as well as the seeming irrationality of its detractors. Another prominent progressive educational theorist went so far as to claim, with "scientific" certainty, that there was no legitimate justification (assuming that the public schools were doing their job) for the existence of private education in America.[24]

While religious schools received ill treatment from educational historians in academia, their defenders wrote their own in-house histories. In an attempt to counteract the often intense opposition to Catholic schools, Catholic historians of the early twentieth century glorified the church school and its leadership. Marvin Lazerson has summarized the main theme of these histories thus: "Started to protect the flock from an alien Protestant environment, despite adversity, [Catholic schools] quickly proved themselves compatible with the American way of life." Rarely did these histories explore the relationship between leaders and followers, internal debates within the Church, or external forces such as economic transformation, ethnicity, or social class. "Catholic immigrants did not need to be convinced of the necessity of Catholic schools," wrote Reverend James A. Burns in his influential book, *The Growth and Development of the Catholic School System in the United States.* "They were of one mind with their pastors and bishops on the subject." Faced with the same progressive objective as mainstream historians—justifying the present through the past—progressive historians of Catholic schooling cast the public schools as godless, and the rise of parochial schools as triumphant and inevitable.[25]

Beginning in the 1960s, revisionist scholars reassessed the "secular" portrait of public school history painted by progressive historians of public and

Catholic schooling alike. Most of these works focused on the origins of the common school movement, trying to show that the transition from colonial theocracy to republican democracy in education was more fluid and mutually reinforcing than had been previously thought. David Tyack and Timothy Smith, for example, focused on the role of ministerial leadership in the common school movement.[26] Likewise, historians of Catholic education questioned the premise that Catholics were "of one mind" regarding the public school, and they urged a move away from looking at official Church policy and rhetoric.[27]

Yet despite the "revisions" away from progressive approaches to the history of religion and public schooling, little has actually changed in the way scholars think about the issue. In 1981, James Sanders lamented that scholarship had stagnated since the 1960s and found it necessary to suggest new directions for research.[28] Twenty years later, F. Michael Perko demonstrated a similar problem in a historiographical review of the field. Minor works had chipped away at the issue, but major work remained undone.[29]

The most recent efforts to explain the relationship between religion and common schools focus on the formative stage of common schools before the Civil War, or on the era of progressive reform following the turn of the century. Relatively little has been written on the critical decades in between. (The period does not even have a decent name.) Considering the significance of these years to the development of modern schooling—a time when vaguely defined, quasi-private common schools blossomed into the "public" schools of the twentieth century, complete with state regulation, rudimentary bureaucracy, and compulsory education laws—the deficiency is striking.

The few excellent works that do exist, however, continue to examine the polemical debate at the national level and the evolution of state laws reflecting that debate. Thanks to the work of revisionists, they no longer assume that public schools were religiously secular, or neutral, but nevertheless they still center on conflict, focusing on the words and actions of leaders. In 1974, Diane Ravitch wrote of the development of the public schools of New York City as the "Great School Wars," recasting the roles but staying true to the theme.[30] In 1987, Lloyd Jorgenson turned the argument slightly, suggesting that the inflammatory rhetoric of extremists not only set the tone but was actually directly responsible for driving religion out of schools.[31] Other major accounts in 1995, 1996, 1999 and 2000 continued the tradition.[32] One recent major book on the subject downplays compromise between religious leaders and public school officials, arguing that any "isolated experiments" were short lived and rare. Instead, it concludes that by 1900 schools had dropped overtly religious trappings "due as much to exhaustion as any thoughtful will."[33]

Another branch of revisionist scholarship, known as the new political history, also has made important contributions to the history of public education. But like educational historians, political historians have left the warfare thesis intact. Using innovative statistical analysis of voter attributes, political historians of the last two generations have shown that ethnoreligious identity played an important role in how people in the post-bellum era voted. Paul Kleppner, for example, has argued that "partisan identifications mirrored irreconcilably conflicting values emanating from divergent ethnic and religious subcultures." He goes on to claim that because different groups had worldviews that were inconsistent at their philosophical cores, their civil participation must have been polarized and extreme. Hitching voting patterns to the words of vocal, and caustic, orators on the school issue, Kleppner argues that religion in public schools was a "frenzy," a "battle," and a "maelstrom of fury."[34] Others are more moderate in their conclusions.[35] Yet people do not always act according to their party platform, nor do they act in similar ways in different contexts. The rhetorical battlefield of politics does not necessarily resembles one's backyard, or one's school.[36]

The way in which recent historians use the work of cartoonist Thomas Nast provides a vivid example of the resilience of warfare thesis. Throughout the 1870s, Nast worked as a cartoonist for *Harper's Weekly* magazine. He is best known today for his images of Uncle Sam and Santa Claus, but he also drew extensively on political matters, including religion in public schools. On February 26, 1870, *Harper's Weekly* published a cartoon by Nast entitled "Our Common Schools As They Are and As They May Become." Nast, like his patron *Harper's*, frequently attacked the Catholic Church for attempting to supplant the common school system with a theocratic one, and this particular drawing targeted the appropriation of public money by the state legislature to several Protestant, Catholic, and Jewish denominational schools in New York City. Nast's cartoon has three panels:

The first depicted his vision of public schools "as they are," a happy circle of racially diverse children attending the same school—one that was "free to all" and had "no sects." Cubberley might have agreed with this vision. Revisionist scholars and their successors, on the other hand, have ungently dissected the naiveté of this vision—pointing to segregated schools for African Americans and Native Americans, no school for Chinese children in California, and so on. To the modern historian, the image appears laughably fictional. In the second panel, Nast spilt his vitriol on the Catholic Church, conveniently overlooking the participation of Protestant and Jewish schools in the school fund as well. The third panel is Nast's apocalyptic prediction for the near future, warning that education could become a battleground of individual interests. The panel resembles many works by Nast in the 1870s that attacked the Catholic Church and captured

FIGURE 1.1 Thomas Nast, "Our Common Schools As They Are and As They May Become." Were any of the three panels accurate? (*Harper's Weekly*, February 26, 1870)

the debate over religion in public schools at its most bitter. But was it any more accurate a view than his treacly one of common schools "as they are," or his conveniently nearsighted depiction of the "distribution of the sectarian school fund"?

Nast's heroic view of happy schoolchildren has been debunked, but his negative vision of religion and public schooling has not undergone the same critical examination. In fact, Nast or Nast-inspired cartoons of battling bishops and crusading common school men grace the covers of Lloyd Jorgenson's *The State and Non-Public School* (1987) and Ward McAfee's *Religion, Race, and Reconstruction* (1998). To be fair to both, each book claims to deal with politics writ large (and does so wonderfully), yet at the same time, both books argue that the bitter tone of *Harper's* cartoons exemplified local reality.[37] Beyond these two examples, Nast's images of conflict over religion in public schools endure, unquestioned, within the pages of other recent histories. The caption in Timothy Walch's (1996) presentation of the following cartoon reads: "Non-Catholics were suspicious of Catholic efforts to reform public education."[38]

FIGURE 1.2 Did Thomas Nast's most popular school image, "The American River Ganges," capture local sentiment or try to shape it? (*Harper's Weekly*, September 30, 1871)

Despite its popularity, the warfare thesis has several major limitations. First, it casts democracy in a rather grim light. Were most local public schools really battlegrounds? Did our nation's most democratic unit of government—the school district—operate by nothing more than "majority rule"?

Or, conversely, were solutions so watered down that they met no one's needs? Was democratic governance so starkly unsuited to social diversity? In the era of small government, high voting rates, and strong local control, the warfare thesis fails the test of common sense. Why would the public support a system that seemed to satisfy no one? Why would so many parents voluntarily send their children to such intellectually militarized zones? How did the public school survive?

The warfare thesis does not make intuitive sense, in part because it relies on inappropriate sources. The most salient theme in Victorian-era American public schooling was not national debate but local control; outside of the occupied South during Reconstruction, national and state educational politics had little to do with actual schools or scholars. At the federal level, the U.S. Commissioner of Education had a tiny office, a mediocre budget, and few tools for educational reform. State offices of education in 1890 averaged two people, the superintendent included.[39] Even in New York, which boasted the nation's most centralized state education office, superintendents rarely exercised control over local ideological matters; in cities, their influence barely registered before the 1890s. Likewise, the statements of leaders in the Catholic Church, prolific Protestant clergymen, and political party polemicists did not necessarily capture the thoughts or actions of common people, who tended to act more according to local circumstance than official church and party doctrine.[40] With few exceptions, the American public school saw its sun rise and set at the local level. Yet as long as historians of religion and public schools rely on the writings of religious leaders and professional school men, and set these against each other in theoretical petri dishes, there is little doubt that they will describe anything but irreconcilable conflict; there is much doubt, however, that they will capture local experience.

Peaceable Adjustments at the Local Level.

This book offers an alternative explanation for how common schools of one state, at least, dealt with the issue of religion. Rather than focus on the rhetorical battles over religion at the state and national levels, it examines how local school districts dealt with religion in practice. In fact, evidence shows that religion was not a major, bitterly divisive issue in local practice in cities or rural districts. Why? Nineteenth-century Americans understood their public school system as being a locally based, political system—that is, as a civil process of organizing and managing tax-supported schools. In New York State, even the laws governing state intervention in local affairs emphasized local discretion. To explain why religion did not usually turn divisive, we must first understand how it functioned in the context of local control at the school district level.

Given that way of seeing the issue, this book develops three explanations for the success of common schools at ameliorating religious differences. First, the strength of the *idea* of democratic control strongly influenced the policies that local citizens developed. (It even shaped the arguments and actions of the leading clergymen who opposed common schools.) Second, the actual process of diffuse, local control proved highly effective at ameliorating religious differences, thereby defusing the dissatisfaction of religious minorities and taking the teeth out of majorities. Finally, the suppleness of the public school system allowed it to bend—sometimes overtly, sometimes subtly—in the various directions toward or away from religious content and theocratic control that district residents pushed.

State bureaucracy and law played an important role in the process as well—an increasing role as the twentieth century approached. Until the 1890s, state law remained largely silent on the question of religion in public schools, leaving it to local districts to decide the nature of that relationship. At the same time, however, state superintendents consistently upheld the appeals of religious minorities against mandatory religious exercises, framing localism in a context of moderate protections of individual civil rights. Beginning in the 1890s, progressive reformers attacked a common school system defined primarily by local control and began a slow but steady process of dismantling localism, democratic control, and religious compromise itself in favor of a professionally managed system. This movement directly affected the traditional emphasis on local control over religion, resulting in a new configuration of more state interference in local religious policies and, at the same time, a repudiation of the principle of protecting minority rights in religious exercises cases. Those elements of local control that survived progressive reform, on the other hand, continued to function as buffers to religious conflict well into the twentieth century.

This book looks at the relationship between religious diversity *and* local control of public schools, not just religion in public schools. This distinction places the emphasis on *how* decisions about school policy were made and allows for a more holistic view of education beyond formal curriculum. Religion in this sense means different things in different contexts—from the actions of members of religious groups to the abstract dogma developed by religious leaders to concrete examples of religious content in teaching. Using religion in context creates a more complex portrait of how religion functioned in the decision-making process at the local level. A woman might be a Catholic, but she could act based on other roles—as a taxpayer, a teacher, a Democrat, or a German-American. Religion in that sense does not reflect official church dogma, and emphasizing the ideas and actions of church leaders and the platforms of political parties fails to capture such rich complexity.[41]

Writing such an argument requires turning the usual historical narrative inside out. The warfare thesis frames history in terms of minor skirmishes in a larger battle of ideas. The words of vocal leaders provide the plan of battle, and the historian arrays the armies accordingly. Details of local practice march in ordered procession. But looking at local circumstance, at the process of local control rather than a few well-known outcomes, without the assumption that it matches the standard generalizations, requires a reverse of the standard narrative form.

The body of my argument has three parts. Part 1 develops the idea of early common schools in New York State as systems of civil control, intended to replace older modes of private and theocratic control of education (though in reality the shift was gradual). It then analyzes the legal framework that defined the relationships between district, city, county, and state levels of governance using quantitative data. Part 2 examines religion and public schools in town and rural school districts. In particular, it explains how religion mattered in terms of taxes, voting, and the drawing of district boundaries. It then looks at religious use of public school buildings and religious exercises in the rural school curriculum, both of these in terms of the process by which locals discussed and decided policy. Part 3 examines religion in urban school systems, detailing how the tension between central governance and neighborhood schooling related to religious pluralism. Here the trends usually described in the warfare thesis begin to take shape, though they appear quite different in the local context. I specifically address two issues: religious exercises and public funding of church-affiliated schools. In the conclusion, I return to the big picture: discussing trends in the relationship between religion and public schools for the state as a whole and speculating over their significance for our understanding of religion and public schools as a national issue.

To make arguments about the process of local control, I use an unusual body of evidence. The durability of the top-down historical approach to religion in public schools probably stems, in part, from a lack of alternative sources. Nineteenth-century local documents are notoriously incomplete to begin with, particularly those from small towns and rural districts. In the case of religion in public schools, however, the vicious nature of the national debate actually encouraged silence. When stories of local compromise crept into national discussion, the spotlight could be disastrous. In Faribault and Stillwater, Minnesota, for example, school boards and church officials reached an agreement in 1891 whereby the public school system rented a church building (formerly a church school), hiring nuns to teach classes. Although both sides showed initial satisfaction, the glare of outside media quickly soured the deal, which ended after only two years. Yet even as the Faribault-Stillwater plan folded, five surrounding communities quietly struck their own compromises.[42] History has thus presented us a paradox: the very nature of religion in public schools, often kept quiet or disguised at the local level, has forced most historians to rely on non-local, polemical data.

New York State offers a tantalizing exception. In 1822, the state legislature invested the State Superintendent of Common Schools with the power to adjudicate all local disputes concerning the common schools. From 1822 to 1913, superintendents issued over 12,000 decisions. A small portion of these has been printed in state documents, and the rest survive, unindexed and still bound in faded red tape, in the New York State Archives. While most of the disputes were over boundaries and taxes, a small percentage was over religion. The state collected other documents as well, including letters received by state superintendents, covering the period 1852–1894, and their replies. These sources allow unusual access to what happened all over New York State, providing a detailed catalog of religious practice in common schools that would otherwise take a lifetime to compile. I have read and analyzed nearly 3,000 legal appeals and over 7,000 letters to the New York State Superintendent of Public Instruction. Pieced together, these bones of contention provide a fossil record of local politics in rural schools and offer the chance to view religion in the context of all of the other issues that locals cared about. Buttressed by local and state government documents, county archives, and newspaper accounts from the multitude of local New York State newspapers, these sources tell a new and important story in American educational history.

There are, of course, certain ironies in using appeals and complaints to the State Superintendent to find evidence of local compromise. Complaints suggest discord; legal appeals, the importance of state-level bureaucracy. Yet while the appeals process shows that the state law and state bureaucracy did matter, *how* they mattered is the key to understanding religion and public education. Aside from their ability to catalog local religious practice and specific instances of state intervention, the documents are valuable taken as a whole. The appeals demonstrate the boundaries of acceptable behavior, and from these boundaries, patterns emerge. From 1865 to 1900, the Office of the State Superintendent received over 3,000 appeals and tenfold that number of letters. The frequency, grouping, and relative number of religious appeals suggest the changing significance of religion as a source of local tension and the specific role of extra-local authority (i.e., the state) in mediating that tension. Periods of few complaints are as suggestive as periods of many.

The appeals and letters alone do not suffice for a state history. Unlike their rural counterparts, residents of urban school districts rarely appealed to the State Superintendent over any issue, including religion. Thus while appeals and letters do provide some information about urban public school policy, I have been forced to look elsewhere. Fortunately, cities, by their nature, kept records and supported an aggressive newspaper industry. I have read the minutes of board of education or common council meetings from eight cities (some in manuscript form) and the published annual reports of fifteen. I also have scoured local newspapers representing different political viewpoints and different regions of the state, including the *Albany Argus*, the Buffalo *Catholic Union,* the *New York Times, The Utica Morning Herald, The Troy Morning Whig, The Troy Daily Press, The Saint Lawrence Republican and Ogdensburg Weekly Republican*, the *Dutchess Farmer*, and others. City school systems also have benefited from some excellent secondary research.

Every state had a unique set of characteristics that shaped its common schools in the nineteenth century, and this study of a single state cannot speak authoritatively for all. Nevertheless, New York State offers a fascinating case study for the study of religion and public education. State histories of religion and public schools typically center on Massachusetts, which had the benefit of Horace Mann's prolific writings; yet with its established Congregational Church, Massachusetts experienced an extremely unusual transition between eighteenth-century theocracy in education and nineteenth-century democracy in education. (The Congregational Church remained the established religion of the state until 1833.) New York State, on the other hand, hosted pockets of settlement that resembled those in many other states. Sections of western New York resembled the frontier towns of the Midwest and West, with their fast-moving populations and temporary boomtowns set against sparse agricultural landscapes. Sections in the lower Hudson Valley and on Long Island, on the other hand, boasted long-established Yankee communities with strong social institutions. Then, of course, New York had cities: Buffalo and Rochester, close cousins to cities farther west with their large German populations, and Poughkeepsie and Albany, which contained established colonial-era families and institutions such as those of Massachusetts and Connecticut.

The uniqueness of New York State also makes it a promising choice for study. New York hosted greater religious diversity than any other nineteenth-century state. Not only did immigrants bring non-Protestant faiths such as Catholicism and Judaism, but New York State provided a fertile breeding ground for offbeat religions and utopian societies, from Spiritualists and Shakers to freethinkers and Owenites. As a result, New York State and especially New York City have benefited from copious historical research into religious and educational history. Much of this attention stems from the fact that New York City was the largest city in the nation, and New York State dominated national politics throughout the nineteenth century. Finally, New York State had the most centralized, powerful state department of education in the nation. If local control survived there, it may have flourished elsewhere. Moreover, New York State's relatively powerful state superintendents left a valuable legacy: paperwork. As a result, the state boasts unrivaled documentation for reconstructing localism in nineteenth-century common schooling, including (as we have seen) the appeals and letters themselves.

Conclusion

Historical writing is as much a process of omission as inclusion, and readers of this book will notice that I have left out several major facets of nineteenth-century education. First, I do not examine secondary schooling per se, including the New York State Board of Regents, which oversaw private and church-affiliated academies that received public subsidies throughout the nineteenth century. Academies and high schools do appear in my statistics, but they were statistically insignificant until the twentieth century. Likewise, I do not discuss the tiny, separate system of common schools for Native American children of New York State, which fostered some interesting (and troubling) relationships between church and state. Finally, though I sometimes make reconnaissance trips into the internal politics and policies of religious organizations and their schools, I keep the focus of the book as sharply as possible on public schools. By making these, and other, omissions, I am able to examine the common school in its most straightforward and representative way.[43]

My hope in so doing is not to resurrect the ghost of Cubberley with its heroic vision of the virtues of public education. Nor, after toppling the warfare thesis from its pedestal, do I propose to replace it with a monument to widespread consensus that ignores ethnic and religious tensions. (In fact, this book provides the most detailed and concise account of local disagreements over religion in New York State to date.) "Peaceable adjustments" did not mean peaceable hearts or pure motives.[44] Nevertheless, the phrase is a useful descriptor of actual school policy and, as we saw at the beginning of this chapter, even comes from a partisan observer. Writing in 1892 during heightened political agitation over religion and public schools, Roman Catholic Bishop Thomas Jefferson Jenkins recognized the yawning chasm between the politics of religion in public schools and the practice of the day. Seeing religion and public schooling interact at the level of the school district to produce peaceable adjustments in New York State suggests a new way of understanding the broader development of public schooling in the late nineteenth century. Of course, schools attracted storms of rhetoric and political opportunism. Given the close association between religion and voting behavior, this should not be surprising. But did these storms of conflict drive school policy? As the following pages argue, in New York State, at least, a particular brand of democratic localism provided significant insulation and grounded schools in the communities they served. As a result, negotiation, modification, and often little more than silence characterized post-bellum school policy toward religion and facilitated the growth of a massive expansion of public schooling in New York State in the context of an intensely democratic, religiously pluralistic society.

Part 1

Origins of the Public School "System"

Today when we talk about the public school "system," we use the word to describe the interconnected nature of public schools—individual institutions that are part of a larger organizational scheme. Thus parents boast that their local school system is excellent, and politicians and pundits propose "system-wide" reforms. This meaning of the word "system" dates back to the colonial era, and it seems particularly suited to twentieth- and twenty-first-century schools. Given the weave of regulations and funding schemes that connects individual public schools to each other within districts, and to larger bureaucracies, most public schooling in the United States today does operate in organizational systems.[1]

Yet alongside this meaning of the word "system," and indeed as old in usage, stands the idea of a "system" as a method.[2] During the American Revolution, for example, debates over *systems* of government described the "how" of decision making; organizational details served that larger vision. It is this meaning of the word that best describes public schools of the nineteenth century. When most school districts comprised a single school, when state offices of education had almost no connection to local schools, and when bureaucratization—even in the nation's largest cities—was still in infant form, public schools could hardly be described as pieces of a larger organizational system. They could, however, be described as operating by the same set of rules, rules that governed the process by which local residents operated their schools: a democratic recipe for the nation's smallest units of government. It is the idea of system-as-method that captures common schools in their formative years.

Seeing the common school system as a method rather than an organization allows us to understand critical factors in the relationship between religion and public schooling. A quiet revolution occurred from 1800 to 1830, in which democratic governance supplanted ecclesiastical and private control of community schooling. As we shall see in chapter 2, the common school system, or method, profoundly altered the relationship between religion and schooling. A common school system centered on local, democratic control at the district level held secular, civil ends above religious ones, and did so by design. Religion could, and often did, factor into schools through local governance. But the common school method usually stopped religious encroachments that attempted to establish a particular religious sect and oftentimes resulted in no religious instruction at all.

Yet even as common schools spread locally, antebellum school reformers fortified a growing state bureaucracy to systematize common schools in the modern sense, thereby undoing local control with state-level regulation. This tension between growing state regulation and local control is a second critical factor in the relationship between religion and common schools. Chapter 3 examines the workings of this relationship in post-bellum school districts, seeing how the issue of religion played out between state and local levels of school administration. While public schools faced increasing pressure to systematize in the modern sense of the term, the process of local control remained fairly intact. As a result, approaches to religious diversity fit into the pattern of local control, not the dictates, or even necessarily the wishes, of the State Department of Public Instruction. In rare instances when locals invited state intervention, the appeals process itself revealed deep-seated beliefs about the role of the state in the public school system as a court of last resort.

Chapter 2

Democracy Trumps Theocracy

The Civil Origins of the Common School System in New York

Understanding the workings of the common school system after the Civil War requires looking to its foundation decades before. The tangled relationship between religion and nineteenth-century common schools stemmed from the late eighteenth century—from seeds sown in the American Revolution. Historians of education and would-be reformers have focused much of their attention on this formative period, and rightfully so. From the formal ratification of the federal constitution in 1789 to the end of the early national period in the 1820s, American education underwent its own revolution—one that redefined the relationships among religion, government, and schooling. Before the revolution, state-supported churches controlled most formal schooling in the American colonies, while religious literature and ideas formed both the means and ends of the curriculum. But these schools primarily served the elite and were by no means a comprehensive, mass system. During the Revolutionary War, however, the grasp of churches over formal education faced a serious challenge from the ideas of the Enlightenment and a widespread emphasis on rational democracy and anticlericism. One by one, states disestablished their churches. Leading figures such as Thomas Jefferson, James Madison, Benjamin Rush, and George Clinton proposed schemes to replace the old colonial model of limited church-based and private education with state-sponsored mass systems to ensure an informed, virtuous citizenry.[1] Within thirty years of the ratification of the federal constitution in 1889, state leaders in New York realized this vision, creating a system of civilly controlled, state-funded common schools to teach a largely secular course in basic literacy and math.

In general, supporters of a common school system meant two different things when they spoke of "religion" in these publicly supported schools. Organized religion, particularly traditional, hierarchical churches such as the Church of England and the Roman Catholic Church, seemed to many revolutionaries to threaten the democratic principles of the American Republic. For leading intellectuals, the high-church emphasis on symbols, liturgy, and ritual smacked of irrational superstition and potential demagoguery. Religion in the organized sense had no place in the mass-educational schemes of the revolutionary generation, except, perhaps, among high church leaders themselves. On the other hand, the religious elements of common culture—real or imagined—did. Benjamin Rush wrote that no one should be allowed to vote or serve on a jury who did not know "reading, writing, and arithmetic." But he also wrote of the importance of instilling the Christian religion in the minds of the young. Thomas Jefferson, who proposed a high wall of separation between church and state, nevertheless advocated a quasi-Christian naturalistic religion as the source of civil virtue.[2] Proposals for common schools in New York aimed to instill "religion" in the masses, but through an essentially secular course of study.

The tension between the religious and civil, secular ends of the common school system of control has run through the history of common schools ever since. In the nineteenth century, Americans resolved the tension locally; the common school "system" provided the means. Scholars have disagreed, however, over just how the issue was resolved. Historians in the first half of the twentieth century seized on the secular design of common schools, arguing that they were virtually secular from the outset.[3] More recent scholarship has emphasized the religion-as-culture argument, looking at references to religion in textbooks,[4] or arguing that in an overwhelmingly Protestant nation, civil control meant religious education for practical purposes, or emphasizing the role of clergy in spreading common schools.[5] Studies of the early national period (roughly from 1789 to 1830) have focused on three issues in particular: To what degree did the founding fathers intend mass education to be religious education? When states did form common schools decades later, how did religion figure into the design? And, finally, regardless of state designs, how did religion fit into early common schools in actual practice? This chapter considers each question, focusing in particular on the common school system of New York State as a method of operating schools for civil ends. In doing so, I argue that the most significant feature of early-nineteenth-century common schools is not that they often contained elements of culture as religion (which one would expect), but that their mode of control and course of study were so startlingly secular.[6]

Religion and Education in the Ideas of the Founders

Addressing the legislative assembly of the State of New York in 1789, Governor George Clinton lamented the effects of the recent revolution on American society, noting the particular evil of the "neglect of the education of youth." To alleviate the problem, he called upon the legislature for action. "Perhaps there is scarce any thing more worthy of your attention," he continued, "than the revival and encouragement of seminaries of learning; and nothing by which we can more satisfactorily express our gratitude to the Supreme Being for his past favors; since piety and virtue are generally the offspring of enlightened understanding."[7]

Clinton's argument and the subsequent acts of the legislature reveal two vital aspects of schooling in the early national period, both of which describe the educational zeitgeist of the times and the ideological foundations of the common schooling that would come later. The idea that the government's primary responsibility was the education of its citizens reflected the common rhetoric (and very real concerns) of state and national leaders that the fragile new republic rested on the solid foundation of an informed, capable citizenry. "The business of education," Benjamin Rush wrote in 1786, "has acquired a new complexion by the independence of our country. The form of government we have assumed has created a new class of duties to every American."[8] Like other founding fathers and mothers who viewed their grand experiment with a mix of euphoria and anxiety—particularly after the subsequent bloody revolution in France—Rush recognized that a republican form of government required an informed citizenry. Reverend Samuel Miller told a Fourth of July audience of New York City elite in 1795 that state aid to mass education was "so plainly and intimately connected with the welfare of all republics that neither proof nor illustration on the subject are necessary."[9] Thomas Jefferson, George Washington, and other leading figures urged a variety of educational schemes to prop up the nation and minimize dissent.[10] Acting further in this spirit than most, Noah Webster codified an American English, wrote textbooks, and even created a "federal catechism" for schoolchildren.[11]

For their parts, some state governments, though financially and bureaucratically impotent in the wake of the war, made constitutional pronouncements about the importance of an informed citizenry, broadly speaking. But they did not inaugurate actual state-sponsored public schools.[12] As we shall see later, Clinton's New York went the farthest, making provisions for primary, secondary, and tertiary education (though such modern distinctions do not snugly fit the times).[13] Concern for the education of republicans also found purchase in the federal government, which ran the post office to encourage the free flow of information and ratified the First Amendment to provide some insurance for the freedom of its content.[14] And although lacking a specific constitutional mandate, the federal government also encouraged schooling through Western land grants, though, like state governments, it did little else to establish actual schools.[15]

In addition to defining a governmental role for education, Clinton's address also showed a particularly "enlightened" attitude toward religion. Invoking divine providence as the reason for the revolution's success, he argued that schooling glorified God and served His purposes for the new nation. "Piety" and "virtue" stemmed from enlightened understanding. In other words, true religion and morality came from education. Here was the essence of eighteenth-century rationalism: reason, not tradition, mediated man's relationship to education, to politics, and to God. By awakening reason, schooling led to moral and civic uplift. That idea was common currency among many leaders of the revolution, from the arch-Deist Thomas Jefferson to the pious John Adams.[16] Clinton himself espoused Deism (if quietly), and that rationalistic approach to religion flourished in some regions of New York State during the early republic, alongside agnosticism and even outright disbelief.[17]

Anti-clericalism, in particular anti-Anglicanism, so suffused the leadership of the founders of the New York State government that legislators explicitly wrote into their 1777 state constitution that the new republican form of government would halt the "spiritual oppression and intolerance wherewith the bigotry and ambition of weak and wicked priests [have] scourged mankind."[18] To this end, the fledgling state sponsored no established church and forbade clergy from holding public office. The motivating factor of such legislation for liberals such as Thomas Jefferson and George Clinton, argues Gordon Wood, was not so much fear of competition as it was fear of sectarian religion itself as the foe to reason.[19] For the more moderate, the desire to separate religion and the state stemmed from a spirit of religious toleration.[20]

If leading revolutionaries questioned an active role for organized religion in their schemes for government, then why refer to it at all in the context of mass education? First, the revolution may have caused setbacks for established churches, but they were by no means eliminated. By the 1790s, a wave of "genteel humanitarianism" swept over the New York legislature, flowing from Quaker and Anglican social reformers, which included calls for mass education.[21] Second, while Deism may have been common among the revolutionary leaders, and in scattered pockets of the state, traditional religious bodies still dominated local life in the North, particularly in Massachusetts and Connecticut. Calvinism would continue to flourish among American Protestant churches for the next several decades, despite the corrosive effects of American democracy. And even for Deists, never mind most Americans,

Christianity in a cultural sense went hand in glove with republicanism, and the concept of virtuous citizenship lay firmly grounded in quasireligious values.[22] In political terms, government gave almost no structure to social life. To use Nathan Hatch's able description of the antebellum period that lay ahead, this was "an age when most ordinary Americans expected almost nothing from government institutions and almost everything from religious ones."[23] Historians differ on the religious significance of the revolution, and on the level of religiosity of American society from then until the Second Great Awakening in the early nineteenth century.[24] Nevertheless, even if most New Yorkers were not full members of churches in this period, the church often lay at the heart of local social, political, and intellectual life, particularly in metropolitan centers, and the rhetoric of government necessarily acknowledged its significance. Clinton's greatest political opponents represented high church influences from the elite of New York City, particularly former Anglicans, now Episcopals.[25]

In colonial times, religion constituted the end as well as the means of schooling: literacy enabled children to read the Bible; higher education prepared ministers; and religious readings, particularly the Bible, were the basic curriculum. After the revolution, that reliance no doubt continued in many places—not only cities and towns established before the revolution but also those "covenanted" communities settled wholesale by colonizing congregations of New Englanders in the early national period.[26] In such communities, churches bore responsibility for local education, organizing schools for children of the parish. The only alternatives were the private schoolmaster or, of course, the family.

A set of regulations by ministers of Flatbush illustrates the interconnection between church and school in a small Long Island town during the early republic. For the schoolmaster, it stated that, "When the school begins, one of the children shall read the morning prayer, as it stands in the catechism, and close with the prayer before dinner; in the afternoon, it shall begin with the prayer after dinner, and end with the evening prayer. The evening school shall begin with the Lord's prayer, and close with the singing of a psalm." In preparation for church, it stated, "[The schoolmaster] shall instruct the children on every Wednesday and Saturday, in the common prayers, and the questions and answers in the catechism, to enable them to repeat them the better on Sunday, before afternoon service, or on Monday, when they shall be catechized before the congregation."[27] In 1784, the state legislature had sanctioned this practice, legally empowering "trustees of every religious denomination to erect churches and schoolhouses." The reason? "It was considered to be the duty of all wise, free and virtuous governments to countenance and encourage virtue and religion . . . and to enable every religious denomination to provide for the decent and honorable support of divine worship according to the dictates of conscience and judgment."[28] Any system of mass education in 1789 would have appeared to require the involvement of churches in some way for its maintenance. The devil lay in the details.

On the one hand, the revolutionary legislature had disestablished the church, barred clergy from office, and established a relatively tolerant, secular government based on fears of sectarian conflict and a clerical stranglehold on social life. Yet with tiny state governments, war debt, and virtually no civic infrastructure, it required those very churches to supply education to the masses. To most leading minds, virtue and morality stemmed from religion, and in fact all but two new state charters required religious tests for office-holders.[29] Governor Clinton's hopes for an education based on reason, not religion, had little hope of success. Instead, he and his successors swallowed their anti-sectarian pride, pinning their hopes on what enlightened understanding might come from church-run education, with the encouragement of the state. As we shall see, the means of this encouragement would shortly trump church control with state-sponsored democratic localism.

A Common School System, Phase One: Failure

State governments in the early national period had few tools with which to encourage education. Deeply in debt from the costs of revolution, lacking political confidence in light of recent agrarian rebellions, and even somewhat suspicious of the "people" in whose name and authority they invoked, most opted to do little in the way of state involvement in education.[30] Nevertheless, while state governments might be poor in money, infrastructure, and power, they were rich in two things: land and the law. In New York, the fledgling state government claimed vast lands unsettled by whites. Moreover, at the helm of a new form of government, the legislature held a virtual monopoly on laws and charters for new educational institutions.[31]

As if in answer to the governor's plea, the New York State Legislature used both land and the law to encourage education.[32] Four years earlier, in 1785 and then again in 1787, the federal government had used land ordinances to encourage schooling in the West, setting aside lots in every checkerboard township for the "maintenance" of public schools.[33] In 1789, the New York State Legislature copied this strategy, enacting a laissez-faire policy of setting aside public lands (known as "gospel and school lands") to raise money for the encouragement of churches and schools. The act directed the surveyor general of the state to "lay out twenty townships, so that each could contain 100 lots of 250 acres each," reserving, near the center, one for the support of a school and one for a church.[34] Using its power over charters, the legislature incorporated the Regents of the University of New York in

1789, based on a preexisting model from 1787 that plainly reflected the anti-sectarian mood of the revolutionary generation. Pulling King's College up from its Anglican roots, the legislature planted the school in care of the state under the supervision of a secular board of Regents, renaming it Columbia.[35] In addition, the act granted the Regents supervisory powers over academies statewide, although for practical purposes those institutions were quite independent and usually sectarian.[36]

The Regents' law did not include schools for the common people, or "common schools," as they were known. This omission is not surprising, given that the Regents system had been devised in 1787 and even earlier (reflecting, no doubt, the prejudices and preoccupations of the leaders of New York, a considerable number of them graduates of King's College), while a state-sponsored plan for common schools had remained a nonissue. The Regents themselves pointed to the deficiency in 1793, recommending that the state encourage schools to teach the "lower branches of education, [including] reading in their native language with propriety; and so much of writing and arithmetic, as to enable them when they come forward into active life, to transact with accuracy and dispatch, the business arising from their daily intercourse with each other."[37]

Demonstrating the typical founder's concern for an informed citizenry, Clinton concurred. Addressing the legislature in 1795, he said, "While it is evident that the general establishment and liberal endowment of academies are highly to be commended, and are attended with the most beneficial consequences, yet it cannot be denied that they are principally confined to the children of the opulent, and that a great portion of the community is excluded from their immediate advantages." He went on to recommend the "establishment of common schools throughout the state" as a remedy. The legislature obliged, establishing annual appropriations for the encouragement of schools in which children "shall be instructed in the English language, or be taught English grammar, arithmetic, mathematics, and such other branches of knowledge as are most useful and necessary to complete a good English education."[38]

The purpose outlined by the Regents, endorsed by Clinton, and enacted by the legislature was explicitly civic. Like religion itself, education was to be encouraged by the state only for the purpose of preserving the state. Education was to be rudimentary and functional, enabling students to engage in the business of life to a degree of intelligence that would inoculate them from demagoguery and superstition. Religious instruction could certainly qualify as teaching another "useful and necessary branch," but only insofar as it served the state's interest in a virtuous citizenry.

The method for supporting these schools reflected a radical break with the past, when either the church or private schoolmasters—not "the people" in a local corporate sense—ruled the schools. According to the 1795 act, the means by which this education would be encouraged was through a combination of financial incentives and a legal process. Financially, the legislature authorized $50,000 annually to go to towns and cities for the support of teachers. The money was to be apportioned to counties on the basis of the number of representatives in the legislature. Within counties, towns divided the money according to their number of inhabitants; at the town level, locally elected commissioners disbursed the money to school districts based on the daily attendance of pupils. To New York City (ever the exception), the act included all religious charity schools in New York City, and, later, all academies.[39]

To monitor and encourage the use of this money and to foster civil, rather than ecclesiastical, control, the legislature coupled a political process to the money. In their support of academies, the Regents did not distinguish between sectarian and civil control; their purpose—encouraging higher learning—could be accomplished by either, without threat to the state; and its clientele, the well-to-do, were not perceived to be at risk for losing their minds to superstition. But the fundamentals of learning for the masses of younger children were an entirely different matter. A common education required civil control. The common school law required participating towns and cities to elect between three and seven commissioners who would be responsible for distributing the state funds and conferring with school trustees on the hiring of teachers and the maintenance of the school. Within the towns (which, as geographic units, resembled counties in other states more than "towns" in the sense of population density and size), the law encouraged inhabitants to "associate together for the purpose of procuring good and sufficient schoolmasters, and for erecting and maintaining schools in such and in so many parts of the town in which they may reside, as shall be convenient." As holders of the purse strings, town commissioners could determine whether or not a particular school district qualified for funds based on the morality of the schoolmaster and the content of the course.[40]

At the heart of the law lay the concept of the school "district," a legally constructed unit of government to manage state funds, to levy taxes, and to operate a school. The idea of the district itself stemmed from struggles in Massachusetts and Connecticut against centralized control in geographically and ideologically dispersing towns.[41] The 1795 New York common school law described a district as the following: First, the district was geographically bounded. Within these bounds residents had elected, by majority vote, to form the district voluntarily and play by the rules of the system. Together the inhabitants would meet annually to elect two or three trustees, whose responsibility was to care for the schoolhouse (if there was one), hire teachers for the winter and summer terms, and preside over disputes between teachers and parents or teachers and students. These elections, and district meetings in general, operated according to traditional English parliamentary procedure, as later canonized in *Robert's Rules of Order*.

It is difficult to assess the effects of this law. A year after its passage, the legislature voted to include academies that offered elementary education under the act. One historian has concluded that the act attracted many established church academies and charity schools but stimulated little new growth in terms of the district system it envisioned.[42] A 1798 abstract shows that 1,352 schools received funding under the law, with an enrollment of 59,660 children.[43] Because the district system was self-selecting, though, it is likely that in those districts that did form, residents were relatively homogeneous, and that the pattern of church responsibility for the education of the parish fit easily within the new system, as long as local politics supported it. The transfer of church control to the new system worked seamlessly in New York City, where a variety of religious denominations already maintained charity schools for the poor and academies for the rich, and where the legislature provided that the district system of governance did not apply.

The 1795 act expired in 1800 without renewal, and many, including Clinton, regarded it as a failure.[44] The law had not encouraged the growth of new schools for which its framers had hoped—probably because the amount of money was too small to be any real incentive to abandon private and parochial responsibility for education, nor did it help at all with the construction cost or rental of school buildings for common, public use. The schools that the law did support were often academies for older children or charity schools for the poor, not common schools for children of the people at large. Moreover, an unpopular state tax levied in 1799 to cover a deficiency in the grant aroused the ire of the people themselves.[45] Although most of the schools it supported probably continued on their own, the state's first experiment in encouraging common schools ended in 1800.[46]

A Common School System Phase Two: Success

The failure of the first law, with its limited funds and consequent focus on preexisting schools, made it clear that any future strategy would require more money. And even before the law's expiration the legislature looked to a longer-term strategy to encourage common schooling, proposing in 1799 a measure to grow a sufficiently large, permanent school fund. By 1811, lotteries and land sales had amassed $150,000 for that purpose, and Governor Tompkins appointed a committee to design "a system for the organization and establishment of common schools."[47] The committee's report demonstrates further evolution of the 1795 attempt at creating a civil process for overseeing common school education and the rationale for the common school system as it would largely remain for the rest of the century. It also reveals the difficulty of that new paradigm set against the religious tradition of the past. For both reasons, it bears examination in detail.

In a report that invoked Rousseau and Montesque, the committee reiterated the founding generation's emphasis on the need for a virtuous, informed citizenry and the role that education could play in creating and maintaining such. The committee began by explaining the various existing conditions of education in the state, and why state aid was necessary to spread common schooling to all children—conceding that even without state involvement, common schooling proliferated. "In a free government, where political equality is established, and where the road to preferment is open to all," they explained, "there is a natural stimulus to education; and accordingly, we find it generally resorted to, unless some great local impediments interfere." Essentially, these local impediments related to population density, and the committee argued that the state had a two-tiered system of education. "In populous cities, and the parts of the country thickly settled, schools are generally established by individual exertion. In these cases, the means of education are facilitated, as the expenses of the schools are divided among a great many." On the other hand, the report continued:

> It is in the remote and thinly populated parts of the state, where the inhabitants are scattered over a large extent, that education stands greatly in need of encouragement. The people here, living far from each other, makes [*sic*] it difficult so to establish schools, as to render them convenient or accessible to all. Every family, therefore, must either educate its own children, or the children must forgo the advantages of education."[48]

The committee recommended that both populations—rural (most of the state) and urban—would benefit from a state system of encouragement based on financial support and legal structure.

The task of stimulating the growth of common schools required finesse. Any "system" that threatened local control over a civil process would fail.[49] The committee's solution, reflected in the subsequent act of the legislature in 1812, was a self-conscious emulation of existing plans in Connecticut and Massachusetts and echoed New York's own 1795 act. All towns were to be divided into districts by elected town commissioners. District trustees, elected by the residents thereof, maintained responsibility for hiring teachers and setting curriculum, as long as it complied generally with the spirit of the law. While the formation of districts was no longer voluntary, participating in the law was. For those who did apply for funds, the law required that they match these funds from local taxes. The district bore responsibility for the school building, as state money could only be applied to the teacher's salary.

Initially, the act again failed. The State Superintendent blamed this on the problem of voluntary participation, and the following year, in 1814, the legislature made town adoption of the plan mandatory, directing town supervisors to levy a tax equal to the state apportionment and requiring districts to comply by building schools. The compulsory participation amendment appears to have stimulated halting, and then explosive, growth. In the first year of the system, 1814, participation was so low that the State Superintendent demurred from reporting the numbers to the legislature. By April 1816, though, the superintendent reported that the previous year saw 2,631 common school districts in 338 towns (enrolling a total of 176,499 students). Describing the effects of the common school system, Superintendent Hawley wrote in a ponderously passive voice that "the number of schools has been increased; many schoolhouses have been built; more able teachers employed, and much interest which ought to be felt in behalf of the common schools has been excited." Hawley's enthusiasm proved perspicacious. Over the next fifteen years, the number of districts and students enrolled would triple.

The superintendent attributed the success of the common school law to two factors. First, the state fund, so much improved since 1795, amounted to an average of twenty dollars per district. "Not to be considered a trifle unworthy of any account," he wrote. The main factor of success, however was not the money itself. "The people of this state are, in general, able to educate their children without the aid of any public gratuity, and if they fail in this respect, it is owing more to their want of proper schools than sufficient means." The act succeeded because it created a means of community control of education and a sense of permanency to the endeavor. "The great benefit of the act consists in securing the establishment of common schools, wherever they are necessary; in organizing them on a permanent foundation, and in guarding them against the admission of unqualified teachers." While undoubtedly many of these schoolhouses were in fact crude log buildings, barns, or other temporary spaces, by creating a common civil method for building schools and managing funds, the act had made possible the construction of publicly owned district buildings and a means for selecting acceptable teachers. The fact that so many districts complied with the law so quickly suggests that New Yorkers by and large approved of the plan, and, for reasons we shall see in chapter 5, had both educational and noneducational incentives to build schoolhouses.[50]

While the common school law effectively ended ecclesiastic control of mass education, it was not devoid of religious influence or intent. Just as the founders had invoked a generic Christian-republican God, so the 1811 committee described the civil purpose of common education in religious terms. In fusion of religious and civil philosophy, the committee described the republican function of common schools as follows: "To rescue man from that state of degradation to which he is doomed, unless redeemed by education, to unfold his physical, intellectual, and moral powers; and to fit him for those high destinies which his Creator has prepared for him, cannot fail."[51] Those "high destinies" meant republican government in this world, however, not salvation in the next.

The subordination of religion to a broader civil, secular purpose of education emerged in plans for the common schools' curriculum. The state common school committee of 1811 recommended that schools ought to include the same curriculum described by the original 1795 act, including "those branches that are indispensably necessary to every person in his intercourse with the world, and to the performance of his duty as a citizen." Among these they included religion and morality, cautiously writing that "Connected with the introduction of suitable books, the commissioners take the liberty of suggesting that some observations and advice touching the reading of the BIBLE in the schools might be salutary. In order to render the sacred volume productive of the greatest advantage, it should be held in a very different light from that of a common school book." With the hope of fostering republican virtue, they stated that the Bible "should be regarded as a book intended for literary improvement, not merely, but as inculcating great and indispensable moral truths also. With these impressions, the commissioners are induced to recommend the practice introduced into the New York Free School, of having select chapters read at the opening of school in the morning. And the like at the close in the afternoon."[52] Moral truths, not Divine Truth; the Bible as a source of republican virtue. The committee, and the legislature, left the matter to school districts to decide for themselves.

The New York City Exception

The committee made an unusual choice by referring to New York City as an example of how common schools ought to use the Bible. New York City schools proved the common school system "rule" with their exception. Since colonial times, New York City had cut a conspicuous figure in state politics, being an exceptional city by international, never mind state, standards. The schools of the city reflected this difference. The state legislature had a strong hand in New York City governance, a joint committee of the governor and the senate appointing the city's mayor and state legislative acts regulating many aspects of city government. Treated in separate legislation from the 1812 common school law, New York City operated schools by an entirely different system from the rest of the state, one which at once mollified church political pressure that emanated from the city and also recognized the entrenched pattern of private or ecclesiastic control over education. Historian Michael Katz has called this method "paternalistic voluntarism."[53] Beginning with the 1795 act,[54] and again in 1813, the state fund went directly to private and church-run charity schools within the city, including the Free School Society (founded in 1805), the Orphan Asylum Society, the Society of the Economical School in the City of New York (for children of West Indian refugees), the African Free School, and "such incorporated religious societies in said city as now support or hereafter shall establish charity schools within said city, who may apply for the same," although none did so until 1820.[55] These schools targeted children not otherwise educated in parochial schools or by private schoolmasters, and they were essentially charity schools for the poor.[56]

Instead of framing a common school "system," the act supported the traditional mode of nonpublic control of education. Broadest in scope and size, the Free School Society quickly dominated the charity school scene in New York City. The society itself consisted of a board of mostly elite New York City businessmen, with George Clinton's nephew—and Mayor of New York—DeWitt Clinton as president. The society's schools employed the cheap and mechanistic Lancastrian system, which used a single teacher to instruct hundreds of children through a minutely detailed curriculum, ability classification, and student monitors.[57] The schools serve as an early example of elite attempts to use education for controlling the poor, and the highly disciplinarian mode of instruction easily fit the society's view of the poor as those lacking self-control and moral substance.[58] Moreover, it demonstrated the growing connection between pietistic pan-Protestantism and urban social reform—though the school retained a distinctly Quaker feel, the members hailed from a number of Protestant sects. For their part, families who patronized the school took advantage of the opportunity to acquire a basic education for free, though their subscription to the society's larger goals is questionable.[59]

Echoes of the religious aspects of colonial education resounded in the curriculum of the society's schools as well as in the private form of governance. The society encouraged not just general religious piety but specific sectarian instruction. In 1814, it reported that "The afternoon of every Tuesday, or third day of the week, has been set apart for this purpose; and the children have been instructed in the catechisms of the churches to which they respectively belong." The children thus instructed included: Presbyterian, 271; Episcopal, 186; Methodist, 172; Baptist, 119; Dutch Church, 41; Roman Catholic, 9. Moreover, on Sunday, the society required children to assemble at its school, thence to be conducted to their respective churches.[60] In turn, rather than dirty their own hands, established churches increasingly relied on the society to educate their own indigent children.[61]

The New York City exception to the state common school system can be explained in two interconnected ways. First, the city system reflected the reality of its social order. In the early national period, New York City (population 75,000 in 1805) already had all of the problems of a major city with virtually no public solutions. Private philanthropy provided all social programs, not just education. More importantly, New York City society contained discernable class differences propped up by church affiliation. A mercantile elite topped the social order, and their Anglican, Episcopalian, Presbyterian, and Old Dutch Reform churches were centers of social status and power. Likewise, even before the first wave of Irish immigrants (usually associated with urban poverty) in 1818, the city already had recognizable slums and a crime problem stemming from poverty.[62] Somewhere in the middle, workingmen belonged to a variety of churches, though a majority joined no church at all.[63] (Universal White male suffrage would not come until 1826.) The entrenchment of churches and their elite members, combined with the city government's commitment to private charity to cure a host of social problems, made anything like the statewide system for education unlikely.

Second, the New York City exception served state political interests. Although a full party system had not yet developed, alliances tended to balance Jeffersonian Democrats, who represented upstate farmers, religious freethinkers or minorities, and New York City artisans against urban Federalists and later Whigs, centered in New York City, who represented the economic and religious elite, as well as former Tory interests in church and state.[64] It is not surprising that New York City's elite got what they wanted—state support of the status quo—while the rest of the state got something else entirely, a democratic system of managing local schools.

New York City's exception did not last, however. In 1822, 1832, and finally in 1840, religious groups challenged the monopoly of the ostensibly nonsectarian but clearly Protestant Free School Society. The final controversy in 1840 sounded the death knell for private, quasireligious control of mass education in New York City. In this famous, and often recounted, "school war," the Catholic Church charged that the Free School Society's management of schools offended non-Protestants and kept thousands of children out of school. The Church called for an even share of the state school fund (and local property tax authorized by the legislature in 1831). Other churches filed petitions as well, staking their claim for public funds should the Catholics succeed. When the city government sided with the Free School Society, the controversy spilled over into the state legislature.[65]

In the legislature, the issue of religious instruction in particular took a back seat to the larger issue of control. The Free School Society, critics claimed, failed to provide a democratic system for managing schools. As a result, centralized, undemocratic control led to religious tyranny. The State Superintendent of Public Instruction charged that the society operated "without allowing to the parents of the pupil the direction of the course of studies, the management of the schools, or any voice in the selection of the teachers."[66] The state assembly's committee on the subject concluded that "Such a concentration of power into mammoth machinery of any description is odious to the feeling, and sometimes dangerous to the rights, of freemen."[67]

The assembly passed legislation disbanding the Free School Society and creating a civil system of control along the lines of the state common school system. Such a system could alleviate religious conflict by placing decision making in the hands of a school's constituents. "The practical consequence" of this process, wrote the State Superintendent, "is that each district suits itself, by having such religious instruction in its schools as is congenial to the opinion of its inhabitants."[68] This pluralistic view of religion's role in mass education allowed as much religion, practically speaking, as any parent in the state would tolerate. The senate accepted the bill in principle but added its own proviso about religious instruction. Moderating the principle of majority rule in religious matters, the senate included a proscription against any *sectarian* instruction in particular—a move reminiscent of the founders' fears of organized religion in general. Expressions of congenial unanimity in religious belief—culture religion—did not threaten the civil ends of the school system; furthering the ends of any particular church did. It was a Pyrrhic victory for the Catholic Church. In its very quest to extend ecclesiastic control over mass education, it had aroused the same fears that had led to the state common school system in the first place. As a result, New York City acquired a publicly controlled system of mass education explicitly exclusive of church control.

State over Church: The Effects of Democratic Control of Education

Thus far I have described the intentions of political leaders and the laws they enacted. I have done this to provide an explanation for why the laws looked as they did, replacing parochial and private control of education with a civil system but simultaneously employing religious rhetoric in its justification. An important question remains. How did the people of New York State react to this legislation? How did they understand the relationship between religion and the local, publicly controlled school? New York City, with the best-documented history of education, operated under a different system and was hardly representative of the state or the future development of American public schooling (though it is sometimes used as evidence for the religious foundation of common schooling).[69] While few local school sources survive from upstate New York in the early national period, a critical one does—reported statistics on Bible reading. Situating these in the social context of the time describes the relationship between religion and common schooling as it was originally understood, as religion and democracy collided in the smallest, most vibrant political unit in American society: the school district.

The legislature intended the common school system to spread mass education across the state by providing a modest financial incentive while requiring compliance. Neither necessarily explains the growth of the system at the local level, however. The state fund was too small to cover teachers' salaries on its own, requiring district matching at the least, in combination with rate bills (tuition assessed from parents by the district on a *per diem* basis). As for compulsory participation, we should not assume that because the tiny state government required towns to do something, that they actually would. In colonial Massachusetts and Connecticut, for example, towns had a long history of intentionally failing to comply with state educational laws, finding it cheaper and easier to pay a fine in penalty. In New York State, proclivity to noncompliance would be even stronger in upstart, upstate communities pushing the frontier of settlement. Rather, the system caught on because it suited the interests of a majority of the state's residents, costing little in tax, aside from the initial procurement of a schoolhouse, and ensuring close local supervision over spending.

New York State saw dramatic developments in the generation following the first disbursement of the common school fund in 1815. The completion of the Erie Canal hastened the growth of New York City as the nation's leading commercial city and drew immigrants from New England and abroad by the millions to the state's fertile farmlands and prosperous towns and cities. Overall, the state's population grew from 1.4 million in 1820 to 2.4 million in 1840.[70] The number of children ages five to sixteen tripled. As the human tide washed into the state, common people altered the political landscape as well as the physical, winning universal white male suffrage in 1826.[71] These settlers filled in the loosely described towns, creating new school districts as they settled, or moving into old ones.

A second significant change took place in religion. Beginning in central upstate counties along the Erie Canal, a great conflagration of religious revivalism consumed the Northeast in the 1820s and 1830s. The "burned over district" of central New York State was hardest hit, but the movement's ideological components—a rejection of Calvinist predestination and communitarian religion and an affirmation of individualistic salvation and social reform—permanently altered traditional American religion.[72] In emerging towns and small cities, religious changes allied urban middle-class culture and evangelical religion.[73] While the fusion of class and religion stalled in rural and small-town areas (where social class itself did not have the same meaning), nevertheless, the revivalist ideology affected churches significantly, paradoxically increasing the role of personal religion in social activism while diminishing the role of churches as centers of moral and social authority in community life. Part of the downward slide of traditional church dominance in community life stemmed from a deemphasis on particularistic religion. In one community, for example, well-to-do families gave money for the construction of churches not of their own faith, including a Catholic one, suggesting that any Christian religion, for them, was better than none at all.[74] Overall, this Second Great Awakening made an indelible mark on traditional religion, "democratizing" American Christianity.[75] It also happened simultaneously with the sharp decline in church control of mass education.

It is important not to overestimate the impact of organized religion and religious revival, however. First, there is a qualitative difference between religion as expressed by formal organizations, churches, and theologies—dogma—from what Winthrop Hudson has called "culture religion." Evangelicals constituted a small minority of the population.[76] For example, while church membership grew tenfold from 1800 to 1850, only 1 in 8 people was an actual church member during the latter year.[77] There were also significant differences among sections of the state, as variations in settlement patterns had mixed consequences for religion and schooling.[78] In one town in western New York, settled by New Englanders, an observer noted, "A very large proportion of the community attend no public worship."[79] Because the West was a tabula rasa, with no established churches or history of ecclesiastic social control, historian Curtis Johnson points out, "These settlers were not content simply to reproduce the religious institutions further east. Western Churches would be built in accordance with democracy and common sense."[80] In short, the changing nature of religion during the formative years of the common school system was very real but probably had greater impact in cities and those places where democratic control either did not yet matter (New York City), where the effects of democratic control could be diluted through bureaucratic systems, or in those areas where the advocates constituted a majority of the voting population.

On the heels of the successful rise of the common school system in the 1810s and 1820s, Protestant social reformers, many of them clergy, called for change. This "common school crusade" sought to improve, expand, and enlighten mass education, pushing a curriculum based on explicit moral instruction, improved teacher professionalism, and increased funding. The movement had the widespread support of Protestant clergy, many of whom were active as leaders at the local level and added a sense of millennial destiny and a notion of an explicitly Christian Republic.[81] In two seminal articles on the relationship between common schools and religion in these years, Timothy Smith and David Tyack have documented the close identification of common school reformers in the 1830s and 1840s with Pan-Protestant, republican ideology. Often ministers were the leading writers and institution builders of the movement. Wrote Smith:

> By their establishment and control of both public and private schools, churchmen stamped upon neighborhoods, states, and nation an interdenominational Protestant ideology which nurtured dreams of personal and social progress. By the middle of the nineteenth century, leading citizens assumed that Americanism and Protestantism were synonyms and that education and Protestantism were allies.[82]

For their part, ministers of established Protestant sects, Congregationalists and Presbyterians, had already begun to face the democratic music in their own churches by adopting methods used by Methodists and Baptists—that is, persuasion and evangelism.[83] Coupled with the political ideology of the Whig Party and the evangelistic zeal of Protestantism and fueled by the inspirational writings of Horace Mann, Pan-Protestant school reform became a kind of middle class "Chicken Soup for the Soul."[84]

Yet while this analysis described middle-class reformers and clergy well, it does not necessarily apply to the realities of schooling in the majority of districts in New York— particularly in the early decades, when the democratic nature of the common school system meant that the schools reflected the religious complexion of rural masses, not the comfy middle class. Jacksonian democracy pushed against established social institutions, especially in smaller communities, where elites were both less ensconced in educational bureaucracy and less likely to identify with revival religion.[85] For these folk, the Pan-Protestant zeal of middle-class reformers was not, apparently, compelling. Common folk in the state's 11,000 school districts (by 1840) did not express their ideas with the same prolific body of writing and associational literature as did common school crusaders. Nevertheless, the sparse evidence of school practice that does exist, when set in context, suggests the will of local, district majorities. Did voters practice what crusaders preached? Two examples in particular provide important evidence of the relative weakness of church influence in schools, and the tension between religiously minded reformers and state voters: the Bible Tract Controversy of 1824 and reported statistics on Bible reading.

Conflict between Pan-Protestant religion and democratic control of schools flared at the state level within a decade of the first disbursement of the school fund. In 1824, Superintendent Yates (Gideon Hawley's successor, and also state attorney general) suggested in an official report that common schools distribute nondenominational biblical tracts as awards for special school competitions and celebrations, probably in response to pressure from the New York Tract Society. He met with immediate protest from the residents of the town of Lebanon, which appealed to the state legislature on the grounds that such a suggestion constituted an inappropriate attempt to foist sectarian religion on local common schools, despite the society's avowed nonsectarian, Pan-Protestant mission. Two Albany newspapers, *The Albany Microscope* and the *Telescope*, sided with the protesters. Soon a hastily formed legislative committee concurred, forbidding any such action in the future, because "conversion of the common schools into channels for [Pan-Protestant Bible tract's] circulation would excite hostility and apprehension of encroachment upon religious tenets."[86] The legislature's rejection of the Pan-Protestant organization's literature, it seems logical to assume, was based upon the assumption of strong political support among the legislature's constituency: voters.

Stronger evidence of the weakness of Pan-Protestantism in early common schools comes from reported use of the Bible. Common school reformers held dear the idea of nonsectarian religious instruction. Such teaching could be accomplished, the argument went, by the practice of reading the Bible without teacher comment and through simple, nondenominational Protestant prayers, particularly the Lord's Prayer.[87] This convenient intellectual fiction—that reading the Bible was a religiously neutral act—rested on the argument that the Bible was not only worthy of study for literary purposes but also contained immutable, moral, republican truths. Said one county school officer from Wayne County in 1843, "Let it be remembered that it is to the Bible we are indebted for the very idea of man's natural equality, upon which rests the temple of freedom." For his part, this county superintendent pressured teachers to use the Bible in a neutral manner, promising that, "wherever the Bible is introduced and treated as the Word of God, its purifying and ennobling influence is seen in teacher and pupils."[88] To common school crusaders in general, Bible reading without note would be like a stake through the heart of the twin monsters of sectarian common schools, built around religiously homogeneous districts, and strictly secular education, which, in their view, tended toward moral degradation and atheism.[89] Spokespeople for the newly emerging middle class, anxious in the face of profound social change, flocked to the Bible as the epitome of the common school education.[90]

How common was Bible reading in the early common schools of New York State? Popular wisdom has long assumed that Bible reading was near universal practice in public schools in some undefined past. Twentieth-century observers saw Supreme Court decisions as "secularizing" the schools that had once been universally religious. Late-nineteenth-century observers, too, looked with disapproval at the lack of Bible reading and assumed that it *had* been universal early in the century; early-nineteenth-century observers, frustrated by the lack of Bible reading, harked back to the days of the "Puritan fathers."[91] Historian R. Laurence Moore has observed that in the language of the landmark Supreme Court Decisions in *Engel v. Vitale,* which outlawed prayer in public schools in 1962, and *Abington School District v. Schempp,* which outlawed Bible reading in 1963, for example, both sides of the debate assumed that Bible reading had "deep roots in the nation's founding principles." Yet even among contemporary scholars, Moore writes, the assumption continues that common schools began religious, only to face later "secularization."[92] The democratic model of New York's common school system in the early 1800s had replaced theocratic control of education, and designers of the system ever held religious ends to be secondary to civil ones. Common school crusaders pushed moral education (both as a natural result of study in the 3 Rs and as an additional subject, with Bible reading as its source), but the design of the common school system remained secular. Did this religious agenda penetrate local districts? Did democratic control at the local level produce what were in essence religious, Protestant schools? For a century, many historians have argued that local control did produce actively Protestant schools, with Bible reading "at the core of the curriculum."[93] Available evidence in New York State suggests otherwise.

Beginning in 1827, state superintendents solicited information on the "common usage" of various textbooks and reading materials in the common schools of each town, including the "New Testament and Bible "(see Figure 2.1). From that time until the superintendent ceased collecting such statistics in 1840, the number of towns reporting the use of the Bible rose slightly and then plummeted, from a high of 216 in 1830 (28 percent of 773 towns total) to a final count of 84 (11 percent) in 1840.

These numbers highlight several important features in the relationship between religion and early common schools. The first is the most obvious: even at its peak in 1830, reported Bible use never reached even a third of towns in the state. Second, reported Bible use declined by 60 percent from 1830 to 1840—precisely the time that reformers in New York and nationwide began their crusade to make nonsectarian Bible reading a centerpiece of a common school education. The most popular text in 1840—used generally in 470 towns—was *Webster's Spelling Book.*[94]

The statistics reveal geographic patterns as well. Table 2.1 compares Bible statistics from 1830, the peak year, and 1836. It shows that in six years, nine counties reported increasing Bible use, ten reported no change, and thirty-five experienced decline. Overall, reported Bible use declined 43 percent in six years and would decline further by 1840 to 40 percent of its 1830 level.

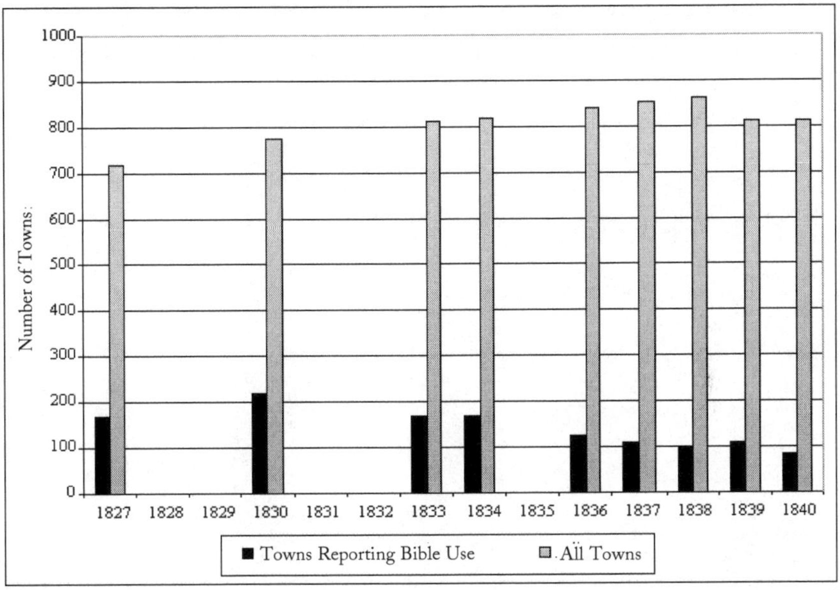

FIGURE 2.1 Number of Towns Reporting "General Use" of Bible and Testament, 1827–1840 (Data not available for some years).
Source: Annual Reports of the State Superintendent of Common Schools of the State of New York, 1830, 1836–1841.

Plotted on a map of the state, these statistics reveal regions of relative strength and weakness of Bible use. Figures 2.2 (1830) and 2.3 (1836) show the number of towns per county reporting Bible use as a percentage of all towns in that county. In 1830, reported Bible use generally corresponded to two areas of the state: that string of counties running up the mid- and upper-Hudson Valley alongside the New England states of Connecticut, Massachusetts, and Vermont; and the "burned-over" district of central New York, which included Oneida, Onondaga, and Otsego Counties. Bible use proved least popular in the most rural and remote sections of the state—western and northern New York State, and the lower Hudson Valley counties along its western side. Yates County, a seeming anomaly in the middle of the western end of the state, had 86 percent of its towns reporting general Bible use. This may partially be explained by the fact that Yates had only seven towns total (as opposed to it southern neighbors, Steuben and Allegany Counties, with twenty-three and twenty-four towns each, respectively). The white hole in the north center of the state, Hamilton County, lay in the heart of the Adirondacks.

TABLE 2.1 Number of Towns Reporting General Use of Bible and Testament, 1830 and 1836, by County, Excluding New York City (n=number of towns with general use of Bible, p=percent of towns using Bible relative to all towns in a county that filed reports)

County	*1830*		*1836*		*% Change*	
	n1	*p1*	*n2*	*p2*	*(n2-n1)/n1*	*(p2-p1)/p1*
Albany	5	56	3	30	-40	-46
Allegany	6	25	2	7	-67	-72
Broome	3	38	1	9	-67	-76
Cattaraugus	4	24	3	13	-25	-46
Cayuga	3	15	1	5	-67	-67
Chatauqua	3	14	3	13	0	-7
Chenango	7	37	2	11	-71	-70
Clinton	2	29	1	13	-50	-55
Columbia	6	38	7	39	+17	+3
Cortland	1	9	2	18	+50	+100
Delaware	4	22	7	39	+75	+77
Dutchess	6	33	1	5	-83	-85
Erie	1	6	1	6	0	0
Essex	7	47	4	27	-43	-43
Franklin	3	30	3	25	0	-17
Genesee	4	18	2	8	-50	-56
Greene	7	70	3	27	-57	-61
Herkimer	4	22	0	0	-100	-100
Jefferson	2	11	2	11	0	0
Kings	0	0	1	17	—	—
Lewis	4	44	3	27	-25	-39
Livingston	3	25	2	17	-33	-32
Madison	3	23	4	31	+33	+35
Monroe	2	13	2	12	0	-7
Montgomery	8	44	3	15	-63	-66
Niagara	2	18	0	0	-100	-100
Oneida	11	44	8	31	-27	-30
Onondaga	8	50	4	22	-50	-56
Ontario	2	15	0	0	-100	-100
Orange	1	8	1	7	0	-13
Orleans	1	13	0	0	-100	-100
Oswego	6	35	0	0	-100	-100
Otsego	10	45	5	23	-50	-49
Putnam	0	0	0	0	0	0
Queens	1	16	3	50	+200	+213
Rensselaer	6	43	2	14	-67	-67
Richmond	0	0	0	0	0	0
Rockland	0	0	2	50	—	—
Saint Lawrence	6	26	1	4	-83	-85
Saratoga	6	30	2	10	-67	-67
Schenectady	3	50	4	67	+33	+34
Schoharie	2	20	2	20	0	0
Seneca	0	0	0	0	0	0
Steuben	6	26	0	0	-100	-100
Suffolk	4	44	1	11	-75	-75
Sullivan	0	0	2	22	—	—
Tioga	7	41	3	16	-57	-61
Tompkins	1	10	0	0	-100	-100
Ulster	8	57	6	43	-25	-25
Warren	2	22	0	0	-100	-100
Washington	7	41	4	24	-43	-42
Wayne	6	40	3	20	-50	-50
Westchester	6	29	6	29	0	0
Yates	6	86	2	25	-67	-71
Total	216	29	124	16	-43	-45

Source: Annual Reports, 1830, 51–59; 1836, 113–15.
Note: Tioga County split in 1836 into Tioga and Chemung Counties.

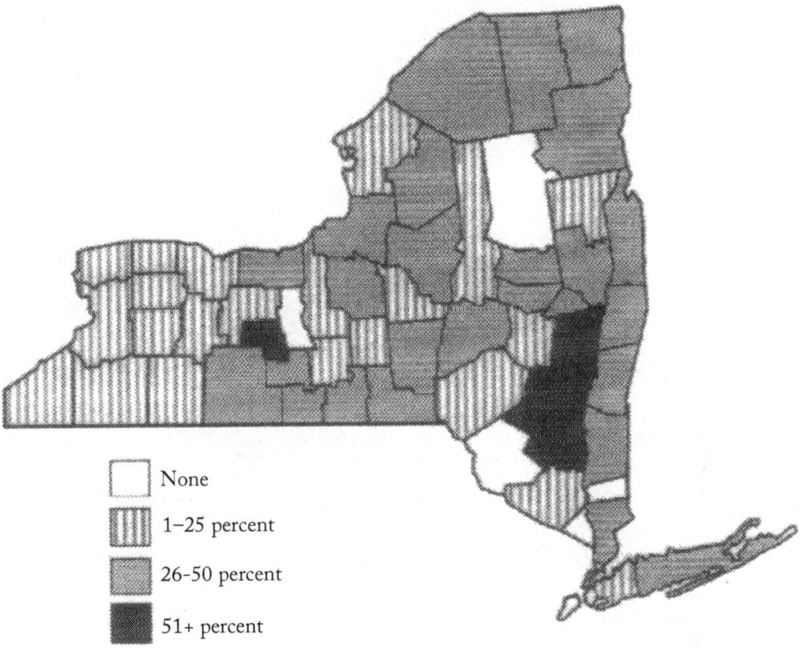

FIGURE 2.2 Percentage of Towns Reporting "General Use" of the "Bible and Testament" in 1830, by County
Note: The following counties were not yet formed in 1830 and do not appear on this map; they have been grouped with their parent counties: Fulton (Montgomery), Schuyler (Steuben, Chemung, Tompkins), Wyoming (Genesee).
Source: Annual Reports of the State Superintendent of Common Schools of the State of New York, 1830, 51–59.

By 1836, reported Bible use retreated in most counties—most notably in those where it had previously been strong (see Figure 2.3 and Table 2.1). A few places, such as Queens and Rockland Counties, actually showed significant increases. Even so, however, the patterns visible in 1830 remained. Several counties in the mid- and upper Hudson Valley and the burned-over district held at between 26 percent and 50 percent (Schenectady increased). The western and northern ends of the state continued to show much lower rates.

Reported Bible use in the 1830s, then, corresponded closely to two geographic areas: the burned-over district and areas along the Hudson River and New England border (which also happened to be the longest-settled regions of the state outside of New York City). Backwaters and areas on the edge of white settlement saw the least reported Bible use. Using regression analysis, a sociologist in 1966 found similar associations. In his study of the late 1830s in Massachusetts and New York State, Charles Bidwell reported that the counties most likely to report Bible use were those with a strong Puritan culture

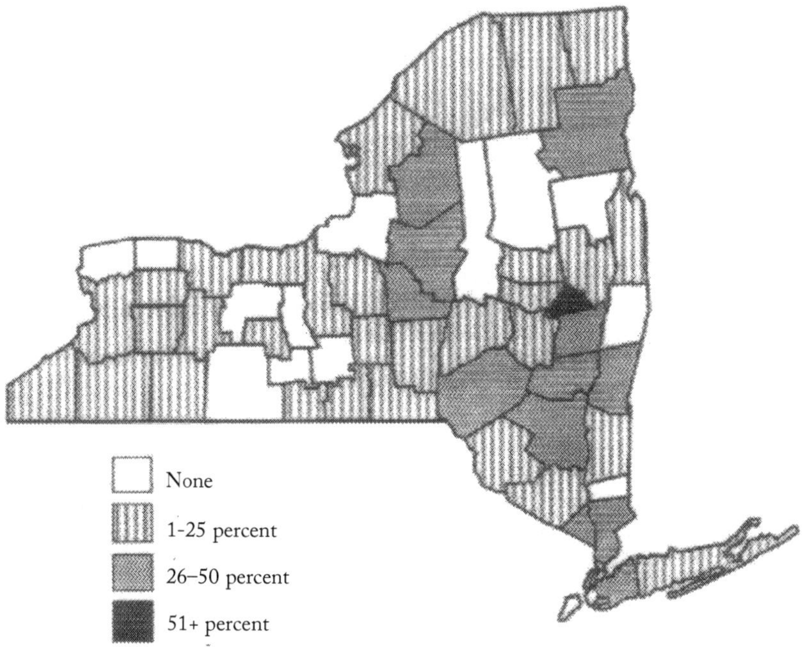

FIGURE 2.3 Percentage of Towns Reporting "General Use" of the "Bible and Testament" in 1836, by County
Note: The following counties were not yet formed in 1830 and do not appear on this map; they have been grouped with their parent counties: Fulton (Montgomery), Schuyler (Steuben, Chemung, Tompkins), Wyoming (Genesee).
Source: Annual Reports of the State Superintendent of Common Schools of the State of New York, 1836, 113–15.

and/or a history of religious revivalism and social reform. Having Yankee settlers per se did not make a significant difference—having Puritans in particular did. Bidwell also found a relationship between use of the Bible and patterns of local control. Bible use flourished in places where anxious middle-class Protestants could command a majority of votes. All depended, however, on the process of local control.[95] Seen as a fairly direct translation of the will of local majorities, reported Bible reading statistics suggest that the effects of religion on early common schools were fairly weak: the "secularization" of the common school in New York State occurred at birth.

Bidwell and I both rely heavily on the assumption that reported Bible reading statistics were a reliable gauge of local practice. As we have seen, historians have not universally accepted this view. The State Superintendent, and the county commissioners who reported to him, did not clarify what exactly they meant by "general use" of the Testament and Bible. One could argue that commissioners reported general use of the Bible only when schools used the Bible as a textbook much like any other. Given the near universal condemnation of "sectarian" instruction in common schools, however, this argument seems unlikely. Teachers probably would not comment on Bible reading, answering student questions as they would with other texts, except in extremely religious homogeneous communities. School commissioners, loud proponents of nonsectarian instruction in their written reports to the state, made no mention of such practice. Comments from some county commissioners suggest that they had a reasonably open understanding of Bible use that fell somewhere between use as a reading text and simple use as an opening exercise. The State Superintendent wrote in 1839:

> It is questionable whether instruction in matters of religious obligation can be carried, excepting so far as the school districts may make the Bible and Testament class books; and there can be no ground to apprehend that the schools will be used for the purpose of favoring any particular sect or tenet, if these sacred writings, which are their own safest interpreters, are read without any other comment than such as may be necessary to explain and enforce, by familiar illustration, the lessons of duty which they teach.[96]

In short, he encouraged using the Bible as a reader but not in the usual sense of a textbook, because the teacher should not be too involved. While we will never know exactly how each commissioner reported his statistics, there is some evidence that the numbers are fairly straightforward. In 1839, the commissioners of Allegany County reported that in two towns (approximately 10 percent of the towns for which they reported information) the Testament was in general use.[97] Five years later, in 1844, a commissioner from Allegany wrote explicitly that "Of the 105 schools visited [in sixteen towns], 9 schools were usually opened by reading a portion of the Bible, followed by prayer; 18 by reading only; 6 by singing, and the residue, 72, in the ordinary way."[98] In other words, only 26 percent of the schools he visited used the Bible for any reading whatsoever—a figure generally consistent with the reported statistics on "general use" from the late 1830s. Moreover, the commissioner understood the "ordinary" way of opening school as having no exercises. For Allegany County, at least, reported "general use of the Bible" was a good measure of *any* use.

The initial infrequency of Bible reading in common schools, coupled with its precipitous decline in the 1830s, suggests that the civil purposes of mass education envisioned by the founding generation succeeded. True, symbolic religious education in the form of Bible reading did constitute a significant aspect of schooling in a minority of school districts. And a softer form of culture religion could be found in popular readers and spellers, including Webster's. But by placing the state's system of mass education in the hands of the people themselves, with a method of governance that ensured a democratic process (forbidding strong religious encroachments), the legislature left religious instruction in the hands of local majorities. While common school crusaders performed rhetorical gymnastics to show that Bible reading offended no one, most New Yorkers appear to have adopted the opposite view: the Bible did not belong in common schools. Mass education, as a common school system, was inherently secular in purpose. Any religious education that occurred in the early common schools of New York stemmed not from the dictation of church leaders or the government but from the piety of the people themselves. And despite the persistence of a powerful mythology to the contrary, that peity did not generally include using the Bible in common schools.

Chapter 3

Religion in *Post-Bellum* State and Local School Governance

In 1876, Mr. B. T. Sheldon of Hyde Park, Dutchess County, wrote to State Superintendent Neil Gilmore in an indignant mood, with a rough hand.

> Has a teacher of a dist[rict] school in the country that has a trustee the right the same as a teacher in the City Schools that is controlled by a board of Public Instruction[?] has he a right to compell his schollares to learne phrases and speak in school if their parents objects to it or write compositions? Has he a right to take the Testament as a reading book[,] some of the states has passed a law that it should not be used in their schools[.] [I]f a teacher will not keep his school according to law how can he be stopped [?] can his certificate as a teacher be taken away from him or what course must be taken [?][*sic*][1]

Sheldon's letter, and thousands like it every year, connected individual districts to the state Office of Education. In this case, the letter voiced concern that the local process was failing and asked what steps might be taken to restrain a teacher's behavior when parents objected. The letter demonstrates a paradoxical understanding of the state's function in local administration. On the one hand, Sheldon did not know the state law concerning Bible reading, even though he seemed aware of the policy in other states. Moreover, he was not certain of what local process might be used to stop a teacher's objectionable practice in general, again not clearly understanding the law. On the other hand, the letter itself demonstrates a good understanding of the state's bureaucratic structure, and a confident use thereof. Like the apocryphal story that physicist Albert Einstein never bothered to memorize his own address (because, he said, he could always look it up in the phone book), Sheldon did not know the law, but he knew where he could find it.

Historians of religious policy in public schools after the Civil War have made much of state law and state bureaucracy, as well as state- and national-level policy talk.[2] Their work has provided a good account of the changes in state law regarding religion and the media-hyped controversy surrounding those laws. What remains to be done, however, is to develop a clear account of the context of state policy, the degree to which hype actually reflected local concerns, and, finally, the overall effectiveness of state policy in actual schools. This chapter builds a foundation for considering these issues by examining the relationship between the state Office of Education and actual district practice. Given that the state system of common schools was, at its core, a local system, how do we make sense of state policy and national debate? If the letter from Hyde Park is any indication, state law did not map cleanly onto local circumstance. To begin to understand the relationship between local schooling and the state, we must try to see the state's educational "system" as Sheldon might have seen it.

In this chapter, I examine three critical and interconnected aspects of the state-local relationship in New York. I begin with the supervisory chain of command that linked New York State to local schools, establishing the degree to which the state Office of Education commanded the attention of local districts. Second, I look briefly at the state bureaucracy as a source of information about religious policy, evaluating it as an educational institution of sorts. Finally, I explore in depth the most significant aspect of the state-to-local relationship in New York: the application of state law to local practice through the appeals process to the State Superintendent of Common Instruction. From these examples, we can see that the state influenced local policy, without a doubt. But it did so in specific ways—ways that gave local districts wide room for movement in settling religious conflicts. In fact, the appeals and other sources suggest that even as it struggled to function efficiently as a system of management, the district may have worked quite well at mediating ideological conflict.

Deconstructing the Dinosaur: State Supervision, 1865–1885

By the end of the Civil War, common schools had become a permanent fixture in New York State. Since the formative decades from 1820 to 1840, the organization of state educational bureaucracy changed several times, as did state educational law. The legislature cleaved the Office of Superintendent of Public Instruction from that of State Attorney General; county-level commissioners replaced town-level superintendents; and New York City's arcane system of a private school society fell—bitterly—to the upstate system of local, democratic control. The most significant state-wide change came right after the Civil War, in 1867, when an overwhelmingly Republican legislature passed a free school law in 1867, which abolished the small fees (called "rate bills") that some districts charged students. The character of common schools changed as well. By 1870, the number of districts leveled off at just under 12,000, the length of school year had grown to thirty-two weeks (hastened by minimum requirements set by law), and the average value of schoolhouses had nearly doubled—from $433 in 1865 to $744 in 1870. Approximately 70 percent of all children ages six to twenty-one enrolled in these schools, though daily attendance was half that.[3]

Despite these changes, however, the fundamental form of the common school system—a political method of democratic, local control—remained intact. One to three trustees, elected by residents of the district owning at least fifty dollars in personal property or having school-age children, ran most aspects of the district school. In large towns, residents could opt for a slightly modified district system called the "union free school district," which unified multiple districts in a multi-room school building under a common board of education, again composed of trustees. In cities, central boards of education vied with ward-level officers for control, but by and large, the ward system prevailed. The educational bureaucracy that held the schools together as a state "system" in the modern, organizational sense of the word played an extremely minor role in the drama of common school policy and practice.[4]

If the state bureaucracy at the end of the Civil War were an animal, then it would surely be a stegosaurus. Not only is the stegosaurus extinct (the usual meaning intended in describing something as a dinosaur), but more to the point, it is widely noted for the incredible disproportion between mass and mind—a thirty-foot long, two-ton body with a brain the size of a walnut. At the close of the Civil War, New York boasted a staggering 11,780 common school districts, 98 percent of them rural. Common schools enrolled over 900,000 students, who accounted for 91 percent of all students in the state.[5] The most distant district in Chatauqua County stretched 350 miles from the state Office of Education in Albany, and the Adirondack Mountains made other districts even more logistically remote. At the head of the state bureaucracy sat the State Superintendent of Public Instruction, elected by the state senate and assembly and supported by three clerks and a deputy. Below the superintendent sat 12,000 districts run by locally elected officials. In between, but really an upward extension of the districts (not a downward extension of the State Superintendent), hovered 111 untrained, locally elected county commissioners, sixteen professional city superintendents, and two representatives of city boards of education.[6]

As the head of a tiny, diffuse bureaucracy in charge of the massive body of common schools, the State Superintendent busied himself with a host of responsibilities. Foremost were the distribution of the state education fund, the collection and distribution of statistics and general information, and the enforcement of the school law. The first power, distribution of funds, proved the most potent tool in prosecuting the other two duties. Trustees who failed to report statistics did not receive their state money, nor did districts that failed to comply with the decisions and orders of the State Superintendent. (The state contributed an average of 43 percent of districts' funds for the teachers' salaries in 1870.)[7] The State Superintendent also had the power to certify teachers for life, a political spoils system that did not survive beyond the 1870s. In order to spread information, the State Superintendent collected statistics from most of the state's districts and published these in annual reports. He and his staff answered thousands of letters, gave lectures, and prepared special reports on various topics. The State Superintendent also acted as titular head of the state normal schools.

In addition, the legislature granted state superintendents an unusual power: the authority to adjudicate local disputes concerning common schools. Rather than take their grievances to the state courts, litigants filed appeals (usually by mail) to state superintendents, whose decisions were final. The appeals process gave state superintendents wide powers in local affairs, though these were curtailed by two factors. First, superintendents could exercise this power only in districts where residents filed appeals, having little power to directly stop illegal or questionable practices when no one filed formal objections. Second, for most of the late nineteenth century, superintendents respected the principle of local control over many matters, including religious exercises. (Superintendents did, however, intervene on behalf of religious minorities who objected to mandatory religious exercises, as we shall see later.) With the exception of the appeals process, and in answering correspondence, state superintendents had no direct connection to the management of the state's common schools.

Below the state Office of Education, the bureaucracy split into two streams: town and city.[8] In rural, small-town, and suburban schools (called "district schools"), county commissioners formed the intermediary layer of authority between the state and the district. Since they were elected directly, however, county commissioners were beholden more to their constituent districts than to Albany. Inspecting schools posed the greatest challenge for commissioners, as the law required them to visit every one of the 100 or so schools in their portion of the county (called a "commissioner district"), though it is likely that they sometimes did not.[9] Their single greatest power of office was to certify teachers, and since the original common school law of 1812, the state required all districts receiving the school fund to employ certified teachers. Nevertheless, common practice and necessity bent the law considerably from its intent. Until 1888, commissioners issued certificates based on whatever criteria they liked, from written public examinations to private interviews to on-the-spot certificates given to teachers after an observation. Moreover, commissioners issued varying certificate levels, from first to fourth grade, based on their assessment of a teacher's mastery of subject matter and pedagogical skills. A certificate also hinged upon the moral conduct of a teacher, though this appears to have been an issue of controversy only rarely.[10] In addition, commissioners adjudicated boundary disputes, organized teachers' institutes to encourage state-approved pedagogical methods, distributed state money, and answered questions about state law.[11] One assiduous commissioner summed up his year's work as, "Thirty days to examine teachers (400 examined); twenty-eight days at the teachers' institute, and teachers' meetings; thirty-four, in hearings; and one hundred and twenty, inspecting schools; not to mention making reports, apportioning school money, and correspondence (the latter over 2,000 enclosures)."[12] Another concluded that, "In accomplishing these duties, I have traveled, in sunshine and storm, cold and heat, over two thousand miles."[13]

Away from rail lines and good roads, some districts barely experienced the commissioner's authority at all, save by post. One Franklin County commissioner described a vivid, if an extreme, example in 1877:

> We left home early Monday morning, with horse, and light skeleton wagon, passed Paul Smith's, or as it has been called, the "St. George of the Wilderness," at about eight o'clock Tuesday morning; two or three hours' drive more brought us to the end of the carriage road, with the deep, clear waters of the Upper Saranac Lake at the left.... After telegraphing home our whereabouts, we exchanged our horse and wagon for a boat, and rowed up the lake eight miles, to "Sweeney Carry." Here we left the boat and took to the woods, on foot, eight miles further, on a trail, or path, which we followed tolerably well, having lost our way only once, which, fortunately, cost us only about one and one-half miles extra travel, and a corresponding anxiety of mind. Tuesday evening brought us to the residence of Simeon Moodie, who gave us a cordial welcome; and to us his pleasant farm, equipped with mowing-machine and modern agricultural implements, seemed to the wilderness what the oasis is to the Sahara. No wagonroad reaches this settlement, and scattered through its valleys, by its rivers, ponds, and lakes, are twenty-five

> children of school age. Wednesday I visited the school. The house, a frame structure, was full up to the average and in good repair. The children gave me a cordial welcome, and evinced a proficiency in their studies and general good deportment that should put to blush some of our would-be model schools. After a day's rest and a feast of fish and venison, we reached home Saturday, thus taking a full week to visit one school."[14]

The farther a district lay from the county seats of government (wherein resided commissioners), the less it felt commissioners' control. In fact, given their busy schedules, commissioners had little time to exercise influence over those schools they could easily reach.

Urban schools did not fall under the authority of county commissioners. Instead, city school charters authorized urban school boards to manage their own affairs, and the city superintendents they usually hired formed the second stream of bureaucracy between the state office and schoolhouse. While urban boards officially stood below the State Superintendent in the chain of command (mainly because Albany apportioned their money and collected their statistics), some considered themselves independent of the state, and big cities operated their own system of appeals. Legislative acts formed city school systems of governance, with no two alike. In a major appeals case in 1887, for example, the city of Binghamton argued that since it drew its authority from a legislative act the same as the State Superintendent (whose position did not appear in the state constitution), its schools were exempt from his authority.[15] Like the commissioners, city boards owed almost nothing to Albany and everything to their constituents.

Urban school boards varied in form and function. They drew members from a variety of sources, from ex-officio officers who held other positions in city government to mayoral appointees to officials elected at large or as ward representatives. Urban schools themselves resembled rural schools in that the ward, like the district, formed a geographically defined community that (in large cities) elected ward-level officials to choose teachers and maintain schools. City schools differed from rural ones, however, in that city school boards proved much more active, authoritative, and powerful supervisors than their rural counterparts, the commissioners. City boards licensed teachers, regulated the use of textbooks, often required symbolic exercises such as Bible reading and flag raising, published daily schedules, and developed curriculum.[16]

Together, the state Office of Education, county commissioners, and city superintendents formed the entire state educational bureaucracy beyond the local level. By design, the system lacked even moderate cohesion. And although benchmark court decisions in the late 1880s and 1890s (including the Binghamton case) upheld the state's supremacy, the Superintendent of Public Instruction almost never challenged city independence.[17] For their part, county commissioners did not work "for" the state office (though Albany officials did send them paychecks) but rather for the political parties and voters of their commissioner districts. As one commissioner candidly wrote, "Commissioners, as a general thing, are looking forward to a re-election, and do not desire to incur the displeasure of any one teacher or constituent, hence the degeneracy of our schools."[18] Overall, the state bureaucracy shared little cohesion, faced competing interests, and demonstrated remarkable smallness in the context of a massive state educational enterprise.

The State as Educator

Because the state bureaucracy relied so heavily on the intelligence of the people of New York to run its own affairs, the state Office of Education made modest efforts after the Civil War at instructing it about state policy. Targeting teachers, the legislature funded an increasing number of state normal schools (teachers' colleges) and, for the great mass of teachers who did not attend normal schools, required annual county-level "teachers' institutes." The legislature intended both policies to improve proficiency in state-approved pedagogy and content. Targeting a more general audience, the state published annual reports by the State Superintendent, periodic updates of the school code, and circulars addressing specific issues. (This effort was neither tightly organized nor thorough. District officers—in cities as well as in the country—frequently wrote to the Superintendent's Office to request updated copies of the school code, annual reports, and accounts of school policy not otherwise published by the state. A few letters describe trustees' absconding with the district's copy of the school code, which they considered a precious document in times of trouble.)[19] State superintendents, for their part, traveled about the state when time allowed to address educational associations and teachers' institutes.

Surprisingly, given their efforts toward informing its citizenry, superintendents made little effort to clarify policies toward religion. Normal schools offered no courses on religious instruction. Likewise, published agendas of teachers' institutes contain no mention of religion as a topic of discussion. At an institute in Onondaga County in 1885, the question of Bible reading came up in a general question-and-answer session. Could a teacher conduct religious exercises without the permission of the trustee? The institute director, a veteran leader of institutes statewide, confessed that neither he nor his assistants knew the answer.[20]

Superintendents occasionally referred to religion in their annual reports, though the high turnover among state superintendents and flip-flop of political party affiliation stifled coherence in the message. In 1874, Abram Weaver, a lame duck Democrat, penned an apologetic explanation for his refusal to grant state funds to "private or sectarian schools," citing such a proposal's unfairness to taxpayers. Two years later, his successor, Republican Neil Gilmour, uncovered a legal loophole that had allowed Grey Nuns to win teacher certification without a formal examination, and reported the ensuing scandal. He finished with an *un*apologetic warning of a Catholic plot to undermine public schools by giving money to "sectarian" schools.[21] Both appear connected to larger political purposes—courting pro- or anti-Catholic voters. Neither provided a specific policy guide for local behavior, however. Later, in 1885, Superintendent William Ruggles, a Democrat, published a clarification of state law regarding religious exercises, which he called a "subject of occasional contention in school districts, and of frequent applications to the State Superintendent for advice and instruction as to the law." Citing a forty-year-old body of case law, Ruggles concluded that the state constitution protected freedom of worship. "Interference therewith, in the way of discrimination or preference, even by legislative enactment is, by the express words of that instrument, prohibited."[22]

For most of the nineteenth century, state superintendents did not go to great lengths to publicize their decisions. The state did produce digests of appeals decisions in 1836 and 1844. These organized select appeals by subject and included do-it-yourself appeals forms as well as detailed descriptions of the process.[23] Not until 1879, however, did a State Superintendent offer an update—a digest of select appeals decisions to reflect the many changes in case law since the 1840s.[24] Like the others, the 1879 digest included specific instructions on how to file appeals. The state probably did not distribute this tome widely (certainly not to every school district). In 1887, a commissioner from remote Clinton County complained of a general lack of access to up-to-date copies of school decisions and the state school code: "A copy of the present school law should be in the hands of the trustees of every district in the State, and rulings of the State Superintendent upon cases of general interest ought to be collected and published, so that school commissioners may have some benefit of the late authorities in deciding questions that come before them."[25] The following year, State Superintendent Andrew Draper obliged in his annual reports, and by 1892, these reports included lists of all appeals, including their subject matter. He discussed appeals over religious matters in detail.[26]

The creeping movement toward wide publication of appeals decisions reflected a nascent tendency in the state educational bureaucracy toward progressive reform. Even as Superintendent Draper made annual reports of appeals decisions, he began a slow assault on democratic localism, including church-state compromises in several cities in the state. Progressive reform meant centralized, bureaucratic control, unified state law, and zero tolerance for local deviations. Nevertheless, the consistently passive stance of state law toward religious exercises endured into the 1890s. What remains to be seen is how much local school districts themselves experienced religion and public education as a district, as opposed to a state, problem.

Appeals to the State Superintendent

As the only forum in which local districts officially interacted directly with the State Department of Public Instruction, the appeals process to the superintendent forged the strongest link between the state and actual schools. The appeals process began in 1822, when the New York State Legislature invested the State Superintendent with the power to adjudicate local disputes in common schools. The move, intended to free the courts from petty disputes and speed the resolution of local problems, gave the superintendent considerable power over local affairs.[27] From that date until the first formal count in 1913, New York State residents filed over 12,000 appeals to the state's chief educational officer. Together, the appeals constitute a remarkable historical source, revealing a critical facet of the relationship between local public school districts and the growing state educational bureaucracy: the connection between local control and state law. The process also offers the most striking example of the weakness of religion as a state educational issue.

Before 1822, it had been common practice for judges in the state court system to consult the superintendent on educational cases, but the office had no power to render decisions directly. Three factors pressured the legislature to grant such power: the need (expressed by judges) for the superintendent's expertise, the interest of the judicial system in ridding itself of petty adjudication, and the interest of locals in having disputes settled quickly. The move gave the State Superintendent unprecedented control over educational matters (compared, for example, to the largely hortatory roles of Horace Mann in Massachusetts or Henry Barnard in Connecticut).[28] With the passage of time and development of precedent, the appeal evolved into a formal, if an exceptional, legal procedure: an early form of the growing nineteenth-century tradition of *administrative*, as opposed to *judicial*, justice.[29] The legal grounds for an appeal were wide and elastic, essentially "any act or decision pertaining to the common schools."[30] Though they usually concerned such issues as taxes, boundary disputes, and teacher salaries, appeals could be brought by persons feeling aggrieved by any decision made by a meeting or public officer of the state. Almost no record of appeals before the Civil War survives, but evidence suggests that the State Superintendent handled slightly more than 100 cases annually, from a low of eighty in 1842 to a high of 184 in 1868. Informal appeals, in the form of letters, numbered annually in the thousands.[31]

As a form of administrative justice, the appeals process both resembled the usual judicial procedure and differed from it dramatically. Like other suits, appeals could be brought by any person and were not limited to whites, males, citizens, or legal voters. Moreover, appeals followed standard procedures for evidence and burden of proof, and the State Superintendent published specific requirements for phraseology in the school code. All appeals had to be verified under oath by a local justice of the peace or county commissioner, had to be filed within thirty days of the offending act or decision, and had to be copied to the defendant, who then had another ten days to file an answer. Usually the State Superintendent would elicit replies and rejoinders from the litigants if he needed further information.[32] State superintendents did, occasionally, refuse to hear appeals that did not conform to this standard procedure, treating these as letters instead.

Yet the appeals process differed fundamentally from that of the state's judicial system. Because the State Superintendent had but one office, in Albany, he could not reasonably require personal appearances to decide appeals. Thus the appeals system rested on correspondence (*ex parte* proceedings) rather than on evidence taken in personal hearings.[33] The ability to litigate in writing made the need for an attorney less pressing, and many appellants did not use attorneys at all.[34] In fact, the correspondence model may have been so accessible that it encouraged petty litigation out of scale with the authority of the State Superintendent. In 1875, for example, L. H. Hanchett, a student in the town of Schroeppel, Oswego County, filed a legally correct appeal over his placement in the algebra standings of his class, and the teacher's right to expel him for protesting it. For those who did use attorneys, including illiterate litigants, legal costs ranged from twenty dollars to over 100 dollars, depending on the complexity of the case and the level of an attorney's involvement.[35] Since many cases were filed by groups of people (sometimes over a dozen), these fees probably were divided evenly or covered by tax in the case of legal expenses incurred on behalf of districts.[36]

While the appeals were more "democratic" in their accessibility than the state court system, the State Superintendent wielded disproportionately strong powers to adjudicate them. By evaluating the legality of acts and meetings, the State Superintendent had the power to stay and nullify proceedings, regulate practice, levy taxes, and remove trustees and other officials from office by declaring them unfit or illegally elected. In one case in Watervliet, Albany County, in 1897, he actually superseded the board of education, appointing the city superintendent himself.[37] From districts that refused to comply, the State Superintendent usually withheld state educational funds or issued warrants to local officials. And unlike those of the state court system, the State Superintendent's decisions were "final and conclusive, and not subject to question or review in any place or court whatever."[38] In short, appealing to the State Superintendent was a double-edged sword, offering a speedy, affordable resolution from which there was no recourse.

As the only forum in which the state authority interacted directly with local school districts, the appeals process created a unique body of historical evidence. Historians of the nineteenth century are familiar with the frequent lack of local sources. Small-town and rural policy often rested on the spoken word and a handshake. Judging by those documents that have survived, when New Yorkers (a nonurban majority until 1880) did generate paperwork, it usually was sparse in detail. State governments, on the other hand, had the wherewithal to collect, to report, and—significantly—to save information. The appeals to the State Superintendent offer the best of both worlds: details of district-level policy and practice collected, labeled, and preserved by the state.

The appeals are not, however, a historian's panacea. The state did not begin publishing indexes of appeals and decisions until 1887, and it did not list brief content descriptions until 1892. Moreover, a tragic fire in the State Education Building on March 29, 1911, consumed all of the superintendent's decisions about the appeals to that date.[39] Since state law literally required the superintendent to keep all decisions in his office, those not published elsewhere were lost forever.[40] Fortunately, for posterity, a superintendent or one of his clerks decided that the appeals documents themselves—as opposed to the decisions—did not fall under the storage clause, and thus kept them elsewhere. This move, probably intended to save space, spared all appeals case files decided from 1868 onward, with an inexplicable gap from mid-1886 to 1892. Now they reside, unindexed and still bound in faded red tape, in the New York State Archive. They are fairly complete and in remarkably good condition. For this study, I have read, indexed, and entered into a database all surviving appeals to 1886.[41]

Who Appealed?

An analysis of this question confirms the widespread utility of the appeals process, but it also portrays differing relationships between New Yorkers and the state governments. The appeals rarely offered information about appellants as individual people. Almost all were men, and the few women who appealed were teachers complaining of a contract violation. Moreover, teaching was the only occupation mentioned consistently in the appeals, with teachers accounting for 9 percent of all appellants. It is much easier to determine where appellants lived, since state clerks listed that information on the docket of each appeal. From 1868 to 1885, appeals came to the superintendent from every county in the state (see Table 3.1). The number of appeals from each county varied greatly, seemingly independent of population. Seneca County (located roughly halfway between Albany and Buffalo), with an average population of 28,466 (population of 1867 plus 1886 divided by two), filed the lowest number of appeals, only five. Chatauqua County, average population 58,297, proffered the most—ninety-one.[42] The county with the highest number of appeals per capita (2.7 per thousand), Hamilton County, was also the state's least populated county, with a population of only 3,288. Overall, New Yorkers from approximately 730 different towns and cities filed the 2,068 appeals in this sample. Plotted on a map of the state, the appeals cover space fairly evenly, though they did cluster in certain counties and towns, with a single large hole described by the Adirondack Mountains (see Figure 3.1). This geographic diversity suggests a process both well known and well used.

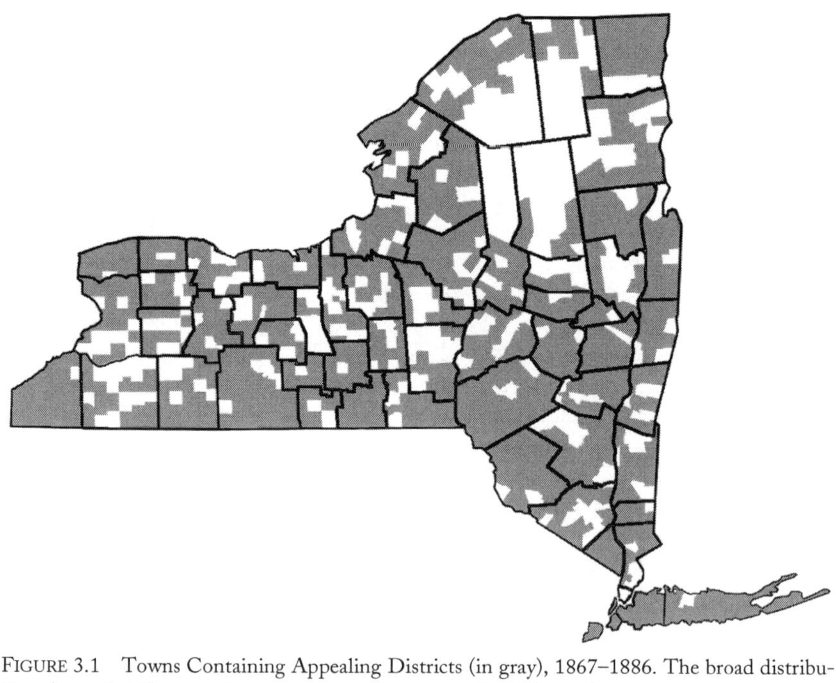

FIGURE 3.1 Towns Containing Appealing Districts (in gray), 1867–1886. The broad distribution shows that the appeals process was well known and widely used.
Source: New York State Archives. *Appeals Case Files of the State Superintendent of Public Instruction*. Series B0496–78, B0496–78A.

TABLE 3.1 Appeals by County and Population, 1867 to 1886

County	*Average Population (1867+1886)÷2*	*Number of Appeals*	*Appeals per 1,000 Inhabitants*
Albany	135197	14	0.10
Allegany	41048	63	1.53
Broome	43708	48	1.10
Cattaraugus	49482	40	0.81
Cayuga	60406	21	0.35
Chatauqua	58297	91	1.56
Chemung	37494	14	0.37
Chenango	39125	22	0.56
Clinton	48305	23	0.48
Columbia	46417	27	0.58
Cortland	25320	30	1.18
Delaware	42180	84	1.99
Dutchess	72198	38	0.53
Erie	187975	48	0.26
Essex	31580	37	1.17
Franklin	30268	20	0.66
Fulton	27749	9	0.32
Genesee	32013	29	0.91
Greene	32203	42	1.30
Hamilton	3288	9	2.74
Herkimer	40912	18	0.44
Jefferson	66276	53	0.80
Kings	455162	14	0.03
Lewis	29628	30	1.01
Livingston	38559	24	0.62
Madison	43309	40	0.92
Monroe	124569	26	0.21
Montgomery	34881	25	0.71
New York City	966343	1	0.00
Niagara	51728	45	0.87
Oneida	109067	70	0.64
Onondaga	105433	50	0.47
Ontario	46429	25	0.53
Orange	62827	25	0.40
Orleans	29366	10	0.34
Oswego	77056	72	0.93
Otsego	50007	39	0.78
Putnam	15013	16	1.07
Queens	74286	61	0.82
Rensselaer	101769	44	0.43
Richmond	33600	11	0.32
Rockland	24239	21	0.87
Saint Lawrence	83495	41	0.49
Saratoga	52524	28	0.53
Schenectady	22213	9	0.41
Schoharie	33132	42	1.27
Schuyler	18642	13	0.70
Seneca	28466	5	0.18
Steuben	71889	80	1.11
Suffolk	48305	36	0.74
Sullivan	32616	40	1.23
Tioga	30418	22	0.72
Tompkins	32571	30	0.92
Ulster	80724	65	0.81
Warren	23154	32	1.38
Washington	47058	32	0.68
Wayne	49599	40	0.81
Westchester	105093	66	0.62
Wyoming	30470	20	0.66
Yates	20213	10	0.49
Total	4455257	2068	0.46

Source: New York State Archives. *Appeals Case Files of the State Superintendent of Public Instruction.* Series B0496–78, B0496–78A.

The most startling feature of appellants is not where they came from but where they did not. In twenty years of appeals, virtually none arrived from major cities (see Table 3.2). New York, Brooklyn, Rochester, and Auburn filed one apiece. Albany and Buffalo filed none. (Only two small cities differed significantly: Poughkeepsie, in Dutchess County, had six, and Lockport, Niagara County, had eight.) *Per capita*, appeals were twenty-three times less likely to come from a resident of a city than a resident of a town district. As far as cities were concerned (seemingly residents as well as school leaders), the state bureaucracy did not apply to local matters, where each city's own appeals processes sufficed.

TABLE 3.2 Appeals from Incoporated Cities,* 1867–1886

City	*Location (County)*	*Population (1867+1886) ÷2*	*Number of Appeals*	*Appeals per 1,000 Inhabitants*
Albany	Albany	76,686	0	0.00
Auburn	Cayuga	17,246	1	0.06
Binghamton	Broome	12,872	1	0.08
Brooklyn	Kings	431,388	1	0.00
Buffalo	Erie	124,818	0	0.00
Cohoes (1869)	Albany	*19,416	0	0.00
Dunkirk (1880)	Chatauqua	*7,248	2	0.28
Elmira	Chemung	16,836	3	0.18
Hudson	Columbia	8,251	0	0.00
Lockport	Niagara	12,511	8	0.64
Long Island City (1870)	Queens	•17,129	2	0.12
Newburgh	Orange	16,366	4	0.24
New York	Kings	966,343	1	0.00
Ogdensburg (1868)	St. Lawrence	*10,341	0	0.00
Oswego	Oswego	20,202	3	0.15
Poughkeepsie	Dutchess	18,140	6	0.33
Rochster	Monroe	70,153	2	0.03
Rome (1870)	Oneida	*10,123	4	0.40
Schenectady	Schenectady	11,912	0	0.00
Syracuse	Onondaga	41,788	1	0.02
Troy	Rensselaer	48,020	0	0.00
Utica	Oneida	28,800	0	0.00
Watertown (1869)	Jefferson	*10,697	0	0.00
Yonkers (1872)	Westchester	*18,892	5	0.26
Total		2,016,178	44	0.02

*City Population=1886 only.
Source: New York State Archives. *Appeals Case Files of the State Superintendent of Public Instruction.* Series B0496–78, B0496–78A.
**Note:* Cities as designated by the Superintendent in the Annual Report for 1887.

Why Did People Appeal?

"Is there any point," asked the inspector, "to which you would like to draw my attention?" "To the curious incident of the dog in the night-time." "The dog did nothing in the night-time." "That was the curious incident," remarked Sherlock Holmes.[43]

Each appeal represents a perceived failure in local government and an attempt to supercede the local process using state authority. Twenty years of appeals to the State Superintendent catalogue the common school woes that New York State residents considered worthy of state intervention—a fossil record of the local bones of contention. Excavating these remains raises important questions: What challenges gripped common schools in an era of democratic localism?[44] Did conflict plague some types of schools more than others? To these ends, the appeals are as significant for what they did *not* say as for what they did. Like the dog that did not bark, the absence of certain issues in the appeals may be as telling as the presence of others.

Collectively, the subjects of the appeals describe the major functions of government on any level: taxation, the conduct of meetings, the regulation of municipal boundaries, and so on. I selected these categories based on the content of cases, not those affixed by judicial opinion (in *West's Digest*, for example).[45] Table 3.3 shows the percentages of appeal by type for the entire period. Reasons for appeal stemmed from the ordinary functions of officers and meetings as representatives of the state. The ratios of the various types remained fairly consistent over the entire period, suggesting that the functions of local government changed little over the period, or at least that their perceived failures did so.

Despite the accessibility and utility of the appeals process, there were some ends for which it was *not* a means. Appeals usually questioned the process of local government (the common school system) but rarely the content of instruction. Thus managerial matters—irregular meetings, taxes, questionable actions by the trustee—account for most of the appeals. In fact, instructional matters that directly concerned what or how children learned accounted for only 1 percent of all appeals, and much of this category questioned appropriate responses to student behavior, not curriculum. New Yorkers rarely appealed issues dealing with ideological differences of opinion. This should not be surprising—the state left such matters to local discretion, and classrooms rarely surfaced as major issues in the media or state politics.

The absence of *religion* in the appeals, on the other hand, is surprising and important. Controversy over religion in public schools engulfed national and state party politics in the 1870s (and again in the late 1880s). *Harper's* cartoonist Thomas Nast drew images of battling bishops and crusading common school men that cast the issue as bitter, divisive, and apocalyptic. Yet religion appeared as an issue in only 1.5 percent of appeals, usually as a complaint about religious meetings in the schoolhouse after hours.[46] The specific instance of religious exercises, including Bible reading in schools, amounted to only 0.5 percent of all appeals.

TABLE 3.3 Appeals by Subject, 1867–1886

Subject of Appeal	*Number*	*Percent of Total*
Proceedings of Meeting	583	28.2
Tax	393	19.0
Trustee's Actions	373	18.0
District Boundary	356	17.2
Broken Contract	139	6.7
Other*	73	3.5
Teacher's Certificate	58	2.8
Previous Appeal	39	1.9
Religious Use of Schoolhouse	22	1.1
Classroom Instruction	21	1.0
Religious Exercises	11	0.5
Total	2,068	100 (99.9)

Source: New York State Archives. *Appeals Case Files of the State Superintendent of Public Instruction.* Series B0496–78, B0496–78A.
Note: Includes actions of other district officers or individuals misuse of school property, and, hard-to-classify cases.

The lack of religious appeals might seem to be explained simply: appeals were not a forum for any ideological disputes—why should religion be exceptional? Yet unlike other curricular and cultural issues, religion had a foot in the legal door. Case law specifically, and repeatedly, ruled that schools could not conduct religious exercises during school hours if parents objected. With the exception of the controversy in New York City in the 1840s, the state legislature remained silent on statewide legislation for religion, honoring the long tradition of local control over such matters. Yet there was a body of case law, based on the decisions of state superintendents, which determined the legal status of religious exercises. From the antebellum era through the 1880s, superintendents steered a steady course, upholding the doctrine first espoused in 1839: prohibiting public funds to church-run schools, and, in turn, protecting the rights of religious minorities in the common schools.[47] Superintendent Rice declared in 1866:

> A teacher has no right to consume any portion of the regular school hours in conducting religious exercises, especially when objection is raised. The principle is this: Common schools are supported and established for the purpose of imparting instruction in the common English branches; religious instruction forms no part of the course."[48]

From 1839 to the turn of the century, state superintendents consistently prohibited religious exercises during school hours, but they did so in a manner that most respected localism. If a single parent objected, then a teacher could not lawfully conduct religious exercises during school hours. But optional exercises before the start of or following school were perfectly legal.[49]

If the appeals process promised at least moderate relief to religious minorities, then how do we explain the lack of appeals? Was the process accessible to those religious minorities—Bavarian-German, French-Canadian, and Irish Catholics, Evangelical Lutherans, and others—who would be likely to appeal, but for whom poverty and illiteracy in English could have been barriers to learning about and using the appeals process? For the very poor, especially those lacking a social network to share cost and responsibility for appeals, the process probably *was* too exclusive. Nevertheless, the process provided accessibility to a wide spectrum of people, including the illiterate, as long as costs could be shared. Moreover, group-based settlement patterns, party politics, and church membership gave those without power access to those who could write, and who did know the law.[50]

Perhaps those same folk, though able to use the appeals system, shied away from its formalism and expense. To test this theory, I have checked a second source: incoming letters to the State Superintendent of Public Instruction from 1873 to 1886.[51] Letters were an even more accessible form of communication with the state than appeals, costing three cents in postage and requiring only literacy. (They did not even require knowledge of the State Superintendent's address, as demonstrated by surviving envelopes labeled only "Superintendent of Public Instruction, Albany, New York.") If the lack of appeals on religious grounds stemmed from the difficulty of the appeals process alone, then far more complaints should appear in the letters, which usually sought advice and complained of various local problems.

In fact, the letters show an even *lower* rate of religious references. Of the 7,000 letters in this study, a mere 0.2 percent concerned religion. In other words, an appeal was twice as likely to concern religious exercises as a letter. The total number of complaints about religious exercises from 1873 and 1874—while Nast penned his cartoons, and the Republican Party waved the new bloody shirt—was ten: seven inquiries about the law and three complaints about actual practice (see Table 3.4). To put these numbers into perspective, I kept a list of the specific subjects of the first 1,000 letters from 1873.[52] Two concerned religious exercises. Of that same group, seven letters complained that the trustee had bought globes and maps for the classroom, and fifteen asked about how to deal with abusive or tardy students. The letter from Mr. Sheldon of Hyde Park at the opening of this chapter may have been representative of the relationship between common people and the State Superintendent, but his concern over religious policy was not. In a forum where legalese did not matter, questions or complaints about religious exercises remained conspicuously infrequent.

The letters strongly affirm what the appeals and other evidence already suggest: New Yorkers considered the problem of religious diversity a local problem, and there was little formal dissention from the decisions that local bodies reached regarding religious exercises. Local control failed to give satisfaction over a variety of issues—taxes, meeting procedures, boundary disputes—but was satisfactory for religion. Why did this pattern persist in the face of such religious diversity, and why for so long? The explanation does not stem from the inaccessibility of the appeals process, which was generally well known (judging by its geographic dispersion, a wide variety of surnames, including many Irish and German, and the relatively supportive position of the state), easily used, and well representative of the general concerns of the people. Rather, the explanation must lie at the local level itself.

LOCALISM'S "APPEAL"

Three possible explanations may account for the lack of appeals and letters about religious controversy. The first concerns the dissemination of knowledge about state policy at the local level. As I argued earlier, the state provided little information about statewide religious policy, and even state agents charged with spreading information appear to have been ignorant of the law. Half of the incoming letters to the superintendent concerning religious exercises were, in fact, letters of inquiry (the state rarely published decisions in appeals) and came from small-town trustees as well as big city board members. In 1873, L. B. Sackett, a lawyer and member of the Board of Education of Poughkeepsie, wrote the State Superintendent, asking, "If you would fur-

TABLE 3.4 Religious Exercises in Incoming Correspondence and Appeals to the State Superintendent of Public Instruction of New York, 1868–1886

Year Filed	*Total Appeals†*	*Religious Exercises Number*	*Religious Exercises Percent*	*Total Letters*	*Religious Exercises Inquiries*	*Religious Exercises Complaints*	*Religious Exercises Total*	*Religious Exercises Percent*
1867	27	0	0.0	–	–	–	–	–
1868	185	0	0.0	–	–	–	–	–
1869	129	0	0.0	–	–	–	–	–
1870	115	2	1.7	–	–	–	–	–
1871	115	0	0.0	–	–	–	–	–
1872	144	1	0.7	–	–	–	–	–
1873	111	0	0.0	1,768	3	1	4	0.2
1874	114	0	0.0	2,252	4	2	6	0.3
1875	114	1	0.9	749*	0	2	2	0.3
1876	117	0	0.0	765**	0	3	3	0.4
1877	132	1	0.8	–	–	–	–	–
1878	121	0	0.0	–	–	–	–	–
1879	120	3	2.5	1,022**	1	2	3	0.3
1880	106	0	0.0	–	–	–	–	–
1881	108	0	0.0	–	–	–	–	–
1882	66	0	0.0	–	–	–	–	–
1883	92	0	0.0	–	–	–	–	–
1884	65	0	0.0	–	–	–	–	–
1885	87	2	2.2	–	–	–	–	–
1886	17	0	0.0	536***	1	0	1	0.2
Total	2,085	10	0.5	7,092	9	10	19	0.3

†This list represents all surviving appeals from 1867 to 1886. The collection is fairly intact, judging by appeal decision numbers, though some gaps exist in every year, particularly 1882 and 1884, and we cannon account for all withdrawn appeals, which were not numbered. Appeals from 1867 include only those actually decided in 1868.

**Note:* Letters for years 1875 are from sixteen of the fifty-nine counties and New York City, which I selected for their variety and their likelihood of having religious disputes. The counties were Albany, Allegany, Broome, Cattaraugus, Chatauqua, Dutchess, Franklin, Lewis, Monroe, Niagara, Queens, Steuben, St. Lawrence, Ulster, Westchester, and Wyoming.

**Letters for 1876, 1879, and 1886 are the same sample plus Cayuga County.

***Only letters from January to June survive in the 1886 records.

Source: New York State Archives. *Appeals Case Files of the State Superintendent of Public Instruction.* Series B0496–78, B0496–78A; *Incoming correspondence to the State Superintendent of Public Instruction.* Series A2004.

nish us with a copy of some recent decision bearing on [Bible reading in schools] or inform us where it can be procured, you will greatly oblige."[53] Thus while the appeals process itself was clearly widely known, either the lack of clarity about the role of the state in ideological disputes or uncertainty about probable outcomes may have discouraged appeals over religion. This explanation does not, however, explain the low frequency of letters.

A second explanation is that religious objectors did not frequent the public schools, opting instead for the expanding network of church schools, or for no school at all. This argument is somewhat stronger. Non-Protestant children were often very poor (the depression of the 1870s made paupers of many Americans), and some parents lacked the wherewithal to send their children to school at all, never mind to complain about what went on there. A letter from a teacher in St. Lawrence County hinted at circumstances: "I have made it a practice to commence [religious exercises] before nine so that I use none of the time of the district. Over half of the district are in favor of having it read and all the rest do not care except about three families and they are very irregular with their attendance."[54]

Children who "opted in" to public schools of the post-bellum era did not experience schooling in the same way that they do today. School terms were shorter, two terms of approximately sixteen weeks apiece in 1870,[55] and school attendance was not mandatory (compulsory school laws were considered "dead letters" until the twentieth century). While most school-age children under the age of employability did enroll in school (especially in rural areas), less than half of them attended on a given day. Almost no children went on to high school. In such a system, with school being far less socially significant than it is now, many parents with children in the schools may have felt less concerned about what happened there, as long as it was nothing outrageous. Explaining the absence of appeals and letters about religious exercises in terms of objectors being absent from public school, or from school being an insignificant experience, sets a useful context, but it is at best only a partial explanation. As schooling became more socially significant, with longer terms, higher attendance rates, and longer student careers, we would expect the number of appeals and letters to increase over the course of the period. In fact, Table 3.4 shows that the number of appeals and percentage of letters did not increase significantly over time (a trend that continued up until 1900), peaking periodically over specific issues but not growing steadily.[56] More importantly, the point begs the question of significance versus insignificance. What made the public school's religious exercises insignificant enough to keep opponents silent?

Some members of religious minority groups, particularly Catholics and Lutherans, found religion in public schools so important that they chose the rapidly growing number of church-affiliated schools in New York State. In some cases, even religious *majorities* abandoned the common school because of its limited religious capabilities. In a predominantly German district in Canisteo, Steuben County, the trustee refused to levy *any* tax to support the local common school (relying on the state school fund alone). Even though they comprised a majority, and could thus control much of school policy, most parents sent their children to a nearby Lutheran school.[57] From a legal standpoint, parents of pupils at private schools would have a harder time establishing their grievance against instructional matters in public ones, if they would even care to do so.

This explanation has two problems. First, it overestimates the capacity of parochial schools in New York State. In 1875, only 13 percent of children enrolled in school attended *any* private school. Because the state statistics did not differentiate between secular and religious private schools, the percentage of these that were actually church affiliated was much lower.[58] By 1890, more reliable statistics counted 10 percent of all children enrolled in school in the state as being enrolled in parochial schools, primarily Roman Catholic and, to a lesser extent, Evangelical Lutheran.[59] In New York City, where 35 percent of the 1875 population had been born in Ireland or Germany[60] (their children born in the United States were, of course, counted as native born), only 11 percent of all children enrolled in school did so in Catholic schools.[61] Second, the alternative-school-system explanation misses the strong non-Catholic opposition to religious exercises in schools. Although religious revivalism and the general "democratization" of American Protestantism since the Second Great Awakening had won many converts, freethinking and nonbelief certainly survived the process.[62] Catholics were not the only opponents to Pan-Protestant religious exercises, despite what religious zealots might have written in their diatribes.[63]

The third, and most persuasive, explanation suggests that New Yorkers did not appeal to the State Superintendent because they were fairly well satisfied with the public school system's emphasis on local control of religious issues: autonomous districts in the towns and school boards buffered by ward control in cities. By *satisfied*, I do not mean to suggest that all parents got what they wanted. But by the same token, they appear to have also avoided getting what they strongly did not want. The relatively large number of appeals and letters on matters of procedure demonstrates that this process did not function smoothly as a mode of governance. Nevertheless, the remarkably small number of appeals and letters concerning religious policy in schools does suggest that the common school system succeeded in mediating religious conflict. Parts 2 and 3 will examine how this process worked in detail.

Conclusion

In the early nineteenth century, the state legislature had designed the common school "system" of New York as a civic replacement for church- and privately controlled education. As method of local democratic control of state-funded, basic-skills education, the system flourished throughout the state, producing generally secular schools (with religious exercises as the exception) and eventually overrunning the last bastion of religiously controlled mass schooling, New York City. Even well after the Civil War, the state's system of common schools endured more as a method of local control than as a bureaucratically connected web of schools. That system rested on the intelligence and skill of local people for its management; if the appeals are any indication, then this management left much to be desired—with one exception. Local control did not give residents call to protest to the state over religious issues. Whatever religious practices did occur in public schools after the Civil War (we have no statewide data until the late 1880s), they rarely raised strong alarm. Likewise, given the absence of any state attempt to codify, publish, and actively pursue its own policy, it is clear that for several decades after the Civil War, state superintendents and a majority of the state legislature concurred with the status quo: religion was a local issue.

Part 2

Religion and District Schools

Like the rest of the country at the close of the Civil War, New York State remained predominantly rural. And until the 1880s, district schools (meaning nonurban schools) continued to enroll the majority of the state's children and employ the majority of the state's teachers. To understand the relationship between religion and district schooling in rural areas, villages, and towns, we must first understand the context in which schooling operated—not only the relationship between the school and its people but also the way in which being a school district defined a "community," and the process by which individual members or factions within that community participated in its management. We also must understand the changing context of American religion itself—linking local religion to local schooling.

Chapter 4 explores the workings of the district school system in the post-bellum era, although its conclusions could apply to rural schooling well into the twentieth century. It analyzes religion in terms of the most contentious local issues: boundary disputes, voting, and taxes. How did these relate to religious policy and practice? While chapter 3 suggests that school districts functioned well at mediating ideological differences, chapter 4 displays the guts of the process.

Chapters 5 and 6, in turn, examine religion as an explicit (rather than an implicit) issue in the district school. Religion affected district school policy in two direct ways: the use of the schoolhouse for after-school religious meetings and the use of the classroom for religious instruction.[1] The schoolhouse—at the heart of many a district, and often its only public space—figured prominently in the relationship between religion and schooling in rural areas. At times the relationship was mutually constructive: local commitment to the expense of a school building often hinged on the assumption that it would be available for religious use. On the other hand, such use sometimes aroused controversy. Interdenominational jealousies contributed to the already common concern that the separation of church and state ought to be reflected in the schoolhouse. Chapter 5 examines the complex issue of religious meetings and tries to untangle the different cords, and discords, of meaning inherent in the parochial use of public space.

Religion interacted with schools as public educational institutions (as well as schools as public buildings) in the form of religious instruction. The decision to have or not to have religious exercises rested at the district level. Years of migration across New York State to, from, and among farmlands and small towns produced a variety of types of settlement patterns and affected the religious practice in rural district schools. In stable, homogeneous districts, religious exercises strongly reflected the religious faith of the community, although religious instruction did not cross common assumptions about the inherently civic purposes of mass schooling. During periods of demographic change, town and county leaders encouraged the formation and maintenance of homogeneous districts to minimize controversy. In mixed districts, the democratic process produced a variety of arrangements, although they tended toward the accommodation of dissenters from majority practice. Whatever the state of religious education in a district, chapter 6 concludes, it generally represented a form of compromise.

Chapter 4

Politics, Religion, and District Schooling

In Part 1, we saw that the district system—originally designed to replace ecclesiastic and private control of schooling with a mass, civil method of managing public schools—centered on democratic control at the local level. After the Civil War, districts continued to act on ideological issues such as religion with wide freedom and discretion, but within the context of an appeals system that purported to uphold legal challenges to religious exercises during school hours. Despite sometimes intense ethnic and religious animosity in society in general, New Yorkers rarely protested to the state over the decisions that their districts reached over religious disputes, even as they frequently and fervently protested other types of decisions. This behavior, discussed in chapter 3, suggests that the district functioned well at mediating religious differences, even as it fared more poorly at administration. This conclusion, however, requires more positive proof: evidence from the districts themselves.

It is quite impossible, at this time, to account for the behavior of each individual district statewide. Such an approach is not necessary, however. While every district—indeed, every school—claimed its own unique character, still schools and school districts resembled others to a large degree, particularly under the general categories of district and city schooling.[1] Foremost, each shared the same set of laws that governed its administration: the common school *system*. Even aside from law, however, the social context of schooling exerted similar pressures on the common school system statewide. Individual ratios and doses varied, but the admixture of factors that mattered to local schooling—political parties, religious denominations, ethnoreligious cultures, formal and informal associations, economically driven conditions and ideas—remained ubiquitous. This chapter concerns the workings of the district school system, common in rural and suburban areas and large towns. For my purposes, the designation of "district" includes "union free school (UFS) districts" as well, a designation that described a multiroom graded school (or occasionally a high school) shared by several small districts that chose to cast their lot together. UFS districts, like regular districts, were usually small, comprised one or a few schools, elected their own trustees (collectively called a "board of education"), and fell under the loose supervision of county commissioners. More importantly, all district schools, traditional or UFS, operated under a similar system of control.

According to their appeals and letters to the State Superintendent, New Yorkers in district schools cared most about three issues: boundaries, voting, and taxes. These subjects attracted the most complaints, and together they describe most of the workings of a local school district. Beyond describing the common school system of New York State, with its entrenched democratic localism and judicially powerful State Superintendent, these factors of district life also interacted with religion and shaped local religious policies. Shining a light on each not only clarifies the inner workings of the district school but also clarifies the manner in which the common school system mediated religious differences among constituents.

The School District, Practically Speaking

In 1866, the State Superintendent reported the following statistics: two-thirds of all children who enrolled in common schools did so in district schools. (Less than half of these children, however, attended school on any given day.) Of the state's staggering 11,780 public school districts, 98 percent were outside of cities. Compared to other forms of schooling, public schools were by far the most common. Of all primary and secondary school enrollment in the state, public elementary and secondary schools claimed 91 percent, academies 3.5 percent, and private and parochial schools 5 percent. The majority of the state's children would continue to live in nonurban areas until 1881 and to enroll in nonurban schools until 1892.[2]

For our purposes, the district had three components: the school (including the teacher), the elected officers of the district, and the legal process that defined the district and dictated the rules by which the residents governed it. Statistics reported by the State Superintendent in 1866 draw the following composite sketch of the typical school in New York State. First, it was a rural, one-room school, housed in a sparse wooden frame building, headed by a single, female teacher. The school district had paid for the schoolhouse itself, at considerable expense, and had probably contracted with a local farmer to build it. On a given day, twenty-three students attended this school, although the number varied considerably, depending on the weather conditions, season, local population, and incidence of disease. The number of children who formally enrolled in the register book was much higher—fifty-three—and probably accounted for nearly all of the district's children between the ages six and eighteen who did not have regular employment.[3] After 1867, parents paid no tuition, since legislation that year required all schools to be free. Textbooks determined the curriculum, and until 1877, parents could (and often did) send their children with textbooks of their choice. The great variety of texts could be accommodated by the pedagogical technique of recitation, in which children sat at their seats (commonly benches) memorizing sections of text. Periodically, the teacher would "hear" children's recitations by asking them to stand at her desk and answer questions (usually provided in the text) by rote, or she would inspect slates and sand tracings written by "abcdarians" learning to write. Subject areas broke up the day, and the week.[4] The school met two terms a year, one in summer and one in winter—traditional periods of convenience for schoolmasters—although schools increasingly shifted these terms to fall and spring to fit the demand of students as well as the supply of teachers.

The teacher for the school had been selected by district trustees: one, two, or three men (or women, after 1880) locally elected to act as custodians of the schoolhouse and chief administrative officers of the district.[5] The selection of the teacher was the trustee's most important function, and elections often hinged on the trustee's advocacy of particular teachers or types of teachers. State law forbade trustees to hire members of their own families except by a two-thirds' vote of the community, but this law meant little in small communities comprising large, extended families, where such a vote was assured. Sometimes voters split over whether to hire a male or female teacher. More common was the debate over hiring cheap *versus* hiring good. Local girls usually filled the former category quite conveniently, as women received half the pay as men for the same work. Female teachers outnumbered male teachers 5 to 1 in rural districts and 10 to 1 in cities.[6] Whether male or female, teachers lacked formal training and education beyond the common school curriculum. Often county commissioners had little regard for the teachers they certified, though they certified them nonetheless. Not to do so was political suicide in an elected office. The Jefferson County commissioner complained in 1871, "There are but very few professional teachers in this district, and I have no hope that their number will increase. . . . I have labored faithfully to keep our schools supplied with teachers of suitable age, experience, and intelligence; but the fatality of marriage to young ladies, and the temptation of better remuneration in other employments [*sic*] to young men, have rendered my efforts almost useless."[7]

In his next year's report, he estimated that, "Over one-fourth of all our teachers had never taught school before, and three-fourths of the whole number were less than twenty years of age.[8]

While trustees varied in their zeal (the office was not paid), their considerable powers included hiring the teacher, drawing up the tax list to pay her salary, and determining students' eligibility for the school (which meant authority over suspensions and expulsions). In general, trustees served as intermediaries between the teacher and parents, and trustees in legal appeals did not show a tendency to side with one or the other.[9] Trustees also selected textbooks and could sometimes turn a profit by contracting with one of the many textbook sellers stalking the state.[10] In areas of controversy, such as religious exercises, trustees usually directed the teacher to do or not do, although sometimes teachers vehemently disagreed. In many cases, parents held the trustee responsible for a teacher's actions. Trustees sometimes fired teachers rather than face a formal appeal and the legal cost to the district.[11] Finally, as custodians of the schoolhouse, trustees took responsibility for repairs and construction, including taking bids and selecting contractors (expenses approved by the district). They took charge of the school after hours, having sole discretion as to its use as long as no damage came to the school building, and also held the keys to the schoolhouse lock.

The law required other officers to help trustees run the affairs of the district, and thus to temper their power. In districts with more than one trustee, each usually held a second position, including clerk, who kept formal records for the district and minutes of meetings, chairman, who ran district meetings, and treasurer, who managed the money. From outside the district, town supervisors kept town funds and supervised expenditures (including authorizing the trustee's tax list). At the county level, commissioners inspected schools annually, issued teachers' certificates (usually *pro forma*), and settled boundary disputes. Commissioners also had the power to dissolve small districts and authorize new ones and condemn schoolhouses or order repairs. Overall, the system created checks and balances, in addition to establishing a hierarchy to which residents could appeal all the way to the State Superintendent himself.

Officers in turn drew their authority from the body politic, which expressed its will at annual and special meetings. The annual district meeting was the most important event in the political life of the district, foremost because it elected trustees and other officers. Meetings ran by parliamentary procedure, and voting practices ranged from shouting ayes and nays to balloting to actually taking names in writing. In one district, common practice dictated that voters stand on a side of the room to indicate their preference. (In a deftly corrupt move, the trustee scheduled one year's annual meeting in a small, crowded barber's shop—standing room only. Because there was no space for people to move for the vote, never mind sit, the chairman called a vote and counted all of those standing as voting on the aye side.)[12] When special circumstances arose, usually the need to repair or rebuild the schoolhouse, trustees called special meetings to win district approval. In times of controversy nearly every eligible voter turned up, and district policy sometimes hung on a single vote.[13]

Because such a large portion of the people in New York State's towns participated in district schools (directly as officers, teachers, and voters, or indirectly as taxpayers, family members, and students), the district "system" was the state's political *lingua franca* outside of incorporated cities. An appeal from Candor, Tioga County, shows how deeply the system ran. In 1877, district ten voted to build a new schoolhouse at a new location in the district. When the new schoolhouse was finished, members of the district assembled for their annual meeting to elect a trustee and commence the school year. At the same time, however, a faction of the district that lived near the previous school site occupied the old school building. Without warrant or official sanction, it met, conducted a school meeting, elected officers, hired a teacher, and commenced its own school. What made school legitimate, the dissenters argued in the subsequent legal suit, was that they had followed the proper form.[14]

As a key element of personal and group identity, religion never left the background of local life in rural and suburban districts. Whether or not it penetrated the schoolhouse in terms of a specific policy, religion colored the management of the district in even its most mundane elements. Religion related to how people grouped themselves residentially, how they voted, what kind of teachers they preferred, or whether they supported common schools at all. In particular, religion interacted with three key aspects of local school management: the drawing of boundaries, voting, and taxes.

BOUNDARIES

Unlike other civil divisions of government like towns or counties, ameba-like school districts changed their size and shape frequently, sometimes dividing in two or consolidating into one. These changes came under the aegis of county commissioners and the districts themselves. Commissioners could alter, consolidate, or divide districts, as long as they consulted the districts in advance. For their part, districts also had the power to divide, to build branch schools, or to consolidate with other districts into "union" districts by majority vote. Occasionally, commissioners and districts locked horns, resulting in appeals to the State Superintendent. Legally, the primary issues in districting were accessibility to children and benefit to the school. In appeals to the superintendent, commissioners and trustees regularly trundled out claims of prohibitive distance from the school, inadequate facilities, mismatches between population centers and school locations, and the need to equalize the tax bases of districts as justifications for altering boundaries. Because districting resulted from a political process, however, other pressures proved equally compelling. Wealthy residents tried to switch to lower-taxed districts, which for their part usually welcomed such additions to the tax base.[15] Political parties massaged district boundaries to maintain voting majorities or confer favors on loyal supporters.[16] Finally, and most importantly, parents and other community members sought to mold districts around ethnic and religious settlement patterns.

The most obvious meeting of districting and religion came when a district comprised a single, religiously defined community. The flexibility of the district definition allowed cloistered communities to operate common schools, as long as they followed the other regular aspects of the law. The Shakers, though not numerically strong, provide the prime example. As an extreme religious sect, Shakers eschewed "the world" as they called it, abstaining from the wicked cocktail of capitalism, secularism, and sex. Although they had to increase their numbers through the missionary impulse (rather than position), two of the three New York communities managed to garner sizeable populations of school-age children in the 1870s.[17] The settlement at Watervliet, for example, boasted a healthy cadre of sixty children under age twenty-one. Surprisingly, despite their differences with the state over nearly every temporal issue, the Watervliet Shakers were able to use the common school system to educate their children. The community operated its own common school, with a duly elected trustee, certified teacher, and state funds.[18] The only unusual aspect of the school was that the teacher, himself a Shaker, did not receive wages, and the district's share of the state fund went to the community itself. Despite its differences with "the world," the Shakers' emphasis on communitarianism found easy purchase in a common school system based on local, democratic control.[19]

Aside from unusual communities such as the Shakers, the district system interacted with religion in subtle ways, though in rare cases as an explicit issue itself. Usually religion related to districting as an aspect of ethnicity. This process stands out most sharply in the context of immigration. By 1875, decades of flooding migration into New York State from Ireland, Germany, and elsewhere had eroded the homogeneous, rural town—if, indeed, it had ever existed. Of every 100 New Yorkers, twenty-five had been born in a different country, seven in a different state, and another fifteen in a different county in New York State—meaning only half of all New Yorkers lived where they were born. Obviously the most dynamic demographic changes occurred in cities, particularly New York, Brooklyn, and Buffalo.

Nevertheless, the diversity of migration touched nearly everyone. Of over 1,000 towns and wards reporting population statistics statewide in 1875, only *six* contained no one born in Ireland. In fact, thirty-seven of sixty counties reported that their population was over 5 percent native Irish, the state average being 11 percent. Foreign-born residents in general constituted at least 10 percent of the population in forty-seven of sixty counties, and at least 5 percent in all but one (Schoharie). One in ten Irish immigrants engaged directly in agricultural pursuits, most as farmers (16,635 of 26,939) and most of the rest as farm laborers (8,266), while statewide, another 41 percent of Irish-born folk found employment as general laborers and servants—occupations that fit town economies as well as city ones. When we consider that the children of immigrants who had been born in the United States were counted as native-born Americans, the numbers become even more impressive.[20]

Religious diversity accompanied this migration. In 1875, the state boasted forty-three major denominations, mostly Protestants, including 180,000 Methodist Episcopals, 111,000 Presbyterians, and 100,000 Baptists. Altogether, New York churches claimed 1.2 out of the state's 4.7 million inhabitants. Religions associated with immigrants, primarily Roman Catholics and Evangelical Lutherans, were significant both for their impressive size and their dissent from the Pan-Protestant ideology that most major American Protestant denominations shared, and that continued to suffuse middle-class school reform. The Catholic Church alone claimed a total of 500,000 members, living in fifty-two of sixty counties, with forty-six of these counties having over 1,000 members. Evangelical Lutherans claimed members in thirty-eight counties, with twelve counties containing over 1,000 members.[21]

The state's largest official religion was none at all. Seventy-five percent of New Yorkers, the state census reported, belonged to no church. This did not mean, however, that all such people did not identify themselves culturally as members of particular faiths. "Nothing is more elusive in church history," wrote one historian in 1971, "than honest statistics."[22] Membership itself as a technical definition varied among religions. Liturgical faiths, such as Catholicism, Episcopalianism, and Lutheranism, counted all of those baptized as infants as quasi-citizens in their nation of faith. Pietistic Protestants, on the other hand, emphasized voluntary membership of adults and made full church membership more restrictive than liturgicals did.[23] In neither case did the state (or national) census count those who considered themselves culturally religious but who were not members of a church.[24] Despite a far lower census report, Bishop Bernard McQuaid of Rochester estimated in this period that fully one-third of the state's population was Catholic.[25] On the other hand, religious leaders often inflated their reports of members to increase the prestige and power of their churches.[26] Either way—inflated or deflated—census statistics suggest that religious diversity affected New York State as a whole, in towns and villages as well as in cities, and included in that diversity were a significant number of decliners from formal religion, skeptics, and outright atheists.

Census data show that migration and urbanization (which went hand in hand) affected demographics at the town as well as the county level. They do not, however, reveal information about individual school districts, and at this time there is no comprehensive reconstruction of rural demographics at the school district level. Letters and appeals to the State Superintendent, on the other hand, provide rich examples of the process by which districting interacted with religion and ethnicity, even if they do not provide comprehensive information on every district in the state. Because school district boundaries centered on population clusters, and because immigrants (native and foreign born) usually settled in groups, the district system may well have been more homogeneous than town population demographic statistics suggest.[27] With the rare exceptions of "covenanted" communities such as the Shakers, religion rode on the coattails of ethnicity as an organizing principle for districting.[28] As a result, the alteration of district boundaries provided one safety valve for the steam generated in heated interreligious rivalry.

In at least some cases, religion remained buried in larger demographic changes and their resulting pressures on district boundaries. Thus a process that would have seemed obvious to firsthand observers proves difficult for historians to spot. In 1872, for example, a large group of people from school district five of Ossining, Westchester County, filed an appeal to the State Superintendent concerning the decision of a district meeting to block the formation of a branch school. On its surface, the appeal—like so many others—bases its claim on the good of the children, and on the inadequacy of the school in both its size and location, to meet their needs. "The school district is a very large district in area," the appellants wrote, "being about 3 miles by 3 miles and that one schoolhouse is not sufficient for the accommodation of the children in said district, and is too far from the most populous portion of said district." The schoolhouse itself sat in the north end of the district, "where reside scattered families on farms, and very few children." On the other hand, population density had shifted southward, to a new neighborhood, containing spillover from the nearby village of Sing Sing, consisting of "small owners of houses and lots." Despite a school-age population of 295 children, the appellants claimed, only twenty-three attended the school on a daily basis. Most of the district's children, residing in the densely populated southern portion, could not or would not make the two-mile trek to school and could not be accommodated even if they did.[29]

The appeal includes a petition, signed by sixty-six residents of the southern portion of the town—and it is this list of names that provides evidence of the role of ethnicity. Of those sixty-six men who requested a branch school, forty-three (66 percent) had uniquely Irish surnames. Another eight petitioners (12 percent) had names that could have been Irish but were also common among either Scots or English, and the remaining fourteen (21 percent) had names that I could not identify at all.[30] The appeal represents an attempt by an Irish neighborhood that did not frequent its district public school to win a public school of its own. In some boundary cases, litigants did mention ethnicity in general terms, though they usually did not offer evidence such as a list of petitioners. The Ossining appeal failed to mention ethnicity as a key issue in the appeal. Were it not for the list of petitioners, the role that ethnicity played would be nearly invisible today.

Usually religion remained even less visible than ethnicity, rarely surfacing as an issue at all, never mind a stated concern, of a boundary appeal. The Ossining case points to one reason. As an aspect of ethnicity, especially among Civil War-era Irish immigrants, religion remained an unmentioned, but, at the same time, key aspect of boundary disputes. In Ossining, an Irish district probably meant a Catholic district. But rather than engulf a district in controversy, the issue of religion found resolution in the broader pattern of ethnically based school districts. In other cases, language proved to be another factor that encouraged tight settlement patterns in rural and suburban settings.[31] Germans, for example, settled in tight communities and operated distinctly German districts when possible.[32] (German language instruction proved a significant market for textbook companies.[33]) As a result of districting and settlement patterns, the "Catholic" district was a common feature of district schooling.[34]

Some Protestants, as well as Catholics, appear to have desired homogeneous districts when changing demographics allowed.[35] In one appeal, Protestants attempted to create their own district separate from a mixed Protestant and Catholic one. Rallying around a teacher they liked (whom the mixed district fired in favor of a more Catholic-friendly one), residents of a new neighborhood known as "Raceville" demanded a separate school district. "All the children of the eighteen families of 'Raceville' and vicinity are all Protestant," wrote the lawyer for the appellants, "while a large majority of the pupils attending the district school are Catholic. There are a large number of families in district ten who refuse to send their children to the district school under the above-mentioned circumstances." As part of their efforts at forming a distinctive community, the residents of Raceville demanded their own common school district. While they awaited a legal resolution, they began a private Protestant school rather than attend the public one.[36]

When districts had achieved relative religious homogeneity, disagreements over the common school's handling of religion probably abated. This does not mean that everyone got along, however. For example, a commissioner of

Onondaga County wrote to the Superintendent in 1880 asking for the removal of Matt Connell, trustee. Like a bad tooth, Connell had caused his district considerable pain, hiring a female teacher without consulting the other two trustees of the district. The other trustees, in turn, hired their own male teacher. "The Irish probably have a majority of the voters in this district; and both teachers are Catholic Irish." But, added the commissioner, citing the factions that supported each side of the fracas, "as you can see the Catholic Irish are not united among themselves."[37]

Why would ethnoreligious groups want their own school districts? For non-English speakers, such as the Germans mentioned earlier, controlling the district meant controlling the language of instruction and hiring a teacher sensitive to the culture of the community (not to mention spreading around the school funds within the district by hiring from within the community).[38] It meant mediation between textbook truth—usually representing the majority point of view—and the points of view of the children and their parents.[39] While homogeneous districts did not automatically produce harmony, they did unite people who tended to share the same values and experiences, particularly in terms of religion.

On a more symbolic, though no less important, level, an ethnic community's control of its own school gave pride and a sense of common purpose. As the attorney for the Protestant claimants in Raceville wrote, "The appellant and his associates have built a church edifice, a church has been organized, where they maintain useful religious meetings—affording those opportunities for Religious improvement which the wants of the people demand. The establishment of the district will give success and greatly aid and encourage *them in their work*. But if denied the district, their affairs in this community will be paralyzed and the community become the moral waste it formerly was."[40] Homogeneous districting in immigrant settlements gave a tangible degree of control to those who, in other aspects of life—such as work or participation in national culture—experienced alienation and occasionally open hostility.

Voting

A primary aim of boundary formation was not mere convenience but the desire to create voting blocks in district elections and meetings. Voting laws proved remarkably democratic, and in small districts, the balance between factions sometimes hung on a single vote. The law entitled three groups of people to vote: those people already entitled to vote in regular town elections who also owned at least fifty dollars in taxable personal property, those renting or owning property in the district, and those who were entitled to vote in regular town meetings who had children attending the district school. The property requirement tended to eliminate transient laborers, although some appeals charged that wealthy farmers would temporarily endow their hired help with fifty dollars cash to display at the annual meeting and order the men to vote in a particular way.[41] An exception to the property requirement allowed parents with school-age children to vote regardless of the value of their personal property. Women won the right to vote in district meetings in 1880 (forty years before they won the same privilege in the Nineteenth Amendment to the federal constitution).[42] New York State provided no apparatus to police voting qualifications, and any voter who averred that he or she was qualified had to be allowed to vote. Illegal voting carried potential perjury charges, but the practice appears frequently in appeals. Not surprisingly, town voting sometimes rivaled urban voting in corruption (people filed 185 appeals from 1867 to 1886 over charges of illegal voting). But, in general, most appeals to the Superintendent over voting tended to deal with technicalities rather than gross violations. Despite its limitations, voting at the district level eased the strains of religious difference in common schools in two ways: by linking local religious concerns to the party system, legitimating controversial voting results by creating a system that seemed "fair," and by encouraging local leaders to consider minority religious concerns as a way to win votes.

Since their beginnings in the 1830s, national political parties catered to ethnoreligious groups more consistently than any other single constituency. This association continued after the Civil War. Voter behavior varied, of course, but generally speaking, Democrats, the party of Catholics, working men, and educational and social conservatives, gave lukewarm support to common schools, with an emphasis on low taxes, local control, and minimal expense. This platform appealed to opponents of public education—including most of the leadership of the Catholic Church—as well as to the poor, who had little use for formal schooling or taxation of any sort, and to the rich, who bore the brunt of local property taxation. Republicans, on the other hand, endorsed school reform, including better facilities, trained (expensive) teachers, and a longer school year. The party drew its support from much of the middle class and from those who stood to gain the most from public schools, from pietistic Protestants and social reformers.[43] In the state legislature, Democrats did their best to represent the political interests of the Catholic Church in particular but of religious minorities in general by espousing a program emphasizing decentralized government, pluralism, and fiscal retrenchment.[44] During a period of Democratic rule in the early 1870s, the state legislature consistently cut common school expenditures after several years of growth.[45] Republican leaders, on the other hand, espoused a reform-minded agenda that included stamping small "p" Protestantism on education, in particular endorsing ceremonial Bible reading in common schools—mainly a Protestant idea—while opposing any direct (Catholic) church involvement in state-supported schools. The presence of religion in party platforms gave a political voice to religious concerns and tied the wishes of believers and nonbelievers alike to a process that legitimated their fears and aspirations and rationally mediated them against opponents.

At the local level, districting played a key role in political balances. Changing district boundaries meant tipping political balances within districts, and political parties, as well as religious groups, did their best to ensure their own success. In one example from 1870, a large majority of residents from district ten (a Catholic district) in the village of Rondout (town of Kingston, Ulster County) appealed to the State Superintendent to diminish their district boundaries, sending several Catholic families to neighboring district thirteen. Although a number of the residents of thirteen also supported the change, arguing that it would better equalize the tax bases of the two, the county commissioner and some other residents of district thirteen opposed it vehemently. "As originally constituted, our District (No. 13) was about equally divided between foreign and native born and it has been only by dint of the most earnest effort and tact that the school management has been kept in proper hands and the school prevented [from] being ruined."[46]

In another appeal, religious districting appears to have been an issue in the election for county commissioner, though in this case that role remained unspoken. Like so many other boundary disputes, the problem in district six, Caledonia, Livingston County, arose because of changing district demographics. "I thought I would write you a few lines," wrote one of the district's trustees, "to let you know the secret of this trouble: first the reason the district got along for the last 40 years is because they were one class of people, mostly Scotch + now they are half Roman Catholic the other half Scotch Protestant and the one class will not give in to the other." He noted in the letter—which did not form a part of the official appeal and thus did not get circulated to the defendants—that he "did not like to say anything about this in the appeal as it would create great feeling in the district." In fact, the "two classes" appear to have coexisted fairly peacefully, no doubt in part because of the efforts of this trustee to minimize conflict. For several years the district had alternated teachers, a Catholic in winter and a Protestant in summer. Now, in a bid to break the political balance, two trustees tried to convince the third to support the county commissioner in altering the district boundary, moving several Protestant families out and creating a Catholic majority.[47]

While the nature of the dispute was religious, politics drove the conflict. The appeal, brought by the trustee just quoted, alleged that the district alteration, supported by the other two trustees, was part of a sweetheart deal with the commissioner. In return for a political endorsement, the commissioner promised to redistrict a wealthy, influential Democrat, along with several Protestant families, out of number six and into a neighboring district. The rich Democrat would avoid an upcoming tax to build a new schoolhouse, while loyal Catholic party members would benefit from a Catholic-controlled district. The Protestant families do not appear to have been party to the arrangement.

The baldness of the deal offended the trustee strongly enough to make him appeal, and he claimed that such a naked attempt at political favors was illegal; however, the appeal suggests two other important points. First, the district had managed to coexist peacefully for several years *before* party shenanigans queered the deal. (Had the deal not failed, there would be little chance of evidence surviving today to record years of compromise before the singular conflict.) Second, the trustee who appealed expressed strong reluctance to publicly point to religion as a cause of the trouble, writing his concerns in an informal letter accompanying the appeal. It was in his best interest, as an elected official, to minimize conflict—both in attempting to preserve the former district compromise and in refusing to play the religion card in his appeal.

Generally, religion as an issue found purchase in larger patterns of ethnocultural politics, settlement, and social organization. Sometimes, however, religious organizations (churches, societies, or actual cloistered communities) participated directly in the democratic process. Such groups could form powerful voting district voting blocks without the aid of political parties, much to the consternation of their opponents. In a mixed district in Groveland, Livingston County, a strong faction of Shakers urged the trustee and collector to defy the orders of a county commissioner to start a branch school. Unlike the Shakers of Watervliet, this community lacked a large cohort of children and resented paying taxes to support worldly state schools.[48] In another case in Lewiston, Niagara County, six priests from the Seminary of Our Lady of Angels voted at the district meeting, upsetting the status quo by electing a Catholic parent who did not meet the property requirement by a vote of 8 to 7.[49] Rivalry among Protestant churches caused similar voting behaviors.[50]

The avowedly non-religious, though not as noisy or numerous as the avowedly pious, also participated in the district system as voters, officials, teachers, and students. Nonbelief defies easy classification, and there was, as there is today, a spectrum of belief from church membership to religion-as-culture to outright atheism, with the vast majority of people lying somewhere in the middle. The difficulty in separating belief from behavior further complicates classification. In school policy, did opposition to religious practice in schools—such as Bible reading, Catholic instruction, or singing hymns—stem from atheism or Deism? Or was it a separate issue from the religion of the individual, relating instead to devotion to the principle of separation of church and state, or simply a desire to avoid religious conflict in school matters?

A spirited annual meeting in district one, Wayland, Steuben County, provides at least one clue. "The people of Wayland just now are divided to a point of almost open hostility," reported the *Rochester Daily Union and Advertiser* in 1880, "not over political issues, for these have become stale and unprofitable with them—but upon the more sacred subject of religion."[51] At a packed annual meeting with every voter present, the district held a tightly contested annual election for trustee between two strongly divided candidates. Unlike other controversies over religion, this one did not fall along Catholic/Protestant lines but united Catholics and Protestants against a common enemy: freethinking. As one partisan observer recalled, "One candidate [was] an infidel of the most radical sort—a believer in "Bob" Ingersol's views.... The other was a Christian gentleman."[52] George Morehouse, the infidel in question, explained it this way: "The bitterness of the whole controversy is caused by the character of their opposition to me as trustee, it being based almost entirely on the ground that I am, in religio-scientific matters, an evolutionist. They gained some votes by privately, untruthfully, unjustly, and ignorantly charging me with Atheism."[53] Hanging in the balance was the power to hire the schoolteacher, who in turn would set the moral tone of the school for the ensuing year. As the *Daily Union* wrote in purple prose, "On this occasion every voter in the village was on hand, armed—if not with a pike and gun—with any amount of enthusiasm in favor of his candidate, and a conflict took place that threw all political strife into the back-ground."[54]

The disagreement had begun a year earlier, when the Catholic and Protestant school leaders compromised over symbolic religious services at the district school. Rather than require Bible reading, which the Catholics opposed without clerical interpretation, the trustee (a Protestant) and the town supervisor (a Catholic) generated a list of appropriate Christian hymns to sing at the start of the school day. The trustee hired a pious Protestant teacher to that end, telling him that the district "wanted a good, moral man and one who would not sit around saloons and hotels, one who would be found in his place at Church on Sunday."[55] The compromise irked the district's strong freethinking population, which opposed the imposition of religious exercises on its children and the trustee's insistence on the religious character of the teacher. One-fifth of Wayland's population had been born in Germany, and the district itself was predominantly German.[56] Not only did a number of these Germans—20 percent of the district's children—attend a nearby parochial school, but most cherished Sunday saloons as part of their way of life.[57] (Native Protestant opponents accused the freethinkers of being part of the whiskey confederation and of being morally debased.) Unlike freethinkers in most of the state, Wayland's had an organization to champion their ideas: the Wayland Liberal League, which sponsored lectures and debates on such topics as "Revivals, Psychology and Superstition." The leader of the league, George Morehouse, led a movement to end the district's religious exercises and to oust the trustee and teacher responsible for them.

At the annual meeting, Morehouse squeaked by his incumbent opponent to win the election. The opposition hastily demanded a revote, which it managed to win, and then refused to allow Morehouse to assume office. Morehouse filed an appeal to the State Superintendent, charging fraud. He won. As the *Rochester Union* lamented, "The church militant was driven by the cold streams of Babel, where its members hung their harps on the willow trees, and thus do matters stand now."[58]

What is most significant about this example is not its delightful characterization of nineteenth-century Christian zeal but the fact that the conflict itself was so modest. In a "battle" so locally important that it joined Protestants with Catholics, the "church militant" limited its action to a revote, as opposed to more drastic means. The Christians' argument in their defense to the appeal rested on their winning the revote at the election (they claimed the first vote was for practice), not on the fact that their opponents were immoral curs (although they did express those feelings in informal letters of support). Furthermore, they accepted the Superintendent's decisions in Morehouse's favor without further incident. Implicit throughout their actions and their defense were two interrelated facets of the common school system: the belief that the voting process legitimated the election of a trustee, and an acceptance of the role of the State Superintendent as a last word in settling disputed outcomes. Despite the seriousness of the issue, freethinkers and Christians alike used technical arguments about voting procedure, not "guns and pikes," as the weapons in their holy war.

Taxes

The common school system provided that local districts raise property taxes to supplement the state education fund, build schools, and cover any extra expenses that the district might accrue. Responsibility for district expense went hand in hand with local control over spending it. Differences of opinion about the importance of common schooling translated into ethnoreligious and socioeconomic patterns of behavior regarding taxation, which often fit into larger political patterns of behavior. As a result, taxation became a central issue in religious disputes, but it also, strangely, acted as a strong force for compromise and reconciliation in the common school district.

Much of the colorful bluster that accompanied religious disagreements over common schools painted caricatures of the participants that turned on the fulcrum of taxes. Alarmist pietistic-Protestant school reformers characterized their main antagonists—Catholics—as stingy opponents of common schools who sought to thwart expenditures for teacher salaries and decent school buildings.[59] Conservative Catholic leaders charged Protestants with being extravagant in their tastes and imperialistic in their confidence that they knew what was right for others. Both charges hit close to the mark. Some Catholic Church leaders did their best to undermine the public schools as they embarked on their own program of church-sponsored mass education.[60] Moreover, the Democratic Party, deeply Catholic, made low local school taxes a central plank of its platform.[61] Pietistic Protestants filled the ranks of school reform organizations that advocated longer school years, better-paid teachers, and new school buildings.[62] The Republican Party, the pietists' main political organ, endorsed these issues in local elections.

These characterizations paint only a partial picture, however. Local property tax touched another nerve even more directly than religion: social class. As they do today, taxpayers paid their school tax as a flat percentage of the value of their property. Although strict Marxian social class classifications fail to describe the economic relations of farming areas of New York State, differences in wealth and social status clearly existed in the social fabric of the town and manifested themselves in district meetings. Wealthy individuals or successful businesses paid large percentages of annual school taxes, sometimes amounting to princely sums of money for expensive projects such as new school buildings. The poor and working classes—laborers, servants, and unskilled and some skilled workers—paid little in tax, but considered any amount dear. The middling classes—small farmers, successful skilled workers, merchants, and those who owned modest property—paid the balance.

Paradoxically, rich and poor often had the same interest in the common school. The wealthy had little personal need for the common school, as they could easily afford private school or tutors, if they even had school-age children. Their zeal—if any—stemmed from party or religious identification, or from the desire to reduce crime and pauperism. The poor and working classes, likewise, could ill afford the lost wages of an able child. They also were much more likely to be Catholic than either the rich or the middling classes. The middling classes, on the other hand, stood to gain the most from well-funded public schools, where they could earn social and economic status through an ostensibly meritocratic educational hierarchy.[63] Moreover, they represented the social heartland from which pietistic Protestantism—as well as the Republican Party—drew its strength.

Taxation created alliances among these groups in district politics. Wealthy Protestants and poor or working-class Catholics sometimes banded together to defeat large expenditures for schools.[64] Catholics and wealthy taxpayers who sent their children to private and parochial schools complained bitterly of the "double tax" imposed by tuition for one school and property tax for the other. Middle-class Protestants pushed in the opposite direction and feared that Catholics would "ruin" their districts by gutting expenditures on teachers and blocking repairs or the construction of new school buildings.[65]

Sometimes the stereotypes of penurious religious minorities did not hold. When they had control over their own matters and saw clear benefits for themselves, religious minorities sometimes supported the common school to a greater degree than the stereotypes would suggest. Recall the two Shaker communities of Groveland and Watervliet. While the former, with few children, blocked the construction of a necessary branch school, the latter, with a large number of children, operated its own common school. In a German village in Adams, Jefferson County, a Protestant religious revival among a rural German community led to their sudden endorsement of public education and the desire to become a school district, when previously they had resisted all schooling for their children.[66]

A strong example comes from the 1873 report of a commissioner from rural Washington County, who lauded the outstanding school of his commissioner district in his annual report of the State Superintendent: "The banner common school district," he wrote approvingly, "as regards length of time in which school was actually taught, was district No. 5, on Morris Hill, in the town of Hampton. This district had thirty-six weeks of school. We call attention to this, because it deserves commendation on its own account. In addition, it is composed mainly of Irish families, the trustee himself being an Irishman. It effectively refutes the slander, that the Irish in this country are opposed to education or are unaware of its benefits."[67] In each case, religious minorities acted in their best interest and not simply as members of a monolithic religious identity or political party. In Hampton, for example, foreign-born residents appear to have been strongly family oriented. Of an adult foreign-born population of 154, 126 were married.[68] (Census reports do not reveal the numbers of children of these couples, since children born in the United States were listed as "native.") In this instance, Catholics may have acted in their interest as parents and patrons of public schools rather than they might have as childless day laborers or as patrons of a parochial school. In another example, self-proclaimed "Americans" from the main business (a paper company) of Hart Lot, Onondaga County, opposed Catholic control of the school board because they spent *too much* money on schools.[69]

Finally, the appeals process to the State Superintendent itself created a common interest among religious minorities and those with property—not only because the Superintendent could overturn grossly discriminatory practices, but because businesses and the rich bore the expense of a district's legal defense. In the Hart Lot case above, where the Hart Lot Paper Company protested illegal Catholic attempts to gain control of the school district, the company itself pushed a program of religious compromise, though hardly out of a spirit of altruism or tolerance. The company reported to the Superintendent that

> this district until last year has been wholly run by ignorant Irish Trustees, and the School has cost us from $1,200–$1,400 every year, except last year when we succeeded in getting in an intelligent American Trustee, who has run the same School—having part Catholic and Part Protestant teachers for little less than $800, and have had a good school at that.[70]

In fact, the company reported having gone to great lengths to avoid an appeal, since it would be doubly troubled to file an appeal on its own behalf and to pay a good portion of the legal defense fees (through property taxes) on behalf of the district.

Conclusion

Boundaries, voting, and taxes: three vital ingredients in the process of local control of district schools. Each issue proved a source of disagreement in itself—not surprisingly. Democracy as a process of decision making was and is ponderous, procedurally messy, and inherently unable to give everyone what he or she wants. As an ever-present aspect of post bellum social life, religion played an implicit role in deliberations over these issues, though only occasionally did it come to the foreground in major local disputes.

While the common school system of New York State generated many unresolved disputes at the local level (necessitating appeals to the state), that very same process worked well at mediating religious differences *before* they erupted as full-blown disputes. It succeeded in several ways. First, the common school system created common interests: mutually satisfactory segregation of districts, politicians in search of constituents, and alliances between Catholics and capital. Second, state superintendents promised legal protection of minorities from blatant abuse during school hours, either in the form of objectionable religious exercises or persecution in other forms. The threat of appeal gave trustees an incentive, regardless of their personal feelings, to moderate at the local level rather than incur the trouble and cost of a legal defense. With the exception of such extreme cases, however, school districts stood far outside of the direct influence of the state educational bureaucracy and had a variety of options that mattered greatly in the local context:

optional or a compromise of religious exercises, the election of trustees, and the selection of teachers and textbooks. At the same time, however, districts all over the state, no matter how remote, replicated the common school system and abided by it. Even those who obviously cheated did so by mimicking the rules. According to the most heated disagreements that reached the State Superintendent's office in the form of appeals or letters, residents almost never acted violently, flaunted the law, or broke it without at least pretending to follow the system.

Chapter 5

Religious Use of the District Schoolhouse

While the district school system contained most religious disagreements at the local level, it did not eliminate discord, nor did it prevent a small number of districts from filing religious complaints, formal and informal, to the State Superintendent. These complaints fell into two categories: after-hours' use of the schoolhouse and use of school time for religious exercises. Both types of complaints stemmed from a common dilemma: how to balance minority rights against majority rule in a democratic, community-based school.

This chapter explores the first of these two issues, religious use of the district schoolhouse after hours, testing the proposition that religious pluralism incited bitter disputes and stifled compromise. In fact, religious use of the schoolhouse provided widely perceived local benefit, even as it led to disagreements. Moreover, when such use did, infrequently, lead to conflict that boiled over the local level, the interests of district residents as taxpayers often superseded their religious affiliation. In other words, the issue became contentious as a tax matter, not necessarily a religious one. As a result, conflict over the use of the schoolhouse for religious meetings cut across ethnic and religious lines, defying the easy characterization that the district school was a locus of Catholic-versus-Protestant religious conflict.

Beneath the question of the use of the school for religious purposes lay two fundamental issues: religious ideas and state policy. The character of American religion—its ideas, its place in society—shaped and encouraged these disputes, even as it played a role in compromise. As this chapter examines religious disputes that over-boiled into a state concern, it places disputes in the context of religious ideas. Staying true to the theme of localism, however, it examines churches in much the same fashion as schools—less in terms of strict dogma or doctrine than in terms of local behavior and belief. State policy, like religious ideas, also defined the character of religious disputes. While religious differences drove people to refuse to cooperate, the common school system gave legal shape to their concerns and provided the axis on which such disputes turned. By the time a conflict transcended local control, it had already taken a legal form that the state could recognize and adjudicate. By the same token, however, the development of the law reflected the needs of the school district, so that state policy toward religious use of the schoolhouse generally followed the trajectory of that practice, from an assumed social benefit to a liability. In both cases—religion and law—the local context remained fundamental to the behavior of school districts regarding school policy.

The Schoolhouse as a House of God

In October 1895, thirteen voters from Rush, Monroe County, submitted a petition to their district trustee. It requested that the trustee block any further use of the district schoolhouse for a Sunday school and religious meetings, claiming that such use damaged the schoolhouse and imposed an unfair tax burden on the district. A larger group, thirty-five voters, issued a counterpetition demanding that the schoolhouse remain open. The trustee sided with the majority. By the spring of 1896, the minority filed an appeal. The State Superintendent sided with the plaintiffs and ordered the schoolhouse closed to religious meetings. In his decision, the Superintendent lamented such occurrences, writing that, "The holding of religious meetings in schoolhouses is almost always the source of dispute in every district in which such a meeting is held, and such disputes are detrimental to the best educational interests of such districts."[1]

The Superintendent's observation fits with the then-emerging (and currently ubiquitous) view of the religious history of public schooling as divisive and detrimental to educational interests. His statement reflected a growing expectation on the part of the state for a more explicit secular purpose for schooling as well as—perhaps—a changing attitude on the part of citizens themselves. Aside from being demonstrably exaggerated, the Superintendent's strident critique also masked a richer, more complex relationship between the use of the public school for religious purposes and the development and support of district schools. True, New Yorkers filed approximately one appeal a year to the Superintendent over the use of their schoolhouses for religious meetings from 1867 to 1898, and they wrote a greater number of informal letters on the subject.[2] But the number of letters and appeals, set against the more than 11,000 districts in the state, is relatively small for what was considered common practice in rural areas. Moreover, those very same meetings had served to prop up public support of district schools for generations—since the founding years of common schools in the early nineteenth century—and continued to do so, even as they led to controversy at the century's end.

Since its inception, the common school system had facilitated local control of schooling, but it did little to help with the cost of building public school buildings at local expense or to regulate their use. The abstract need for an educated citizenry did not provide the sole incentive for constructing and maintaining such buildings in a state that was, at the end of the Civil War, predominantly rural. Public spaces were in short supply in thinly populated areas, and schoolhouses often served as the only nearby public space, particularly for groups that could not afford to build their own alternatives. Moreover, schoolhouses tended to be centrally located, loosely following population centers to accommodate the maximum number of children. As a result, schoolhouses commonly served a variety of municipal functions (serving as district meeting places and polling centers, for example). After a great flood swept through district nine in the town of Kingston, Ulster County, the schoolhouse became a temporary hospital and depot for medical and food supplies.[3] But schoolhouses served other purposes as well, hosting major community events and visitors, such as traveling performers, revival preachers, singing schools, lectures, and other functions. Occasionally other community members objected to this use—particularly when it damaged the school building or used district-funded fuel for the stove. Others objected on principle. In 1867, several citizens from Bolivar, Allegany County (population 959), refused to pay for repairs to the schoolhouse, protesting the use of the building for "public exhibitions, accompanied by a jaw bone band, with clown and negro performance, calculated to attract large crowds of auditors from a distance."[4] The expectation that schoolhouses would be used as community centers stimulated school construction, helped earn the support of those without children in the school, and led to generous appropriations for extras, such as large rooms, organs, and pianos. In Crown Point, Essex County, the district voted to build a schoolhouse with an extra floor, not intended for a classroom but to be permanently rented by a fraternal organization and theatrical club.[5]

This sense of community ownership stemmed from the obviously local nature of school administration, and also from the realities of district finance. Until the Free School Act took effect in 1868, rate bills covered the part of tuition that the small state fund did not. This meant that the parents of children attending the school had a large responsibility for the cost of the actual instruction that their children received. Nevertheless, the entire community bore the cost of the school in two ways. First, the cost of building the schoolhouse touched all residents of the district. It required a majority decision to build a new school, but then all were responsible, through proportional property taxes, for its construction. Second, all residents of the state paid the statewide tax to support the school fund. After 1868, when the Free School law came into effect, local tax covered the cost of tuition formerly borne by the rate bill, actually increasing the interest of all of the district's taxpayers in school matters. The community as a whole literally and intellectually owned the schoolhouse; its use reflected the needs of the community as a whole, and not just that of the young scholars whose work papered its walls.

As a major social institution in local life, organized religion also permeated the schoolhouse as a public space. Religious denominations commonly used the school when they lacked a church—sometimes even when they had one—and, in addition, citizens used the schoolhouse for practices that might best be labeled "culture," rather than "religion," such as holiday celebrations and funerals. In some cases, even people outside of a district's boundaries would contribute money by private subscription to the construction of a schoolhouse for such purposes.[6] A trustee from Rodman, Jefferson County, explained why:

> Most of the [private donations] was raised outside of the District and the understanding was at that time that by permit of the trustee or trustees the school house should be used for holding funerals and meetings when not wanted for school purposes[.] [A]nd it has been used since that time for holding meetings, Sunday schools, singing schools, debating schools, and sometimes for exhibitions at the closing of the term of the school and also for the holding of a Christmas tree and there has been occasions when shows have been permitted to show in the house... such as the illustrations of astronomy... and also showing Cities, Mountains, Lakes, Rivers, Gulfs, Railroads, Steamboats, Animals, Birds, and also the portraits of noted men and some battle scenes in the late rebellion.[7]

Even though congregations owning churches commonly allowed others to share the space, rural villages sometimes lay several miles from any church building, making attendance difficult, particularly in upstate New York's notoriously bad weather.

The practice of using the schoolhouse for religious meetings was as old as the common school law itself. Appeals and letters about religious meetings usually described the practice as having persisted since time out of memory. Some mentioned local arrangements having persisted from thirty to as much as fifty years previous—since the formation of districts themselves—before turning sour in the decades after the Civil War.[8] In the years of settlement and consolidation before the war, the use of the schoolhouse served the civil and ecclesiastical needs of raw communities in need of public meeting space. The expansion and transformation of American Protestantism at that time strengthened this need. The vast majority of school districts may have rejected Bible reading in the classroom in the 1830s (as we saw in chapter 1), but by the 1840s and 1850s church membership in particular and the Pan-Protestant ideology often associated with Bible reading in general had gained considerable ground.[9] Grassroots religion exploded in size and significance. By the eve of the Civil War, community leaders in rural as well as urban areas commonly associated the establishment of religion with the march of civilization and the social good, whether or not they themselves belonged to a church.[10]

In addition to meeting the spiritual needs of the people by hosting funerals, holiday celebrations, and other broadly inclusive cultural activities, the local schoolhouse met the specific needs of this rapidly changing American Protestantism. Beginning in the early nineteenth century, new Protestant faiths sprang up like spring wildflowers across the nation, particularly as massive human migration pushed westward away from previous seats of ecclesiastic control. By disestablishing religion, federal and state governments nudged the process along—severing traditional church hegemony and civil authority. New ideologies of human efficacy, social reform, and democracy offered alternative visions to Calvinism and complemented political reforms in the "age of the common man." As a result of these intellectual and social upheavals, grassroots religions—which relied on less formal, less coercive, and less liturgical methods—flourished, and itinerant preachers stalked the countryside like holy arsonists, lighting the fires of religious revival meetings and winning mass conversions.[11] Baptist, Seventh Day Adventist, and Methodist churches enjoyed dramatic growth in membership, with Methodism emerging as the nation's single largest denomination by 1850.[12] No place felt these effects more strongly than New York State, where migration, capitalism, and ideology blended to spread pietistic Protestantism to the middle class in small towns and cities and to farmers in rural areas.[13]

These new religions required meeting places for revivals as well as for weekly church meetings. In colonial times, New York had imposed taxes on all citizens for the support of churches. The disestablishment of religion in the first state constitution of 1889 forced churches to fend for themselves and made the construction of new churches for new denominations particularly difficult in sparsely populated areas that did not boast sufficient means. Mass conversions required public spaces; the pious required pews. But in raw settlements with few resources and no public space, where would these pews be?

The common school system provided an answer. It offered an alternative to the old state aid to religion by ensuring thousands of public spaces spread evenly across the state, following pioneers into their new settlements, with construction costs paid by all residents in common. In fact, the arrangement resembled the old colonial church tax, though now it served explicitly educational purposes first and religious ends second. In rural areas of modest means, the common school offered the only space capable of housing any religion, save for distant churches or exceptionally large living rooms. This problem was particularly acute for Sunday schools, because children were less capable of making long journeys than their parents. The contemporaneous rise of common schools and pietistic Protestantism was no mere coincidence; each supported the other as adequate common school buildings gave the faithful a place to worship.

The use of the schoolhouse favored new religions over old ones, particularly the anti-formal faiths, including Baptists, Seventh Day Adventists, and Methodists.[14] (Appeals and letters to the Superintendent about religious meetings in schoolhouses, in fact, mention only these three groups by name.) In formal churches, spiritual authority, as well as spiritual practice in worship, followed hierarchical channels of authority. Formalist faiths, such as the Roman Catholic and Episcopal churches, insisted on ordained priests and consecrated suitably beautiful churches. Newer, anti-formalist churches, on the other hand, settled for much less in terms of leadership and aesthetics, with congregations forming themselves and then acquiring clergy—sometimes on a part-time or rotating basis. Methodists even strained the meaning of a congregation, meeting frequently in smaller units called "classes" led by laymen and laywomen, and holding protracted revivals and "love feasts" in addition to regular Sabbath worship.[15]

In fact, the particulars of Methodism often made the schoolhouse a more attractive site for religious meetings than a church—unless the congregation owned a church itself, and sometimes even then. Commonly, rural Protestant congregations shared a church building until each faith could construct its own, alternating Sabbaths and days of the week, or simply sharing ministers and celebrating interdenominational Protestant masses. Sharing worked when faiths were able to schedule regular preachers or agree on common services. For Methodists, as well as for other anti-formal evangelists, irregular schedules and fervent, lengthy meetings made sharing difficult, if not impossible. A series of so-called "protracted meetings" in a schoolhouse in Penfield, Monroe County, in 1879, for example, lasted six nights a week for six weeks.[16] For similar reasons, a group of Methodists in Candor, Tioga County, in 1870 did not join other faiths in using the local Baptist church, choosing to maintain its use of the schoolhouse. Although school repairs forced the group temporarily to the Baptist church (a quarter mile away), it returned as soon as possible to begin a series of "protracted" nightly meetings at the schoolhouse—meetings it could not have held at the Baptist church.[17] In another example in Wellsville, Allegany County, in 1879, religious societies of various denominations built a church for use by all as an alternative to the schoolhouse (used for thirty years prior); the town's largest faith, Methodist-Episcopals, held the deed. As soon as the new church opened, however, a faction of Methodists split from the main body, named itself the Protestant Methodists, and returned to the schoolhouse. Although the Methodist-Episcopals offered to let the faction have a regular weekly slot, the Protestant Methodists preferred the schoolhouse where they were now the sole denomination.[18] Even when they did own a church, Methodist bodies used nearby school buildings for their lay-led "class meetings" and revivals and then attended their regular church on a weekly or monthly basis.

Appeals and letters to the Superintendent suggest that the use of the schoolhouse for religious purposes continued to be widespread in the decades after the Civil War (see Table 5.1). Appeals about the practice continued to come to the state infrequently but consistently through the 1890s. They came from all over the state, cities as well as towns. Overall, the appeals and letters show the practice to be only slightly more controversial than religious exercises.

A lack of other reliable sources, however, makes it difficult to assess whether these complaints represent most or all such arrangements (supporting Superintendent Skinner's 1896 lament that they were always contentious), or whether many more existed that either stopped without controversy or endured with their districts' blessings. Federal and state censuses did not collect data on nonchurch meeting locations. The New York State Census of 1875, for example, shows 6,243 edifices for the state's 6,320 religious organizations, but it does not clarify where the other seventy-seven organizations did meet. Moreover, it claims a parity of organizations and edifices in counties where appeals and letters show schoolhouses in use.[19] The 1890 and 1900 federal censuses collected data on the meeting places of religious organizations but to save space did not publish these data fully, instead listing meetings in halls, schoolhouses, and homes as one category. In both cases—state and federal censuses—data came from central church offices by correspondence and were then checked against published "yearbooks" of various denominations. In such a scenario, bodies without churches would likely be undercounted, particularly splinter organizations such as the Protestant Methodists of Wellsville. The Methodist classes that met in schools, for example, would not be counted at all, except as members of a more distant church.

The use of the schoolhouse for religious meetings could prove mutually beneficial for the district and religion alike. Religious societies and congregations invested in larger school buildings and finer furnishings. Congregations using the schoolhouse sometimes bought organs, kept in the schoolhouse, for district as well as religious use. In cases where the district was divided on

TABLE 5.1 Religious Meetings in Incoming Correspondence and Appeals to the State Superintendent of Public Instruction of New York, 1868–1898

*Year*****	*Total Appeals*†	*Religious Meetings*		*Total Letters*	*Religious Meetings*			
		Number	*Percent*		*Inquiries*	*Complaints*	*Total*	*Percent*
1867	27	2	7.4	-	-	-	-	-
1868	185	0	0.0	-	-	-	-	-
1869	129	1	0.8	-	-	-	-	-
1870	115	0	0.0	-	-	-	-	-
1871	115	0	0.0	-	-	-	-	-
1872	144	0	0.0	-	-	-	-	-
1873	111	1	0.9	1768	1	2	3	0.2
1874	114	2	1.7	2252	0	11	11	0.5
1875	114	0	0.0	749*	2	4	6	0.8
1876	117	1	0.9	765**	0	2	2	0.3
1877	132	0	0.0	-	-	-	-	-
1878	121	2	1,6	-	-	-	-	-
1879	120	1	0.8	1,022**	0	4	4	0.4
1880	106	2	1.9	-	-	-	-	-
1881	108	0	0.0	-	-	-	-	-
1882	66	0	0.0	-	-	-	-	-
1883	92	0	0.0	-	-	-	-	-
1884	65	1	1.5	-	-	-	-	-
1885	87	1	1.1	-	-	-	-	-
1886	17	0	0.0	536***	0	1	1	0.2
1892	110	2	1.8	-	-	-	-	-
1893	75	1	1.3	-	-	-	-	-
1894	104	0	0.0	-	-	-	-	-
1895	102	0	0.0	-	-	-	-	-
1896	104	0	0.0	-	-	-	-	-
1897	100	2	2.0	-	-	-	-	-
1898	116	3	2.6	-	-	-	-	-
Total	2,796	22	0.8	7,092	3	24	27	0.4

†This list represents all surviving appeals from 1867 to 1886 at the New York State Archive, and those published in the annual reports of the Superintendent of Public Instruction from 1893 to 1898. The collection is fairly intact, judging by appeal decision numbers, though some gaps exist in every year, particularly 1882 and 1884, and we cannot account for all withdrawn appeals, which were not numbered. Appeals from 1867 include only those actually decided in 1868. Likewise, appeals from 1886 are obviously incomplete. While annual reports from 1887 to 1891 and 1898 to 1904 do contain some mentions of religious appeals, they are not comprehensive, so I do not include them here.

**Note*: Letters for years 1875 are from sixteen of the fifty-nine counties and New York City, which I selected for their variety and their likelihood of having religious disputes. The counties were Albany, Allegany, Broome, Cattaraugus, Chatauqua, Dutchess, Franklin, Lewis, Monroe, Niagara, Queens, Steuben, St. Lawrence, Ulster, Westchester, and Wyoming.

**Letters for 1876, 1879, and 1886 are the same sample plus Cayuga County.

***Only letters from January to June survive in the 1886 records.

****Before 1887, year filed. After 1887, fiscal year reported on by Superintendent (lags published date of annual report by one year).

Source: New York State Archives. *Appeals Case Files of the State Superintendent of Public Instruction.* Series B0496-78 and B0496-78A; *Incoming correspondence to the State Superintendnent of Public Instruction.* series A2004.

whether to repair an old schoolhouse or build a new one, the interests of local congregations could swing the vote in favor of new construction.[20] Common interests between religious bodies and the district school created local political blocks that tempered conservative opposition to the common school system and may help explain the relatively minor opposition to common schools, despite the fact that the state mandated school construction and maintenance without ever having appropriated funds. Whether or not they accepted the lofty goal of an educated citizenry, by the 1870s, many native New Yorkers could look back on past or current benefits of the common school system to the school district's religious life by the very existence of the district school.

Religious Meetings as a Source of Controversy

Even as religious use of the schoolhouse sometimes propped up the common school as a local institution, it also wore it down. Over the thirty years from 1867 to 1898, New Yorkers filed approximately one appeal a year to the State Superintendent over controversies stemming from the use of the schoolhouse for religious purposes after school hours, and they probably wrote more than ten times that number of letters.[21] Although relatively small in number, these complaints show that use for religious purposes caused both literal and figurative wear and tear on the district school, damaging physical property and straining district goodwill. And unlike religious disputes over curriculum and governance, these disputes cut across religious, ethnic, and political lines, dealing directly with questions of public support of religion in specifically local contexts.

Why did decades' old arrangements for the religious use of the schoolhouse wither after the Civil War? For many districts, the context of the issue had changed. As newly settled communities matured, religious societies built churches to keep pace with increasing church enrollments. While the use of schoolhouses for religious meetings continued into the twentieth century, the need grew less pressing as more churches and better transportation improved accessibility to parochial spaces. Likewise, rough and ready rural Protestant denominations, (such as Methodists, Baptists, and Seventh Day Adventists) underwent facelifts in the 1850s and 1860s, seeking middle-class respectability by building commodious churches, renting pews, and hiring educated, professional clergy.[22] Finally, immigration and modernization brought dissenters from the mainstream American Protestantism, such as Catholics, Lutherans, and freethinkers, who evinced skepticism at the supposed confluence of civil interest and religious convenience. In this context, religious groups had less need for school buildings, and their neighbors had less toleration of their use for public space.

Throughout the whole of the nineteenth century, state educational law left after-hours' use of the schoolhouse at the sole discretion of the trustee, as long as such use was for ostensibly "educational" purposes.[23] The vagueness of the statute left state superintendents wide latitude in defining what constituted appropriate use, and they varied in their interpretation, beginning in the late 1880s, depending on their political outlook. In general, state superintendents tolerated meetings, bowing to the reality of rural district life. As observed in a state-published digest of legal decisions in 1887, "Frequently in rural districts, the schoolhouse is the only suitable place in the district for holding a meeting of any character, and such policy had greatly promoted the convenience as well as the intellectual and moral activity of the district."[24] Defenders of meetings frequently played to this tune, averring the hardship of finding alternative meeting places. Nevertheless, objectors could block such use if they could prove that it damaged district property, a criterion that all superintendents accepted in their decisions against meetings. In some cases, superintendents blocked meetings when plaintiffs could show widespread opposition within the district—a civil harm resulting from meetings.[25] Until 1896, when Superintendent Skinner interpreted "educational purposes" in strictly secular terms, all plaintiffs from religious meetings attempted to show evidence of damage to district property, whatever their real motivations.

The damage was real enough. Appeals and letters complained of broken chairs and desks, stolen materials, graffiti, and carved desks and benches. Some meetings left tobacco quids and spittoons, and brown stains from the less accurate use thereof. During a series of meetings in Penfield, Monroe County, the pious piled schoolbooks in the windowsills to make more room. Frequently opening the windows when things got hot, they let little snowdrifts pile on the books, causing twenty dollars' worth of damage.[26] More serious damage included broken locks, doors, and hinges, resulting when religious groups with overactive senses of entitlement broke into locked school buildings. Yet the most grievous and bitter (and probably most common) form of damage to a district was the theft of district firewood.

Charges of damage, however, do not sufficiently explain complaints—formal and informal—about the use of the schoolhouse for religious meetings. After all, most appeals challenged long-standing arrangements, ones that, presumably, had caused normal wear and tear for years. By using damage as the standard by which it judged the use of the schoolhouse, the law provided opponents with an opening for blocking use *even if* the trustee or religious groups repaired the damage. Certainly taxpayers would normally be wary of damage to public property, but appeals to the Superintendent demonstrate an unwillingness to let arrangements continue, not just demands that damage be repaired, and thus they reveal attitudes about the practice of religious meetings in the schoolhouse itself. Aside from general complaints about damage, local controversies over religious meetings flared for two reasons: the changing context of local religion and disputes between local religious groups. These usually stemmed from self-interest.

The changing material context of American religion had a strong influence on the toleration of religious meetings in common schoolhouses. Statewide, the quest for respectability of Protestant churches had led to impressive gains in numbers and wealth of church edifices from 1860 to 1890. While the number of churches grew by 50 percent during that period, the value of these churches grew an astounding 400 percent. Among Methodists, the largest Protestant denomination in the state and by far the most frequent defendant in appeals and letters about the use of the school, the number of churches grew by 44 percent, while the value of these churches tripled.[27] An appeal in 1874 described the effect of this growth at the local level: "Previous to the building of our [new] church," read a petition signed by twenty-two residents, "there was no objection to the employment of our schoolhouse for religious meetings, although it resulted in great damage to our house."[28] In appeals and letters, opponents and defenders of meetings frequently debated the accessibility of church buildings—both groups recognizing the weakening legitimacy of the school building as a place for religious meetings in the face of alternatives. Even churchgoers evinced a notion that the use of the schoolhouse ought to cease when a church became available.[29] Thinking as taxpayers rather than as members of particular sects, New Yorkers had increasingly high expectations after the Civil War for the ability of religion to fend for itself and lower toleration of added taxes for its support.

Material objections usually quibbled with the type of religious use rather than religious use per se. Occasional use for religious or quasi-religious events, such as funerals or Sabbath meetings, rarely appears in appeals or letters complaining of material damage to the schoolhouse, except in cases where another church building stood nearby. Instead, the majority of material complaints concerned specific behaviors: nightly meetings and revivals, which were particular to Methodists and, to a lesser degree, to Seventh Day Adventists (a Methodist spin-off from the 1840s). A letter from Mrs. L. E. Wood in 1886 may explain why. "We have always been having Sunday school and some meetings in the school house; but there is now a denomination calling themselves Free Methodists who have settled a minister, built a parsonage, and taking the school house for their church, had some keys made so they could get in when they chose, and they hold meetings every night for four and five weeks at a time, even in time of school, using the school wood."[30] Mrs. Wood's letter implied her favorable opinion of Sabbath meetings, but not the heavy use of nightly meetings and (what seemed to her to be) an excessive sense of ownership. For those denominations that did not engage in the fervent class meeting or revival, particularly members of Protestant churches seeking respectability, such heavy use may have strained their feelings of charity in cases of actual damage.

Although less common than material complaints, some letters and appeals reveal that religious people argued over the use of the schoolhouse for religious reasons as well. The demographic changes that swept New York after the Civil War—only half of the residents of a given town were born there—brought diverse interests to districts that may well have been, before the Civil War, relatively stable. "The schoolhouse belonging to our District has been used steadily as a place of religious worship by the Methodist-Episcopal denomination during the past fifty years, perhaps longer," wrote Horace Butts to the Superintendent in 1875. "We do not know, and never have known, of any objection, on the part of the district. But the present trustee dislikes the present minister, and locks the school-house, also forbids it to be used while he is in office."[31] Like others in his office, State Superintendent Draper expressed dismay in 1892 that such matters should affect schools, declaring in frustration, "It is not a part of the duty of this Department to determine religious controversies" and promising, "it will not assume to determine them."[32] Nevertheless, being the center of the district made the school building a lightning rod for local religious disputes—not only as the place of Protestantism changed in community life but in occasionally stormy local confrontations as well—and letters and appeals to state superintendents necessarily brought the state school system to bear on district-level religious discord.

Instability among a district's faithful led to disputes over the use of the school building, both among Protestants and between Protestants and Catholics. In each case, the objection was not based on a belief in a strict separation of church and state but on two competing versions of self-interest. Among Protestants, disputes arose when one group enjoyed access to the schoolhouse when others did not, and in such cases the outsiders either demanded equal access or threatened that if their group could not enjoy fair use of a public space, then no other group should either. The latter proposition fit Catholic and atheistic objectors to a "T," since neither group could enjoy the privilege of such use anyway.

Yet while nativists were fond of blaming Catholics and foreigners for religious controversies surrounding schools, most appeals and letters about religious meetings came from natives or Protestants complaining about other Protestants. Most complaints referred to damage, particularly from class meetings and revivals, and they were filed by English surnamed appellants and writers. In some instances, however, Protestants appealed as Protestants, for religious reasons, and local school disagreements showed signs of religious motivation.

As anti-formal Protestant faiths benefited from their populist appeal in sheer numbers of members, so they suffered from the fractious, chaotic nature of such an affiliation. Local feuds within denominations contributed to fights over the schoolhouse far more than Catholic-Protestant conflicts or extremely rare examples of cross-denominational Protestant conflict. A typical example of a school's feeling the fallout of an interdenominational Protestant conflict comes from Italy, Yates County.[33] In 1870, Philo Conklin led a group of residents in a bitter appeal from the actions of their trustee:

> The schoolhouse is remote from any church and the Methodist-Episcopal Society has had a class there for thirty years or more, and the schoolhouse has been the place where they held their meetings and Sunday schools. Last fall two of the members got dissatisfied with the preacher in charge and their only known grievance was because the preacher would not appoint one of them Class leader. They said if the Preacher was sent back hear [sic] another year they would leave the Church. He was sent back and they got up a paper stating that they were free from sin and the Methodist-Episcopal Church, that theire [*sic*] names were registered in the Lamb's book of life on high and so on. Then they went around—even on Sunday—to the most ignorant ones of the class, and those that they could influence, and had them signed theire [*sic*] paper to leave the church and some signed it that did not make any profession or belonged to the Church; they got some twenty names they said that they would break down and run out the old class. They then set up a class and called themselves Free Methodists, they got a preacher and appointed a meeting on the same hour that we had Sunday school.[34]

Eventually, the trustee, a member of the Free Methodists, closed the schoolhouse to the Methodist-Episcopal's Sunday school altogether. Events continued to turn sour (the Sunday school eventually met in a barn), until finally the Methodist-Episcopals wrote an indignant appeal to the Superintendent. In its conclusion, the appeal posed three increasingly interesting questions: "First—is it lawful or right to use the School House for any other purpose than common school? Second—is it right to open the house for one society and close it against another when the inhabitants belong to both societies? Third—in the view of the division in the District on this matter, would it not be better to close the house to all Except common schools purposes?"[35]

What makes these questions interesting is their progression. Before the appeal, the Methodist Episcopals of district six, Italy, used the schoolhouse for religious purposes without discord or (it would seem) a second thought.

Suddenly put in the position of outsiders, they questioned the legality of such use, then the justice of the common school system that allowed them to be excluded, and finally the wisdom of allowing anyone to use the school building at all. As Superintendent Skinner would do thirty-six years later, the Italy Methodist-Episcopals recognized the potential for conflict inherent in religious use of the schoolhouse. But theirs was an exceptional situation. The problem was not diversity of opinion, which usually did not cause conflict among different sects who shared schools and church buildings on Sundays throughout the state, but the bitter, unbending vision of the religious faction in power that inflicted the power of the majority upon a minority.

Catholics could understand the idea of being outsiders, being conspicuous dissenters from American Protestantism and sometimes objects of hostility. Moreover, as the backbone of the Democratic Party, they joined other district watchdogs over unnecessary school expense without sharing the Republican penchant for Protestant piety. Nevertheless, despite contemporaneous and contemporary characterizations, Catholics made little formal hay of Protestant use of school buildings, except in complaints about damage. In Clinton County (25 percent Catholic in 1875), one trustee wrote, "It is the custom in this section of [the] country to use school houses for public worship in localities where they are not able to build and sustain a church."[36] The absence of appeals and letters from or concerning Catholic opposition is even more striking than the relative silence on the issue in general.

The few appeals and letters that did come from Catholics do not differ from other material objections to the state, nor from those of so-called "infidels," who ranked equally low in the estimation of their opponents in disputes. (Indeed, until Superintendent Skinner's 1896 decision, what other type of complaint could Catholics and nonbelievers make when the state condoned meetings?) The appeals did differ, however, in the character of the replies that they garnered—replies that reveal a lack of understanding on the part of those who did use schools for meetings. Both Catholics and nonbelievers faced open derision in appeals documents of their opponents. One district trustee sarcastically defended his opening the schoolhouse to Methodists, writing, "This Respondent admits that all good and religious meetings and Christian exercises such as congregations to gather for social prayer and the preaching of the gospel whether in the Humble Cottage of the School House [*sic*] in this district or in the Spacious Churches in the City of Albany is a very and "Great Annoyance" to Infidels and Roman Catholics, a very few of wich [*sic*] this school district is annoyed with."[37] A trustee from another district targeted Catholics, infidels, and Democrats together, claiming that the appeal "was gotten up principally to avenge those who favor religion, education, and good morals."[38]

Despite the added rhetorical hurdles that Catholics and nonbelievers faced—having to deflect arguments that they were hostile to religion as well as the usual burden of proving material damage to the schoolhouse—their appeals and letters are most notable for their conspicuous infrequency. Among pietistic Protestants, the issue was not so much the damage caused by Sabbath meetings—after all, these groups derived benefit from the meetings greater than the cost of the damage, which was borne by the district as a whole—but by other details of use. For Protestants, controversies arose over the exclusive use of the school by one group, or the exceptional type of use characteristic of Methodist revivals and class meetings.

EXPLANATIONS

Why was there only one appeal a year, on average, targeting religious use of the schoolhouse? The law itself provides the most obvious explanation. Statute and case law left religious meetings at the sole discretion of the trustee, permitting such use unless appellants could show evidence of damage to the schoolhouse. If Catholics, nonbelievers, or anyone else for that matter failed to prove damage to the schoolhouse, then they would likely lose their appeal until 1896. Even after that date, however, there was hardly an explosion of appeals over the issue. If religious meetings did no actual damage, on the other hand, then opposition to the practice would probably be tepid at best, since no one suffered any direct harm. In fact, in an age when government and religion teamed up on other social issues, such as poverty and health care, there was little impulse toward strict separation of church and state for its own sake. Perhaps the appeals represent all or nearly all of the examples where use of the schoolhouse resulted in damage. This seems unlikely, however, given the type of damage described in those that did.

A second explanation is that the common school system contained local disagreements over the use of the schoolhouse—differences of opinion that may have been widespread but remained at the level of local contention rather than erupting into major controversy or extra-local conflict. Chapter 4 shows that certain aspects of the common school system worked in this fashion: districting policy could generate homogeneous districts, voting procedures could legitimate controversial decisions or policies by creating a system widely accepted as just, and tax policies could keep district voters directly in touch with expenditures while creating local alliances between the rich and religious outsiders by discouraging litigation. The effects of districting are obvious in the context of religious use of the schoolhouse. Homogeneous districts would be less likely to disagree over which religion, if any, would have access to the school. Likewise, the process of taxation, which made local taxpayers responsible for their own schoolhouse as well as any legal costs from an appeal, made residents conscious of their wallets at least as much as their souls, and made Protestants more likely to object to meetings and more likely to mollify religious minorities or dissenters. Both districting and tax policy would help explain why most complaints over meetings came from Protestants, not Catholics.

Voting also played a role in conflicts over religious meetings. The idea that democracy offered the fairest means of settling disputes ran deep in school districts, and democracy itself—as an abstract concept—legitimated the entire common school system. Describing midwestern school district residents, Wayne Fuller wrote, "They wrestled with such intricacies as bond issues, taxes, and contingency funds, and if they had greater confidence in democracy than other groups of Americans, it was because democracy was no abstraction to them."[39] This characterization applies to nineteenth-century New Yorkers within district schools as well. Faith in democracy related specifically to the religious use of the schoolhouse. The law gave trustees sole discretion over use of the schoolhouse, yet trustees often used district voting as a tool for resolving differences of opinion.

> "Notice"
> A Special Meeting will be held at the Millgrove School-house
> January 23, at 7 o'clock pm
> (The question to be voted on is this)
> Shall the School-house be opened for Public Worship, Preaching
> the Gospel, etc. and the house be warmed for such purpose with
> school wood as often as such appointments may be made?
> Every Voter in this School District is respectfully requested to be
> present at the appointed meeting and show his colors.
> By order of the Trustee.
> W. W. Skive, Clerk[40]

This notice, hand copied into a letter from Portville, Cattaraugus County, typified the use of voting to authenticate (and in some cases to determine) the decisions of the trustee. Appeals and letters from Granger, Clinton, Wellsville, Middletown, Parishville, and other towns describe trustees' calling (or attempting to call) special meetings to democratically determine whether the district school would be open for religious meetings.[41]

Majority rule did not provide districts with an easy solution for differences of opinion. Minorities obviously not only lost such votes but also may have rejected the concept that voting was a fair way to determine a practice that was inherently unfair. In such cases, they could appeal if the school suffered material damage, and they would, presumably, win. All of the evidence of voting to settle schoolhouse disputes comes from the appeals and letters of those who did not accept voting as a legitimate way to settle the matter. And there is no way to know if those examples of voting reflected common practice. Yet the fact that trustees called meetings in many cases means that they had reason to assume that all of the residents of their districts would accept the outcomes—that is, even opponents of religious use of the schoolhouse would accept the practice if it came as the result of a democratic decision-making process.

Conclusion

It is difficult to determine which specific aspect of the common school system best kept disagreements over religious use of the schoolhouse contained at the local level—taxation, voting policy, or homogeneous districting. Perhaps there just was not that much controversy at all. What is apparent is that the practice of using the schoolhouse decreased over time as the need for public space, the tolerance of voters, and even the state's opinion of the practice diminished. While this winnowing process occasionally jumped to the level of state intervention, for the most part, it remained local.

In this light, the 1896 appeal from Rush, Monroe County, that opened this chapter takes on a new significance. The case led Superintendent Skinner to articulate the criticism that religious use of the schoolhouse always led to conflict. In fact, the case provides evidence of a different sort. The appeal came after a failed attempt at a local peaceable adjustment: a district-wide referendum. The losers of the vote did not accept that attempt at local mediation, arguing that the decision of the trustee, and the majority, was an unjust imposition on the public. The defendants argued that the religious use of the schoolhouse had, in fact, enhanced the schoolhouse, providing a cabinet organ, lamps, and window shades that were available for school use. Moreover, their Sunday school and religious services met the educational intent of the law, which required that trustees allow use of the schoolhouse for only educational purposes or singing schools. In short, the religious use of the school provided singular benefit to the district. The appellants countered that the very use of the school for such purposes did harm by "embarrassing the instruction of the pupils," a nonmaterial argument about the rights of the minority to not be subject to an intangible establishment of religion—an argument that carried the day.[42]

Altogether, the case tells a complex story. While unusual in the fact that it went all the way to the state for resolution, the controversy of district seven, Rush, represents a broader process. It tells of competing understandings of the use of the schoolhouse for religious purposes. Viewed by users—

usually Protestants—this practice benefited the district spiritually and materially, as it had done for many years. Viewed by the objectors—usually other Protestants—the practice violated the intent of the common (or public) school by introducing a spirit of religious favoritism that made itself clear in the classroom by the material evidence of its presence. The use of the district schoolhouse for religious meetings had always had a Janus-faced relationship with common schooling—building interest and a sense of ownership in the school while sometimes generating controversy and discord. Over the nineteenth century, the benefit and cost seemed roughly balanced, but by the end of that century, that balance had shifted, in the view of the state at least. The social benefit of religious use of the schoolhouse no longer outweighed the costs to district harmony.

Chapter 6

Religious Exercises in District Schools

Introduction

Religious instruction is probably the oldest and most enduring curricular issue in American education.[1] As we saw in chapter 1, the New York State Legislature engaged the issue directly in the early nineteenth century when it created a civil system of mass education to replace the older forms of ecclesiastic control. A civil system did not necessarily mean strictly secular schools. Taking a safely neutral view on the issue, the legislature left decisions about the religious character of school instruction to the democratic determinations of individual districts—except in New York City, where the state legislature intervened directly to prohibit "sectarian instruction" but allowed Bible reading without comment.

Throughout the nineteenth century (indeed until the late twentieth), the state government followed this laissez-faire path—with one exception. Beginning in 1839, state superintendents consistently upheld the doctrine in appeals decisions that district schools could not engage in denominationally specific or "sectarian" religious instruction.[2] Such instruction harked back to the day of ecclesiastic control and threatened the ability of district schools to draw all of a district's children. During the nineteenth century, superintendents interpreted this to mean any formal religious exercises, but their interpretation did not technically make religion in public schools illegal; it just made exercises during school hours illegal if someone objected. Within the context of this tradition of case law, school districts developed a wide array of arrangements, from Bible reading without comment, to nondenominational prayer, to singing popular hymns, to (in about half of all post-bellum districts) nothing at all.

After the Civil War, changes in the religious character of the nation, and in New York State, created new challenges for the common school system. Immigration brought increasing numbers and strength to the Catholic Church. The Civil War enhanced the place of religion in American public life and led many leading Protestants to equate Americanism with Protestantism, or at least with Christianity. And finally, new religions, and new scientific challenges to religion, sprang up even as old religions garnered new strength.[3]

Governed locally and charged with making good citizens out of a community's children, district schools reflected their constituents' ideas about the place of religion in public schooling. What happened when these ideas clashed? Religious ideas, tied to absolute concepts of right and wrong and good and evil, seemed particularly prone to disagreement. Some leading American Protestants, for example, regularly referred to the Catholic Pope as the "Antichrist," and Catholics as "Papists." Devotional Bible reading, popular among American Protestants, was itself an un-Catholic act, a celebration of the individual's unfettered relationship to God, and a bitten thumb at the Catholic Church's insistence on clerical interpretation. *Harper's Weekly* cartoonist Thomas Nast depicted Irish Americans as gorillas and Catholic priests as dangerous enemies to American public schools.[4] Conservative Catholic leaders, on the other hand, labeled Protestants "heretics," and leading bishops in New York State used the threat of excommunication as a tool to coerce Catholic parents into parochial schools.[5] Pope Pius IX's 1864 *Syllabus of Errors* railed against freedom of conscience, religious toleration, separation of church and state, and public education by the state. Five years later, Pius declared himself infallible, much to the chagrin of moderate American Catholic leaders.[6] Arguing that only religion could truly make a citizen good, militant religious leaders from all sides drew lines in the sand at the schoolhouse door, endorsing various types of religious instruction at public expense.

Most historical accounts of religious exercises in schools have followed the paradigm set by vocal religious and political leaders. Examining doctrines, dogmatists, and demagogues, chroniclers of religious instruction in public schools typically describe the issue as polar and irreconcilable.[7] These accounts make four common assumptions. First, they assume that people thought and behaved in harmony with spiritual and political leaders. Second, they argue that regionalism mattered little. "There might be isolated experiments [at cooperation]," writes one historian, "but they were not likely to be embraced in a country where Protestants outnumbered Catholics five to one."[8] Third, histories of religious exercises in public schools usually examine urban schools, probably for lack of alternative sources, assuming that urban experience at least moderately represented public schooling in general. Finally, scholars embracing the "new political history" have equated ethnoreligious voting trends with groups' full endorsement of extreme political positions on schools, implying that polarized voting behavior reflected actual school practice.[9] Given these assumptions, one can easily view the common schools as being hardly common at all, reflecting various forms of religious tyranny either by overzealous majorities or scheming minorities.[10]

This chapter offers an alternative interpretation. Renewed piety may have gripped the people of New York after the Civil War and led to new demands on schools to reflect religion in the curriculum, but these demands either petered out at the local level, or the common school system usually managed to mediate among them. While not always satisfying to everyone, local school policies were a far cry from the black-and-white polemics of religious leaders or the piquant art of Thomas Nast. When dealing with religious instruction in their own district schools, district residents acted on a variety of motivations that stretched beyond religious affiliation.

Surveys from the late 1880s and 1890s suggest that roughly half of all district schools conducted some form of opening religious exercises, usually Bible reading without discussion. Yet religious exercises excited little controversy in appeals or letters to the State Superintendent (see Table 6.1). In fact, a district was twice as likely to complain to the State Superintendent about religious meetings after school hours than religious exercises during the school day. To put it a different way, one in five districts in New York State appealed to the Superintendent over some local dispute from 1865 to 1905. One in 1,000 did so over religious instruction. This dearth of complaints is at once provocative—because Bible reading, dynamite in the national political arena, seemingly failed to ignite passions at the local level—and frustrating—because there are so few appeals and letters that do exist to offer clues to explain the paradox.

Like previous chapters, this one examines the process of local control of district schools to understand how religious exercises functioned as a local issue. It begins by developing the main ideas used by religious and civil leaders to promote or oppose religious instruction in public schools. The chapter then sets these ideas against district school practice itself, fitting religious exercises into the context of the common school system—a method of school management that emphasized district autonomy and democratic decision making. Finally, the chapter examines the rare instances when controversy spilled over the local level to appear in letters and appeals to the State Superintendent, trying both to explain why those particular examples turned so divisive and why this happened so infrequently. These local controversies fell into specific time periods. From 1867

TABLE 6.1 Religious Exercises in Incoming Correspondence and Appeals to the State Superintendent of Public Instruction of New York, 1868-1903

*Year*****	*Total Appeals†*	*Religious Exercises*		*Total Letters*	*Religious Exercises*			
		Number	*Percent*		*Inquiries*	*Complaints*	*Total*	*Percent*
1867	27	0	0.0	-	-	-	-	-
1868	185	0	0.0	-	-	-	-	-
1869	129	0	0.0	-	-	-	-	-
1870	115	2	1.7	-	-	-	-	-
1871	115	0	0.0	-	-	-	-	-
1872	144	1	0.7	-	-	-	-	-
1873	111	0	0.0	1,768	3	1	4	0.2
1874	114	0	0.0	2,252	4	2	6	0.3
1875	114	1	0.9	749*	0	2	2	0.3
1876	117	0	0.0	765**	0	3	3	0.4
1877	132	1	0.8	-	-	-	-	-
1878	121	0	0.0	-	-	-	-	-
1879	120	3	2.5	1,022**	1	2	3	0.3
1880	106	0	0.0	-	-	-	-	-
1881	108	0	0.0	-	-	-	-	-
1882	66	0	0.0	-	-	-	-	-
1883	92	0	0.0	-	-	-	-	-
1884	65	0	0.0	-	-	-	-	-
1885	87	2	2.2	-	-	-	-	-
1886	17	0	0.0	536***	1	0	1	0.2
1892	110	0		-	-	-	-	-
1893	75	0		-	-	-	-	-
1894	104	0		-	-	-	-	-
1895	102	0		-	-	-	-	-
1896	104	0		-	-	-	-	-
1897	100	1		-	-	-	-	-
1898	116	1		-	-	-	-	-
1899		2						
1900		0						
Total	2,796	22	0.8	7,092	3	24	27	0.4

†This list represents all surviving appeals from 1867 to 1886, and published thereafter. From 1886 to 1892, the state published only a sample of appeals, not a comprehensive listing of all. The collection is fairly intact, judging by appeal decision numbers, though some gaps exist in every year, particularly in 1882.

**Note*: Letters for years 1875 are from sixteen of the fifty-nine counties and New York City, which I selected for their variety and their likelihood of having religious disputes. The counties were Albany, Allegany, Broome, Cattaraugus, Chatauqua, Dutchess, Franklin, Lewis, Monroe, Niagara, Queens, Steuben, St. Lawrence, Ulster, Westchester, and Wyoming.

**Letters for 1876, 1879, and 1886 are the same sample plus Cayuga County.

***Only letters from January to June survive in the 1886 records.

****Before 1887, year filed. After 1887, fiscal year reported on by Superintendent (lags published date of annual report by one year).

Source: New York State Archives. *Appeals Case Files of the State Superintendent of Public Instruction.* Series B0496-78 and B0496-78A; *Incoming correspondence to the State Superintendnent of Public Instruction.* Series A2004.

to 1880, residents from eight districts appealed over religious exercises. After 1885, religious exercises disappeared from the appeals process (and emerged in the 1890s only as a tangentially related issue: the wearing of religious garb by public schoolteachers, discussed in chapter 9).[11]

Pedagogy for a Pious Nation

In 1879, longtime Long Island school commissioner Thomas Mount announced his retirement. "I have been school commissioner for twelve years," he explained. "My service has extended from January 1864 to the present time, three years excepted." Now, in his final official report to the State Superintendent, Mount penned an impassioned manifesto. He expressed particular concern for religious instruction, arguing that religion was the source of all morality and, ultimately, all citizenship. "When we educate the mental [faculties], at the expense or neglect of the moral and religious faculties of a man, we are only turning him around instead of moving him forward. In society and the State, the result is revolution, and not progress. We must educate to good or we educate to evil." An experienced school leader, Mount displayed awareness of the problems of religious education in an inclusive public school, qualifying his recommendation: "I mean not sectarianism nor bigotry," he assured the Superintendent. "I mean a knowledge of the relations existing between man and his Maker, and a proper observance of them." Nevertheless, he offered no specific means to teach religious ideas without offense, instead enjoining the state, to his final sentence, to "Teach them—teach them unhesitatingly as knowledge relating to any science; then will the system of education be a safe one."[12]

Mount's faith that religion could, and should, be taught without being "sectarian" or unfairly biased revealed a common dilemma for district schools in post-bellum America. Many Americans, and many New Yorkers, experienced the Civil War as a profoundly religious event. In the decade before the Civil War, American religions enjoyed rapid growth in members and importance. The war not only consolidated these gains but propelled religion into a new position in American life. Most Northern clergy supported the Union cause when war began in 1861. From the start, Northern and Southern clergy alike invoked rich biblical language to justify the prosecution of war as Divine will, as well as to predict victory for their sides. For religious leaders—Catholic, Protestant and (though few in number and low in profile) Jewish—the war provided a new opportunity to be public figures, and victory bestowed a newfound civil authority. Brooklyn's Henry Ward Beecher and other leading Protestants gained national recognition.[13] Even New York City's Archbishop John Hughes, the boogeyman of anti-Catholic, anti-immigrant nativists in the antebellum North, emerged as a respected spokesman for Catholic concerns before his death in 1864—due to his unflinching support of the Union cause.[14] Among soldiers, the army hosted major religious (Protestant) revivals, and soldiers themselves organized Bible study groups and built churches. For those women and men who remained at home, religion justified hardship, consoled loss, and mobilized action in charitable organizations such as the Sanitary Commission, the Christian Commission, and freedmen's aid societies.[15] For many Northerners, writes one historian, "the link between Union victory and God's plan was almost complete."[16] For Northern religious minorities, such as Catholics and Jews, service in the war provided proof of full citizenship, paid in blood.[17] Attempting to forge this consensus, Congress coined the phrase "In God we trust" on U.S. currency.

Renewed interest in religion, and particularly in its seeming connection to American civic identity and Union victory, brought new pressure to bear on Northern public schools. In the decades following the war, religious enthusiasts sought to include religion as a key curricular component of public education, arguing that good citizenship required religious belief.[18] "Piety is not to be put on like a holiday dress, to be worn on state occasions, but it is to be exhibited in our conduct at all times," wrote Cardinal James Gibbons in *Our Christian Heritage*. "Our youth must practice every day the Commandments of God, as well as the rules of grammar and arithmetic."[19]

Protestant and Catholic leaders alike endorsed religious instruction in public education, but they differed dramatically in their proposals. Some Protestant leaders vigorously pushed Bible reading without comment in public schools, which they insisted could offend no person of faith, whether Protestant, Catholic, or Jew, because the Bible was nonsectarian. Many public school leaders, such as Commissioner Mount from Long Island, adopted this view as well, arguing that religious education could avoid "sectarianism and bigotry" and dismissing dissenters' protests that it displayed both.[20] The National Teacher's Association (later the NEA) resolved in 1869 that "The Bible should not only be studied, venerated, and honored as a classic for all ages . . . but devotionally read, and its precepts inculcated in all the common schools of the land."[21]

The Catholic Church leadership, on the other hand, demanded public funding for church-run schools, challenging the very concept of the common school system. In 1866 the Second Plenary Council of Baltimore urged priests to redouble their efforts to provide a religious education for Catholic children. "Religious teaching and religious training," the council declared, "should form part of every system of school education." Bishops were to oversee the movement, so that "schools [would] be established in connection with all the churches of their dioceses."[22] New York's *The Catholic World* emphasized the civil aspects of this vision in 1870, writing that "The children of Catholics must be trained up in the Catholic faith, in the Catholic

Church, to be good exemplary Catholics, or they will grow up bad citizens, the pests of society."[23] Though most religious and many civil leaders could agree on the general principle of religious education, historians David Tyack and Elisabeth Hansot conclude, "For a majority of the pan-Protestant school promoters and Catholic leaders, compromise on religion in public education proved impossible."[24]

Throughout the 1870s, Catholic leaders pushed for state funding of their own church-controlled schools but never clearly articulated a position on religion in public schools. In 1871, Rochester's Bishop McQuaid accused public schools of teaching Protestant religion when they conducted religious exercises and of teaching atheism when they did not.[25] Buffalo's Bishop Ryan employed similar logic, stating flatly in 1873, "Public schools are either godless or sectarian; by law they are godless, in fact, they are mostly sectarian."[26] Neither clarified whether religious exercises could be truly nonsectarian for all faiths, or whether the common practice of reading the Douay (Catholic) version of the Bible in all-Catholic public schools was acceptable. Concessions along those lines would hurt the Church's arguments in favor of church-controlled, publicly funded schools.

There were notable exceptions to the push for religious education in public schools and the division between militant Catholic and Protestant versions of this vision. While many skeptics avoided stirring the bog, by the 1880s, U.S. Education Commissioner William T. Harris made a splash by coming out in favor of no religious instruction at all in public schools. Harris feared the coercive nature of state-sponsored instruction and also cited the essential differences between academic and religious instruction. The former, he argued, required critical thinking and reason; the latter required unquestioning faith. "It seems to me clear," he wrote in an article for the New York-based *Independent*, "that it is better to separate religious instruction from secular instruction and to place it in a different school, a school connected to a church."[27] The New England Conference of the Methodist Episcopal Church resolved in 1875 that while Bible reading in public schools was desirable, "when enforced by legal sanction, [it] is an obligation inconsistent with our republican form of government, and the principles of our Protestant religion, and the teaching of the Bible itself."[28] Even Henry Ward Beecher opposed compulsory Bible reading for children whose parents objected—liberty of conscience being more important to the state than the benefits of religious education.[29] Nevertheless, this "civil" view of common schooling, held among lay Catholics and Protestants, as well as many Jews and nonbelievers, remained relatively obscure in the discourse on religion in public schools until the late 1890s.[30]

New York State law did little to address the issue directly. At no time before 1894 did any law exist regarding the conduct of religious exercises in common schools throughout the state; while the legislature did periodically enter religious tussles in New York City and Brooklyn, it remained mute on statewide legislation for religion, honoring the long tradition of local control over such matters.[31] After a careful study of the law, a Manhattan lawyer concluded in 1889, "The question of what is to be taught in [public] schools is left exclusively to the trustees of each school district or to the board of education in each city."[32] This legislative silence was not entirely neutral: the legislature did defeat attempts to provide state aid to parochial schools, thus rejecting the Catholic Church's proposal for religious mass education in church-run "public" schools. Nevertheless, it enacted no legislation specifically prohibiting such arrangements until the entire state adopted a revised constitution in 1894. That constitution prohibited aid to "any school or institution of learning wholly or in part under the control or direction of any religious denomination." It also blocked funds to any public schools "in which any denominational tenet or doctrine is taught," thereby outlawing denominational instruction in public schools.[33] The constitution did not, however, specify whether interdenominational instruction, particularly Bible reading and prayer, constituted "denominational sects or tenets."

Instead of legislative acts, case law—based on the decisions of state superintendents—determined the legal status of religious exercises in New York State. From the antebellum era through the turn of the twentieth century, superintendents steered a steady course, consistently construing the common school system as legitimately common, ruling in favor of minorities in appeals cases over religious exercises, prohibiting public funds to church-run schools, and, in turn, protecting the rights of religious minorities in the common schools who objected to offensive religious exercises.[34] State superintendents did so, however, in a manner that most respected localism. If a single parent objected, then a teacher could not lawfully conduct religious exercises during school hours. But optional exercises before the start of or following school were perfectly legal.[35] And unlike legislative acts, case law held authority only on a case-by-case basis: superintendents usually had no power over a given district's policies unless an aggrieved resident filed an appeal.

Left to their own devices, New York district schools responded to the movement for religious instruction in a variety of ways, from avoiding religious exercises to optional exercises before school to mandatory exercises during school hours. Set in their local context, these decisions reveal a complex set of motives and policies that moves beyond the irreconcilable positions of religious leaders, politicians, and school reformers. Just as the schoolhouse often provided a physical community center, it also served as the symbolic heart of a district—a testament to both the district's civic cohesion and its ideological division. A look at how districts responded reveals that the former—civil cohesion—usually trumped the latter, so that districts arrived at relatively peaceable adjustments at the local level far more frequently than they found themselves embroiled in the bitter conflicts that required outside mediation.

Evidence of religious practice in district schools comes from a number of sources, but the most useful comes from appeals and letters to the Superintendent, and, to a lesser degree, from unofficial statewide surveys. Appeals provide details of the specific form and function of religious exercises in district schools: what they looked like, and how teachers, trustees, parents, and other district residents felt about them. Surveys, though limited in their scope, show the popularity of exercises statewide, providing quantitative evidence to support the qualitative descriptions from letters and appeals. Moreover, the surveys reveal the ideas and anxieties of the surveyors themselves. Together, appeals, letters, and surveys offer a colorful glimpse into the practice of religion in district schools.

Religious Exercises in Practice

In practice, religious instruction in post-bellum district schools never reached the elevated status of "knowledge relating to any science," for which Commissioner Mount and others campaigned. Instead, religious instruction boiled down to morning religious exercises at the start of school: brief, symbolic, and rote, involving ritualistic exercises, not classes on specific religious theories; religious instruction never stood as an equal with the regular course of studies. Often called "chapel exercises," religious exercises mimicked the rituals of church worship, including prayer, Bible reading, and singing hymns. They reinforced the practices of denominational (usually Protestant) sects without referring to any particular one.[36] Conducted in the district public school, they conveyed a strong message that good citizenship and morality rested squarely in the Christian tradition.[37]

What did religious exercises in district schools look like? The most popular was reading passages from the Bible (usually the King James version); sometimes schools combined this with a prayer.[38] Teachers used these exercises to open the school day, either officially at 9:00 A.M., or unofficially at 8:45 A.M., and conducted them for approximately fifteen minutes.[39] Objectors described the practice in detail. In district eight in Arcade, Wyoming County, "the teacher read a chapter of the Bible and prayed and ordered the scholars to put their books under [the seat] and bow their heads."[40] In district one in Hurley, Ulster County, the teacher read a chapter of the Bible and "compelled students to cross and fold their hands behind their backs, the pupils standing during the whole reading."[41] In district 3 in Saugerfield, Oneida County, the teacher required students to kneel during the reading and prayer.[42]

Sometimes the children sang religious or patriotic songs during the opening exercises. A less common but potentially more genuinely nondenominational practice than Bible-oriented "chapel exercises," singing religious hymns offered a greater chance of finding common ground. In Wayland, Ulster County, for example, Catholics and Protestants agreed on a list of hymns to use as opening religious exercises in the common school as an alternative to Bible reading and prayer. (A group of freethinkers mobilized against the process, electing a trustee who shut it down.)[43] Song books for schools in the post-Civil War period reflected an increasing use of singing to encourage district "harmony" in opening exercises. From 1870 to 1880, these steadily changed from explicitly Protestant hymns to more vaguely religious, strongly moralistic, and patriotic songs.[44] By 1891, the State Superintendent endorsed musical education in general, vowing to encourage it through all the means at the department's disposal.[45]

Why did districts choose to offer religious exercises? One reason was practical. American teachers today can attest to the daily struggle required to bring a class to order after the bell rings. While students in nineteenth-century district schools did not change classrooms during the day (there usually being but one), they nonetheless arrived to school at 9:00 A.M. after a vigorous journey—by foot, sled, bicycle, or, if they were lucky, hitching a ride on a horse or buggy—of up to a mile and a half.[46] Religious exercises enforced a unifying moment of silence and backed it with sacred significance. "I believe [Bible reading] marks a definite change from free conduct to study conduct," reported the city superintendent of Fulton in 1903. "It is the best help in the discipline of a school."[47] Exercises conferred upon the teacher a few moments of infinite authority, at least in theory, not only teaching the fear of God but exploiting it to quiet the children. "The morning exercises give dignity to the school," explained another. "The Bible reading inspires in the pupils an attitude of respect, if not reverence, and the day begins on a higher plane." In an age when most writers considered a "good" teacher to be one who kept effective discipline, religious exercises must have held strong pedagogical appeal.[48]

Moreover, religious exercises fit in well with a pedagogical revolution that occurred in the 1870s: graded schools. In a study of a rural school in Wisconsin, historian Herbert Kliebard found that the decades from 1865 to 1900 saw a major change in the organization of curriculum and instruction, a change that New York experienced as well. During those years, the traditional form of common school teaching, in which students learned individually, at their own pace—marching through textbooks, monitored and occasionally heard by their teachers—crumbled like old chalk. In its place emerged a graded system, which grouped students by age, set a standard pace for learning, and envisioned a course of study beyond what textbooks defined as "instruction." This change pressured school districts to buy uniform textbooks (required by law in New York in 1877) and to build union schools with multiple rooms. By 1887, writes Kliebard, grading pupils in urban and rural schools had gained national acceptance.[49]

The change to a graded curriculum (even within one-room classrooms) encouraged and sometimes required teachers to offer group, or *ensemble*, instruction in addition to the textbook curriculum.[50] Several county commissioners mentioned these changes in their annual reports, noting that many teachers were now offering some subjects "as general exercises, the whole school taking part." "I find now," reported a commissioner from Rensselaer County, "blackboards in daily use, and a more general discussion of ideas between teacher and scholar in connection with the daily lessons. The pupils have lost their diffidence, and take a decided interest in the general exercises."[51] The new pedagogy required teacher-led group activities by grade level but also encouraged teaching to the class as a whole. Religious exercises provided a convenient form of such instruction, easily suiting a classroom of disparate grades while also fitting the pedagogical exigencies of the day. By 1902, the state Department of Education published a recommended curriculum guide for public schools that included opening exercises, though it did not specify what they should be.[52]

Advocates of religious exercises spoke explicitly of the moral benefits that religious exercises provided. Order, good behavior, and religious exercises seemed to go hand in hand. "I would like to here state that I do not belong to any church whatever, nor never did," declared George Flint, former trustee of school district ten, Rodman, Jefferson County, "but I had rather see my children go to Sunday school and to meeting instead of running about the streets and that instruction from the Bible is a part of children's education."[53] The details of the religious exercises mattered little, as long as they maintained some religious quality and remained nonsectarian. In a laudatory annual report in 1871, for example, a county commissioner from Jefferson County highlighted the religious piety inculcated in his county's schools: "Much attention has been given to the manners and morals of the pupils; chapel exercises of some sort are held in nearly every school, and good order, neatness, and gentle manners are everywhere in rule."[54] The *some sort* is revealing, as is another example from a graded union free school in Mount Morris, Livingston County. Teachers there reported that their principal had ordered them to conduct some form of exercises daily in their classrooms, saying that "if they could not conduct chapel exercises, they were not fit to teach school." The details of the exercises did not concern him. He told them that they "could read a chapter of the Bible, or a poem, or some such matter as they thought interesting, but it would be best if they made up their minds to conduct the exercises."[55] In both cases, the idea of a solemn, religiously oriented exercise mattered more than whatever specific form it might take or content it might contain.

Many evangelicals insisted that religious exercises be mandatory. In case law, superintendents ruled against religious exercises in district schools during school hours throughout the nineteenth century but at the same time permitted such exercises outside of regular school hours.[56] Indeed, religious exercises outside of school hours barely differed from the long-established, legally permissible practice of allowing religious meetings in the school house outside of regular hours.[57] Despite the permissibility of before-school exercises, however, advocates of religious exercises pushed for exercises during school hours.

Opponents to mandatory exercises were quick to charge that Protestants wanted to use the coercive power of the school to proselytize to non-Protestant children. During the Civil War, for example, Protestant officers took advantage of their "captive audience" of Catholic soldiers, refusing visits from priests unless a majority of the men were Catholic, preferring to evangelize them instead.[58] Given the missionary tradition in American Protestantism and the desire among Protestant moralists to curb "immoral" behavior in other people's children, this charge probably contained some truth.

From the point of view of classroom instruction, however, there was a strong practical incentive in making religious exercises mandatory. Advocates intended religious exercises to instill piety and order in the class, but optional exercises put teachers at a decided disadvantage. "There has been some trouble between the Protestants and Catholics in regard to the reading of the Bible in District No. 3, Town of Mentz," wrote County Commissioner Daratt. "It appears the teacher met the pupils before 9 o'clock—with the consent of the trustee—and required them to lay aside their books while she conducted the exercise. Mr. O'Neils' children came and claimed they had a right to study while the teacher was reading. The teacher claimed that if she allowed them to, other pupils would disregard her wishes."[59] In a union free school district in Orangetown, Rockland County, the board of education insisted that Catholic children be present during religious exercises and act "with decorum," even though they were not required to participate. In an appeal to the State Superintendent, parents demanded that their children be allowed to wait outside until after the exercises. This the board refused, arguing, "This interference causes much disorder outside of the room, and the subsequent entrance of these pupils causes a loss of time and disturbance to class work."[60] In both cases, symbolic religious exercises failed in their pedagogical utility unless they could be made mandatory for all children and could lead teachers to adopt a coercive policy rather than abandon the practice.

Mandatory exercises also fulfilled the symbolic intention of religious exercises more effectively than optional ones by wedding religion directly to the district school—the heart of the community. The district school often served as the only public space in rural areas, hosting most public events, both social and civil. Even beyond its function as a building, the district school as an institution served as a strong symbol of the district's linkage to

American civil society. Residents paid taxes to build and support it, sent their children to it, and enjoyed the power to govern it in the smallest, most democratic unit of the American system of government. Religious exercises need not offer thoughtful, deep instruction in religion, as long as students and the community felt their presence in the school. By literally framing the school day as an opening ceremony, religious exercises served as a powerful symbol to the community: a declaration of common civil identity as a Christian republic.[61]

As time passed after the war, demographic and economic changes swept over district schools, and anti-immigrant agitators such as Josiah Strong urged New York Protestants to clutch at symbols such as the Bible in schools.[62] A nationwide depression ravaged the state in the 1870s, and again in the 1890s. Many New Yorkers headed westward, or to cities, to find work, and the rural school district experienced demographic displacement. In 1870, a Tompkins County commissioner lamented the effect on district schools:

> Many of the schools are very small in comparison with what they were formerly. I not infrequently find schools now with less than twenty scholars in attendance, where a few years ago seventy-five or eighty were registered. The farms have been enlarged, and young men with their families have sought homes in the West. The location of many of these sparse districts is not such that they can be united with other districts, without making it very inconvenient for some to attend school. How this difficulty can be met, and those schools which are now struggling for an existence be relieved, I know not.[63]

Even those who held jobs found their wages cut by growing corporations, while agricultural prices, generous to farmers in the decade before the war, entered a downward spiral. Amid these disorienting economic changes, demographics shifted as well. For some native Protestants, the two calamities were directly related. Immigrants (many non-Protestant) competed with natives for jobs and political power—not just in cities but in emerging mill towns and on farms.[64] In 1872, a commissioner from Oneida County described the changes in economics and demographics in rural district life over the last thirty years:

> There were then comparatively few foreigners on the farms in rural districts. The settlers were mainly from the New England states, and nearly all had large families. Seven, eight, and nine pupils, registered at the winter school, for a single family, was a common occurrence. There were but two academies then, where there are a

> dozen now. The thousand occupations for agents, and traveling agencies for trade, for insurance, patent rights, and publications, had yet made no drafts upon the country for young men and for boys yet in their teens.
>
> The descendants of those farmers have but small families. From four- to seven-tenths of the farming population now supplying our schools are foreigners. The wealthier classes send their children to higher schools, at ages ranging from twelve years upward; while the children of these foreigners are permanently withdrawn from school at an average age of fourteen.[65]

"There is a constant tendency in society toward centralization," wrote another commissioner in 1885, "in which the rural schools diminish, and village and city schools increase. I have no hesitation in saying that there are as many children attending school in this commissioner district as there were twenty-five years ago; but their location has changed."[66]

Finally, Christianity in general—Protestantism and Catholicism alike—though enjoying increasing membership and status, also faced its own spiritual crisis. Darwinism threatened the foundations of Judeo-Christian tradition, particularly the literal authority of the Bible.[67] Contemporary observers noted with alarm the seemingly growing opposition to religion, not only among "freethinking" intellectuals but also in the population at large. Henry King Carroll, director of the Division of Churches for the Eleventh U.S. Census, estimated in 1893 that "one out of every twelve persons is either an active or passive opponent of religion."[68] Challenges to religion touched rural areas as well as cities. "For every overt village freethinker," wrote a recent historian of the period, "there must have been dozens who responded to organized religion in the way of passive resistance."[69] A writer for *The Forum* concluded in 1886 that "Christianity appears to many of the wisest to be at the present day in deadlier peril than it has been at any time during the eighteen hundred years of its existence."[70]

Awash in this sea of change, concerned Protestants could look to the Bible as a buoy for Americanism as well as Protestantism, and they chose the public schoolteacher as their lifeguard.[71] Moreover, as Protestantism increasingly became a "creature of culture" from the turn of the century, more Americans could identify with symbols of Pan-Protestant piety, whether or not they belonged to any church or were otherwise evangelically inclined.[72]

It would be a mistake, however, to associate the appeal of religious exercises solely with defensiveness and retrenchment within American Protestantism, however. In a more optimistic, proactive sense, symbolic religious exercises fit into Protestantism's missionary, reformist tradition as well. In addition to encouraging good behavior, religious education could—in some Protestant eyes—combat the negative aspects of social change that surrounded them in small towns as well as big cities: poverty (then commonly understood as a result of vice), crime, corruption, and (for the more zealous) Catholicism.[73] One expert on criminal behavior, for example, wrote in 1900 that he had never known an instance of a habitual criminal or recidivist being a member in good standing in a Protestant Evangelical church.[74]

How could brief, daily exercises accomplish the lofty goals of Protestant reformers? In spiritual affairs, Protestants frequently referred to their religion as being inherently "reasonable," in the sense that it relied upon (and survived) man's reasoning. Retiring Commissioner Mount of Long Island argued that keeping religion out of schools thwarted reason, since any deep intellectual inquiry into human knowledge would end up at the doorstep of God. "Any one is mistaken," wrote Commissioner Mount, "who supposes that the American mind of the nineteenth century will rest satisfied with drinking the turbid waters at the mouth of a stream of knowledge by whatever name it may be called, without tracing those waters to their source, withersoever they might lead him."[75] Though advocates of religious exercises differed in whether they viewed the Bible as the literal word of God, a guide for a moral life, or simply great literature, they generally agreed on the positive educational results that would result from religious exercises.[76] Leading advocates argued that the reasonable mind could garner the eternal truths of religion from symbolic exercises even without teacher comment and interpretation. The New York State Superintendent tried to explain this concept in 1903: "The influence of the Bible upon the mind of a child, if daily read in his hearing, cannot but be inspiring, and the unconscious influence of familiarity with its teachings, by all analogy, would certainly tend to the development of good moral character."[77] If the teacher read the Bible at the start of the school day, it was hoped, would not the children think it was true?

Surveys and Surmises

How common were religious exercises? The same forces of localism that discouraged state interference in district affairs (rendering state compulsory education and uniform textbook laws "dead letters" and exerting political pressure against legislation concerning religious instruction) prevented the state from collecting data on local religious practice. Instead, surveys came from religious crusaders with holy axes to grind: the New York Synod of the Presbyterian Church and the Chicago Women's Educational Union. Despite their best efforts, however, the surveyors made only moderate headway into the tangled world of the district school. Their questions were amateurish, their data inconsistent, and their reporting confusing. Nevertheless, they are all that we have.

In 1889, the New York Synod of the Presbyterian Church conducted the first statewide survey on religious practices in public schools since superintendents stopped collecting such statistics in 1840. The survey capped a four-year study of the issue of religion in public education—a study that included reports from eight nations (including the United States) and that sought as its ultimate goal to wed nonsectarian religious instruction to moral education in New York public schools. Its questions reflected the concerns of the committee, including its assertion that religious instruction could be "positive" (that is, overtly Judeo-Christian) without being sectarian. The committee drafted a circular with twelve questions in all and sent these to the state's twenty-five city superintendents and 114 county commissioners. Much of the survey is useless to us today. First, forty-three (38 percent) of the state's commissioners did not respond, and another three sent in responses too illegible to be used. Many of the questions caused confusion for respondents, because the survey committee never defined "positive" religious teaching—a problem that the committee itself admitted.[78] Finally, the committee did not report its results consistently, using phrases such as "many," "most," and "a few" to describe answers.

Despite these problems, several questions provide useful, if confusing, data. Although the committee's unskilled reporting made the responses difficult to interpret, the responses did help depict the relative popularity of various types of religious exercise in district schools (see Table 6.2). The committee did not publish clear statistics by county or numeric (even estimated) accounts of school practice. Nevertheless, comparing the percentages of types of answers suggests that districts that did offer religious exercises engaged in Bible reading approximately twice as often as in prayer or singing hymns. This statistic mirrors the relative frequency of Bible reading as the focus of policy *talk* about religious instruction in schools, as opposed to prayer and hymns, and indeed the place of the Bible in Protestant nationalist symbolism.

Can questions 2–4 in Table 6.2 help determine the percentage of district schools that actually conducted religious exercises? The imprecision of the data in the survey defies any standard statistical analysis. More importantly, commissioners themselves may not have been a good source of such information. As we saw in chapter 2, county commissioners rarely visited a school more than twice a year, and usually only once. Moreover, even if they did see religious exercises—or a lack thereof—on a given day, we cannot know to what extent the teacher was altering her daily routine to please the commissioner. Writing the conclusion to its survey of district schools, the Synod's Committee on Religion and Public Education expressed vague disappointment with its findings. "The vast majority of the answers to these three ques-

TABLE 6.2 District School Results of the New Synod's Survey, *Religion and Public Education*, 1889[1]

Question	*Number and Percent of Commissioners Responding by Answers They Gave*[2]									
	At least two-thirds		*Fewer than half*		*None/Don't Know*		*No response*[3]		*Total*	
	n	%	*n*	%	*n*	%	*n*	%	*n*	%
2. (a) In how many schools is the Bible read?	31	27	23	20	14	12	46	40	114	100
(b) In how many is it read daily?	28	25	20	18	20	18	46	40	114	100
3. (a) In how many is prayer offered?	13	11	31	27	24	21	46	40	114	100
(b) In how many is it offered daily?	12	11	30	26	26	23	46	40	114	100
(c) Is the Lord's Prayer only used?	13	11	16	14	39	34	46	40	114	100
4. (a) In how many are Christian hymns sung daily?	12	11	32	28	24	21	46	40	114	100
(b) In how many occasionally?	6	5	17	15	45	39	46	40	114	100

[1] *Source: Religion and Public Education: Reports of the Committee on Religion and Public Education, Presented to the Synod of New York of the Presbyterian Church in the United States of America, at its Meetings in Auburn, 1887 and in Poughkeepsie, 1889,* 30–32.

[2] Only sixty-eight of 114 commissioners responded to the survey at all. Percentages are rounded and do not always total 100 percent. This table is an approximation of the vague statistics presented in the document. I have combined the original categories as fairly as possible.

[3] Includes three illegible responses.

tions, 2, 3, and 4, were purely conjectural even in the case of those who answered affirmatively, and whose papers elsewhere indicate warm interest in the subject. Plainly," they surmised, "the subject is entirely unfamiliar to most of the Commissioners in the state."[79]

Given that one-third of commissioners did not respond to the survey, I see two ways of using the data to determine the extent of religious exercises in district schools. The first is to take the Synod's findings at face value, assuming that they are accurate and representative. If this is the case, probably a little more than half of all district schools engaged in religious exercises. If category one (at least two-thirds) is weighted as .83 ((.67 + 1.00) ÷ 2), category two (fewer than half) as .25, and none is weighted as zero, then approximately 41 percent of all district schools read the Bible daily. A more generous approach would weigh category one as 100 percent (meaning all schools in those commissioner districts used the Bible daily) and category two as 50 percent, resulting in 56 percent of all district schools using the Bible.

Yet there is good reason to believe that the sample was not entirely accurate or representative. County commissioners were locally elected officials. Their answers to the Presbyterian survey implicated them in a larger debate which, as we have seen, could be bitter and divisive. The Presbyterian committee lamented the fact that many of the commissioners seemed not to care about the issue of religious instruction. "Indeed, 'I don't know' is so frequent an answer," wrote the committee, "as to indicate very clearly the indifference of a large number of these public officers to a vital part of our educational system."[80] Indifference, however, might not be the best explanation. A commissioner from Westchester offered an alternative: "I am of the opinion that no religious teaching, strictly speaking, is given. The harmony of most of our school would be materially disturbed were such teaching given in them." In fact, a minority of the New York Synod's own committee expressed similar concerns, writing, "In the circumstances peculiar to this country, the State will 'best foster the interests of religion pure and undefiled by declining to insist upon distinctive and extended religious instruction in the schools which are under her care, and which are supported by public funds.'"[81] Commissioners excited about the Presbyterian cause of universal Bible reading would have been much more likely to respond to the survey than those who saw the questions as a trap to be avoided in their districts, or those who found the whole question irrelevant. If we consider "no response" as being a more likely indicator of little Bible reading in a commissioner district (say 25 percent), then the generous figure of Bible reading in 56 percent of district schools drops significantly, to 44 percent. The stricter view would put the number at 35 percent—only a third of district schools.

Nine years after the Presbyterian survey, the Chicago Woman's Educational Union (CWEU) conducted a state-by-state survey as part of its reform effort for universal Bible reading in public schools. Perhaps because of its more ambitious scope, the CWEU asked fewer questions and presented even less data than the Presbyterians. Questions included:

1. Were portions of the Bible read regularly in all of the schools under their care? If not, in any part of them?
2. If read, for how many years had it been the custom?
3. If not, was it formerly read there? For how many years?
4. Did the school board rule on the subject?

The questions suggest two features of the CWEU's crusade: indifference to forms of religious exercise other than Bible reading and a desire to set Bible reading in a historical perspective by asking how old the practice was. The former represented the specific nature of the union's reform agenda: putting the Bible in public schools. The latter historical questions—it hoped—would strengthen its claim that the Bible was in fact the nation's book and had served as a traditional bulwark to public education and national identity. To find answers, the CWEU mailed the questionnaires to state superintendents, county commissioners, and city superintendents.[82]

Given the survey's place in a larger, strongly partisan book entitled *The Nation's Book in the Nation's Schools*, the resulting data shine with a suspicious veneer. Consider, for example, the finding that fifty-five city superintendents and county commissioners in New York State claimed that *all* schools in their jurisdictions read the Bible daily (a claim that the Presbyterians had been unwilling to make nine years earlier). On the other hand, the reluctance of state officials to participate in a survey on religion remained consistent. Forty percent of all state officials surveyed did not respond, similar to the 34 percent rate of nonrespondents in the Presbyterian survey (see Table 6.3). Unfortunately, the data failed to differentiate between district and urban schools (the CWEU did not distinguish between the responses of city superintendents and county commissioners). This lack of precision makes other comparisons to the former survey inappropriate.[83]

Like the Presbyterian survey, however, the *Nation's Book* survey lends itself to several different conclusions about the overall use of the Bible in New York State public schools. If we assume that the survey was accurate and representative and weigh the categories of the survey as "all schools" = 1.00, "nearly all" = .67, "some" = .33, and "none" = 0, then approximately 72 percent of all public school districts in New York State, urban and nonurban combined, read the Bible in 1898. If we include nonresponses as districts in the "some" category, then the percentage slips to 57 percent of all public school districts. A more rigorous standard would put the percentage somewhere below half of all districts.

TABLE 6.3 Combined District and City School Results from *The Nation's Book in the Nation's Schools*, 1898[1]

Question	*Number and Percent of Commissioners and City Superintendents Responding by Answers They Gave*											
	All Schools		*Nearly All*		*Some*		*None*		*No Response*		*Total*	
	n	%	*n*	%	*n*	%	*n*	%	*n*	%	*n*	%
1. Number of schools where portions of the Bible were read regularly in all the schools under their care?	55	35	12	8	13	8	14	9	63	40	157	100

[1] *Source:* Elizabeth Blanchard Cook. *The Nation's Book in the Nation's Schools* (Chicago: Chicago Woman's Educational Union, 1898), 16, 31–33.

Opposition to Religious Exercises in District Schools

Opposition to religious exercises came from a variety of sources. The most vocal, well-articulated, and widely published came from freethinkers and Catholics—strange bedfellows indeed. At the local level, some Catholics and freethinkers expressed the same views as their leaders, although (as we shall see) not quite so articulately. Some Protestants opposed religious exercises on civil grounds, or because they might violate individual rights of conscience.[84] "It would be poor policy and poorer Christianity for those in authority to force their opinions on a district either one way or another," wrote a county commissioner in 1903. Others opposed exercises because they did not go far enough. "It is my opinion," countered a superintendent from Medina, "that the mere perfunctory reading of the Scriptures at the morning exercises has no ethical value whatever. In fact, it lessens the respect of pupils for the Sacred Book."[85] One of Brooklyn's leading Protestant lights, Bishop Horatio Potter, told a diocesan convention in 1874 that he "wished to throw out an earnest warning to all Christian people that if they look to the mere reading of a portion of Holy Scripture in the public schools for any effectual religious training, they will lean on a broken reed, they will be deluded by a vain hope."[86] Aside from these, the most influential opinions on the issue at the local level probably came from those who had no strong feeling either way but instead concerned themselves with the civil purposes of the district school. Though their views did not appear in published diatribes, trustees, teachers, and district voters seem to have often chosen to avoid religious instruction altogether, in many cases probably to protect the conscience of the objectors rather than impose the will of the supposed "Protestant majority." (The large number of districts without religious exercises and the low number of letters and appeals suggest this.) They did so for complex reasons. In cases where religious ideologies would not yield to civil concerns, residents filed appeals.

In most cases, controversies over religious exercises began with Catholic parents who objected to religious exercises as a violation of their rights of conscience. Usually they appealed or complained about their children's exposure to, and participation in, mandatory Protestant ("nonsectarian") exercises. A parish priest writing on behalf of parents in Fairport, Monroe County, explained their objection to school prayer:

> Our school is sectarian in tone and manner of opening and closing the school exercises. Catholic children must be there in the morning at a quarter before nine to begin prayer according to the *modus operandi* of the Baptist Church of prayer—
>
> Now I appeal to you to correct this if you can and let those poor children go to school for instruction but not for to become

> Baptist [*sic*]. These children are taught to pray as at here in the church they worship.[87]

Other parents complained that "nonsectarian" Bible reading offended them, because it was the King James Bible, not the Douay Bible (the only English translation approved by the Catholic Church), that was read. "Your petitioner being a Catholic and averse from religious scruples [objects] to having his children instructed in such version," claimed an appeal in 1870.[88] Some parents withdrew their children from school altogether in protest, others only while they fought to change the policies.

Parents also detailed, and detested, the punishments that teachers and trustees occasionally meted out to children who refused to participate in mandatory exercises. In 1870, the trustees of district eight, Watervliet, expelled Catholic children for refusing to participate in exercises.[89] A Cayuga County Catholic mother of three school-age children described her situation to the State Superintendent in 1874. "Sir, my children are being abused in school because they refuse to put down their books while the Bible is being read. They have not disturbed the school in any way. But they are *Catholic* and so the trouble." She also provided heartbreaking details:

> The Trustee's name is Oscar Gutchess and his sister teaches the school. At first he came to the school and hulled [*sic*] my daughter Lizzie out doors a cold freezing morning after the child had walked nearly two miles. I have also to [*sic*] more children attending the same public school who have been treated in like manner and an older son went and the first morning Miss G—sent for her brother who came with his hired man and dragged the boy (John O'Neil) out and scratched his face so the blood flowed down his cheeks. This was continued for several days and began about the first of January.
>
> Since the sixth of this month [January] the teacher has not heard their lessons. This morning I went and seen the teacher and trustee and they both said that until the Children should put down their books their lessons would not be heard.[90]

The mother, Julia O'Neil, concluded her letter by appealing to the notion that public schools must necessarily be religiously inclusive, and that religious exercises failed the test. "Now Mr. Weaver if you say that this is justice in a public school which we (Catholics) support I will take my children and send them elsewhere, and if you believe this is my side of the story send this letter to Oscar and Celia Gutchess (Trustee and Teacher) of School District No. Three Mentz and let them correct all errors."[91] The county commissioner got wind of the situation as well and wrote to the State Superintendent for advice.[92] Though emotionally evocative for readers today, incidents such as this proved to be quite rare in the decades after the Civil War. In fact, after 1874, no letter in my sample mentioned the abuse of students who declined from religious exercises, nor did any appeal complain of abuse after 1872.

Only one appeal mentioned conscientious objection to religious exercises from non-Catholics. In this case, however, the opponents did not appeal to the state over the issue of exercises but over an illegal election that centered on the issue. In 1879, Catholics and Protestants in district one of Wayland, Steuben County, devised a set of religious exercises for the public school that offended neither group, essentially, hymn singing. Freethinkers, however, objected to the whole idea and organized a campaign to elect a trustee who would block it. The freethinkers won the election but were forced to appeal when the Christian officers of the district illegally declared a revote. "As far as character and honors go," wrote the actual winner of the election, "we court comparison." Such extreme action among freethinkers was probably rare, however, given that this appeal from Wayland was the only record among letters and appeals of any such activity. There is no evidence that freethinking children were ever punished for objecting to exercises.[93]

In another unique example, taken from a letter, a pocket of Spiritualists in Friendship, Allegany County, opposed religious exercises by subverting their intent rather than their form. Spiritualism, which spread its first roots in New York State in the 1840s and 1850s, challenged traditional Christianity by positing the existence of a parallel spirit world, with which mediums could communicate.[94] After winning a close election, the Spiritualist trustee hired a teacher who, opponents charged in a letter to the State Superintendent, "Uses every occasion to ridicule Religion, the Bible, and uses her influence to instill unbelief in the Bible in the minds of her schollars [*sic*]." Rather than end the school's traditional religious exercises (Bible reading at the start of the day), the teacher read the Bible "in School hours for the purpose of contradicting it." Friendship Christians now found themselves on the defensive regarding Bible reading, asking a question usually posed by Catholics, "Are we obliged to send our Schollars [*sic*] to such a teacher or keep them from school entirely?"[95] The State Superintendent shared their indignation, responding that, "If the teacher to whom you refer is guilty of the acts you mention, I think that her moral fitness to teach is a proper matter for investigation by the school commissioner, who is authorized by sub 7 sec 13 title 2 of the code . . . and if the charges are sustained to annul the teacher's certificate."[96]

Not all opponents to mandatory exercises necessarily objected to optional ones before school hours, however. And case law permitted exercises outside of school hours (much the same as it permitted religious organizations to use the schoolhouse in evenings and on weekends). Michael Larkin, a Catholic parent from West Hurley, Ulster County, charged that the school trustee and teacher unfairly required his children to stand during daily readings of the King James Bible. But, he assured the superintendent, "your petitioner has no objection to the reading of said version of the scripture in said school but prays that his children and others as their parents so wish may be permitted to stay away 'till such reading is ended." If his children could be required to be present during the reading, he asked that at least "they be permitted to remain in their usual seats and not be compelled to stand or fold or cross their arms or take any unusual attitude or position."[97] Whether Larkin's appeal displayed his true feelings on the subject or just his recognition of the legal limits of the satisfaction that he could gain from appeal, however, is hard to determine.

Larkin's appeal, the dearth of letters and appeals on the subject, and logic itself suggest that optional exercises were less objectionable than mandatory ones. That is not to say, however, that they were popular. Because the law consistently upheld optional exercises, dissenters were forced to work within the local system to stop or prevent them. In Moira, Franklin County, a new teacher introduced optional Bible reading and prayer to the district school in 1885. One Catholic parent objected. "On inquiry," wrote the trustee, "the teacher found that there were but very few Roman Catholics in said district and continued to read the Bible and engage in prayer at the opening of school every morning, doing both before nine o'clock and giving any one present...an opportunity to absent themselves." In response, the parent took his child out of school. Together with another Catholic parent, he later challenged the election of the trustee who hired the teacher, hoping to end the teacher's contract and the exercises she had started.[98]

In a similar fashion to the Christian opposition to the Wayland Liberal League, opponents to optional exercises also could resort to the Machiavellian technique of fabricating events to justify an appeal otherwise destined to lose. In 1878, George Fox, a Catholic parent from Arcade, Wyoming County, appealed to the State Superintendent to charge that his nineteen-year-old son had been punished and then expelled from school for refusing to participate in Bible reading and prayer. When he had first learned that the teacher was conducting exercises, Fox had complained to the teacher and trustee. As he explained in his appeal:

> Finally the trustee and teacher agreed to forget and forgive all past differences and the teacher who had abused and mistreated your petitioner's schollar [*sic*] and children on that account should treat his schollars as well as she did the other schollars attending her school and use no partiality in school among her schollars and that

> she might pray in school by ringing the bell for prayer just before the time of commencing the school and after prayer have five minutes intermission then ring the bell for school.

But the next day, claimed Fox, the teacher expelled his son for noncompliance with the exercises. The evidence in the case weighed heavily against Fox's claim, however. The trustee described quite a different situation:

> Densie Slocum [*sic*], teacher, has not been partial in this term of school—nor cruel as a teacher. She is an experienced and successful teacher, has taught thirteen terms previous to this term, One term in Lima Seminary, this state, one term in Oramel graded school Allegany Co. and the other terms in Cattaraugus Co. N.Y. and McKean Co. Pa. [*sic*] Never had any trouble in any of these schools. Has had in some of these schools large numbers of Catholic children and no complaint, always treating all impartially.[99]

The trustee's defense portrays a teacher with long experience in considering the needs of Catholic students in a variety of schools in two states (suggesting the spirit of cooperation among those districts as well?). The child had been expelled, wrote the trustee, because he could not control himself during school hours and had been repeatedly warned to behave by both teacher and trustee. The expulsion probably had nothing to do with his refusal to participate in exercises, as the continued enrollment of Fox's other two children suggests. Fox's appeal appears motivated more by spite than by actual religious persecution. Nevertheless, the time that he took to appeal to the State Superintendent demonstrates his clear resentment of the exercises on religious grounds.

Conscientious objectors such as George Fox, Michael Larkin, and Julia O'Neil, who pinned their arguments on the notion that their district common school must not violate their religious beliefs, resented the notion that the school could mandate participation in such exercises. As Fox wrote, "[I] being a Catholic, did not think it was proper and right for [the teacher]to . . . impress the schollars [*sic*] with her particular tenet . . . in school, as the common schools were open to all—and not designed in any sense to be sectarian or a place where any sentiment should be taught."[100] They appealed when the process of local control failed to redress their grievances (and as a result created a historical record of their concerns and actions). Like champions of religious exercises, their arguments are linked to broader currents of thought expressed by writers and spiritual leaders. Viewed in contrast, these arguments appear irreconcilable—one side insisting on "the nation's book in the nation's schools," linking the survival of Americanism to

Protestantism, and the other side insisting that religious exercises could not exist in schools "common" to all. What such a construction misses, however, is the context of these arguments, including those in the few appeals and letters over the issue that reached the state level. In fact, the disputes that reached the state level were extremely unusual by virtue of making it so far. Most disagreements over religious exercises in district schools, if they existed at all, never left the district level.

Local Control and Religious Exercises

What kept differences over religious exercises local? Aside from the conscientious arguments for and against religious exercises, a third view of the issue predominated in common school districts. This view placed district harmony above the zealous prosecution of religious ideas. In one study of the ideas of educational leaders, historian Robert Michaelsen called this the "civil view" of religion in public education.[101] A few national leaders expressed this view—William T. Harris and at moments Henry Ward Beecher—but few local documents do it justice. Its evidence exists as actions; its form to us today is only a shadow. (And, like the shadows visible to mortals chained in Plato's metaphorical cave, it is wavering, distorted, and hopelessly imperfect.) As we saw in chapter 3, pressures for harmony were often hardly altruistic. Nevertheless, the impulse to make common schools accommodate difference, in religious terms, probably shaped much district policy toward religious exercises, reconciling Protestants, Catholics, Darwinists, Freethinkers, Spiritualists, and others to the schools they shared.

Compromise did not mean the same result in every circumstance. For the Christians of Friendship, Allegany County, a respectful teacher would have been enough. Julia O'Neil, Michael Larkin, and George Fox wanted to make exercises optional. For Catholic parents in Moira, the introduction of religious exercises was unacceptable—optional or not. Moreover, a compromise for one group did not give satisfaction for all. Recall the Wayland Liberal League's rejection of the Catholic and Protestant compromise to sing religious hymns. Local context determined the meaning and significance of compromise, as well as its success or failure.

We will never know all of the stories of local reconciliation that occurred in the state's 11,000-plus districts for the very reason that reconciliation obviated the need for appeals and letters to the Superintendent and stunted the growth of succulent stories for newspapers and magazines. Instead of looking for direct evidence, however, we can look to the *process* of local control. Chapter 3 examined the way religion wove through the fabric of district politics in general. Next, I offer examples of how local control related to religious exercises in particular. One can appreciate the degree to which pressure to reconcile predominated in districts by seeing it at work even in appeals themselves (which are, at heart, evidence of the failure of reconciliation). In most of the cases I mentioned in this chapter thus far (and in other cases I will mention later), trustees, teachers, parents, school commissioners, and others tried—though unsuccessfully—to prevent offense to angered religious minorities. These particular efforts usually failed because one or a few unyielding individuals eschewed compromise, despite the process.

Not surprisingly, the role of various levels of the state bureaucracy in settling district disputes over religious exercises grew increasingly indirect the farther that layer was from the district itself. The State Department of Public Instruction had a direct hand only in the fourteen districts that appealed from 1867 to 1899. Nevertheless, the existence of state law exerted indirect pressure on the policy of local districts, affirming the beliefs of those who objected to mandatory exercises and offering a potent sting to the threat of appeal. In 1885, for example, State Superintendent William Ruggles published a detailed description of the department policy on religious exercises in his annual report to the legislature.[102] In the report he cited many decisions, including the 1839 decision by John C. Spencer that "Neither the common school system, nor any other social system can be maintained, unless the conscientious views of all are respected." Ruggles concurred, averring that, "The principles laid down in these early decisions have been followed by every one of my predecessors in office, no distinction having been made between Scripture reading and prayers, but each having been held, in separate and distinct appeals, to constitute no legitimate part of the business of the public schools."

Whether or not they were aware of state policy, parents, teachers, trustees, and commissioners heard about it when they wrote to the Superintendent in confusion or outrage. In one of many examples, George Heald of Pleasantville, Westchester County, wrote to Ruggles's successor, Superintendent Andrew Draper, in 1887 to ask, "Is there a law forbidding the reading of the Scripture in the Public School, or does it make it Optional with the Board of Education?" Draper referred him to Ruggles's statement of 1885—affirming the state's position of protecting minorities from mandatory exercises.[103] For trustees interested in keeping the peace, state correspondence could carry the weight of law. As William Gallup, trustee in Victor, Ontario County, explained in an 1872 letter, "We are having a little agitation on that subject [of reading the Bible in our public schools] here and desire a 'thus saith the authorities' on that question."[104]

The next layer of bureaucracy, county commissioners, also could play a role in encouraging compromise, although they normally displayed little direct involvement in district affairs. As we saw in the Presbyterian survey results, many commissioners remained "indifferent" (or wisely oblivious) to the issue of religion in public schools. Nevertheless, they did play a minor role in helping to settle disputes. Using their power to alter boundaries, commissioners sometimes created homogeneous districts along religious lines.[105] In mixed districts, commissioners could remove morally offensive teachers, as the Superintendent suggested in the case of the Friendship Spiritualists, though such drastic action appears to have been rare.[106] More commonly, earnest commissioners attempted to play the role of ombudsmen. Before Julia O'Neil protested her children's persecution to the Superintendent, her county commissioner wrote a letter describing "trouble between Protestants and Catholics" and asking for advice.[107] Likewise, in 1874, a commissioner from Westchester sought the text of an 1872 appeals decision on Bible reading, no doubt to contribute legal information to a local dispute.[108] In the controversy in Moira, when Catholic parents objected to the addition of offensive—but legal—optional religious exercises, the commissioner had intervened unsuccessfully on behalf of the minority, advising the trustee to hire a different, less objectionable teacher.[109]

The most accessible public school officer in disputes over religious exercises was, of course, the trustee. Because of the powers of the office, it fell on the trustee's (or trustees') shoulders to set district school policy. In some of the aforementioned cases trustees provoked controversy by promoting offensive exercises. In the three cases that follow, however, trustees attempted to block such exercises, standing up to unyielding teachers and parents who insisted on their rights to use the school for religious instruction. In each of these cases, all from the same year, the trustee's perceived responsibility to the district as a whole led to conflict with teachers who considered religious instruction a personal crusade.

Dansville, Steuben County

At 8:50 A.M. on May 5, 1879, Hattie Clymo commenced her fourteen-week summer term as teacher in district eight, Dansville, by reading a brief passage from the Bible and reciting the Lord's Prayer, asking students to repeat it back line by line. This six-minute exercise touched off a conflict between her and the district trustee that would outlast the term itself. At the heart of this disagreement lay two irreconcilable beliefs. Clymo believed that a proper school, by definition, included religious exercises—though she readily admitted that these needed to be optional and before school hours. Hannibal Poore, the trustee and a professed atheist, held the opposite view, "considering religious exercises no part of the duty of District School Teachers."[110] Events escalated as the summertime mercury rose:

May 16—Hannibal Poore directed Hattie Clymo to stop using "regular school hours" for her exercises. She continued with her exercises.

June 2—Poore forbade Clymo "using regular school days." She contacted the county commissioner, who told her she had a legal right to conduct the exercises before 9 o'clock, so she continued.

June 16—Poore visited the school to prevent the exercises personally. Clymo led her class off to the woodshed and conducted her exercises there. Poore remained to observe the day's lessons, writing afterwards in the teacher's register, "Religious exercises should be omitted. Success of teacher is good in other respects." That night Poore instructed his son to be present for, but refuse to participate in, the exercises. Clymo ejected the boy two days in a row.

June 21—Poore changed the lock on the schoolhouse door and posted a sign that read, "The schoolhouse will be open at nine o'clock for school purposes on all regular school days." The next morning, Clymo held exercises on the steps until the trustee arrived at nine to unlock the door. He told her to not use school grounds for religious exercises. The following morning, Clymo held exercises in the highway.

Several days later—Poore found the lock on the schoolhouse mysteriously broken and removed; Clymo resumed exercises in the schoolhouse. Poore put on a new lock, which was also mysteriously broken, with exercises again resuming in the schoolhouse. Poore bought a third lock; the exercises moved back to the highway.

June 27—Hattie Clymo filed an appeal to the State Superintendent, asking that Hannibal Poore be removed from office. In his answer, Poore requested that Clymo be ordered to cease the exercises.

In the appeal documents, Poore and Clymo rehearsed arguments that would sound familiar to early-twenty-first-century students of religion in public schools. Clymo claimed that she had a right, as the teacher, to conduct religious exercises, despite what the trustee said. She wrote, quoting an 1858 appeals decision on trustee powers, "His actions show 'only a stubborn determination to follow out his own purposes, without regard for the legal or equitable rights of the teacher, and for the wishes and interests of the inhabitants of the district.'" Clymo also circulated a petition among the inhabitants in her favor. In essence, she argued that omitting religious exercises in the public school actually violated the rights of parents and teacher. Moreover, she charged, Poore's locking the door until precisely nine o'clock forced children and teacher alike to wait in "sun or rain" without protection.[111] (She did not mention the same lack of protection for children who might be forced to absent themselves during these "optional" exercises.)

Poore displayed acute incredulity. He wrote in his defense, "Not believing that you would take cognizance of the matter, or give it any importance, I do not wish to put you to the trouble of reading or considering any explanation or reply to the matters contained in said appeal." Assured by the Superintendent that the charge was indeed serious, Poore later penned a more detailed response. First, he defended his religion. "My religious views, which have been thrust upon no one, are and at all times have been the same as when I was elected to [this] office, and were doubtless well-known to the people of said district then, as now." More to the point, Poore wrote that he and others of the district considered "religious exercises no part of the duty of District School teachers—as such," and he cited case law to back his position. Clymo's petition to have him removed, he charged, had been signed by a large number of nonresidents.[112]

Poore's dual role as a parent and a trustee complicates the significance of his position in the Dansville appeal. On the one hand, his actions as a trustee appear drastic—disallowing any use of the school property for optional exercises, even when the majority of families in the district supported them. These actions, while perhaps unusual, do suggest the strength of the trustee's sense of duty to protect religious minorities. Viewed as a parent, Poore appears quite reasonable. He objected to the religious indoctrination of his children and observed—as twentieth-century plaintiffs would in several U.S. Supreme Court decisions—that so-called "optional" exercises could nevertheless be coercive.[113]

Cohocton, Steuben County

While Hannibal Poore and Hattie Clymo sparred over the propriety of optional religious exercises in Dansville, residents of district five of the neighboring village of Cohocton confronted mandatory exercises run amuck. The trouble began in the winter term of 1878–1879, when the principal teacher of Cohocton's three-department graded school attempted to improve and expand religious education. First, he doubled the length of mandatory morning exercises from fifteen minutes (the usual length) to thirty minutes or more. Second, he invited the ministers of the village's two churches to participate in these exercises every Monday morning. Not surprisingly, residents complained to their trustee.[114]

The trustee claimed in later testimony to have responded quickly and decisively. "[I] immediately investigated said matter and finding that the same occupied too much time requested the said teacher to either discontinue said exercises or hold them before nine o'clock." When the teacher refused, the trustee dismissed him at the end of the term, hiring a replacement who did not conduct exercises. He also hired a new intermediate schoolteacher, Myron Morris, who agreed to keep his mandatory exercises short. These actions did not satisfy most of the district, however. In a packed annual meeting, a large majority of voters ousted the trustee in favor of Conrad Shults, who ran on a platform of ending all exercises for the sake of district harmony.[115]

This peaceable adjustment to district policy might never have been recorded in an appeal had not the new intermediate department teacher, Myron Morris, felt aggrieved at his dismissal at the end of the summer term. True to his election promise, Shults had not rehired Morris for fear that his religious zeal might offend parents. "I could not in justice to the district and my own opinion hire anyone who would not agree to dispense with chapel exercises during school hours." Learning that his contract would not be renewed, Morris appealed to the State Superintendent, claiming that the trustee previous to Shults had hired him for a full year, and that he (Morris) would gladly have stopped exercises during school hours had Shults ordered him to do so. Perhaps with the memory of the Dansville dispute in mind, Shults seems to have feared that Morris would have conducted optional exercises in any case. His instinct was probably correct. With the appeal still pending, Morris left New York State and headed for the West to begin his ministerial studies.[116]

The importance of district harmony appears more explicitly in this appeal than most. None of the appeal documents mentioned religious minorities, or conscientious objection to religious exercises per se. All town leaders involved—Shults, his predecessor in office, the town supervisor, the postmaster, and two prominent citizens—shielded the identity of objectors, instead accepting responsibility for all district members in a strong affirmation of the civil view of public education. One resident, J. M. Reynolds, wrote that he "verily [believed] that the act of Mr. Shults in hiring another teacher will greatly harmonize the dissatisfaction existing in said district and therefore fully [endorsed] the acts of Mr. Shults in so doing." In his letter, Town Supervisor William Harris explained, "Indeed, I have no doubt but that the course of action pursued by Mr. Shults in declining to hire Mr. Morris was greatly for the district's benefit—and I am free to say that a majority of the people of our district are of the same opinion." Thomas Warner, "Manufacturer and Wholesale Dealer in Pine and Hemlock Lumber, Lath, Shingles, etc," wrote on his office stationery, "I will venture to say that Mr. Shults will be sustained in all charges he has made by three-forths [*sic*] of the district or except the faction that has attempted to force upon the trustee Mr. Morris in the interest of a particular church."[117]

New Bremen, Lewis County

In 1875, the school of district three, New Bremen, Lewis County, suffered from a deservedly bad reputation. Physically, the two-department school stood close to a busy road that posed danger to students and vehicular traffic. More importantly, ill tempers and low morale gripped students and residents alike. "The reputation of the school as being the worst in the county derived more from the parents than from the children," explained the trustee, "as not a term went by that some trouble was had with trustee, teacher, scholars, and inhabitants, the latter faulting the teachers during school time." In 1873, the constable had had to arrest an aggressive local minister for cuffing a student on school grounds. Two years later, the constable and justice of the peace again made an arrest—this time in class—of an unruly student who had attacked the trustee. A November 2, 1875, encounter in the upper department suggests the state of things. As the trustee arrived at 9:45 to paint the blackboards, he noted the presence of a strange young man in the upper department in the company of a female student. "I went to the seat and asked him if he was a schollar [*sic*] here, and he answered, 'no, I come to see the girls.' I told him that the visitors should not disturb the school and not sit with the schollars, then the girl spoke to me and said, 'this is not your damn business.' " In response to this low morale and open hostility, the trustee used extreme measures to run the school, including a rule that the teachers must lock their doors at 9:15 to bar late students from attendance.[118]

While available evidence does not point to religious differences as a source of district animosity in general (the district contained four to five major denominations), disagreement over religious exercises exacerbated the situation, leading to a showdown between the teacher and trustee. After a series of disagreements between Edward Thomas, the trustee, and Florentine K. Bradman, the teacher, Thomas fired Bradman for refusing to cease conducting religious exercises. Bradman, in turn, filed an appeal to the State Superintendent to be reinstated and to have Thomas removed from office, charging that the trustee was godless, tyrannical, contentious, and unfit for office. While the appeals documents focused more on Thomas's qualities as a trustee than on the legality of religious exercises, the case nonetheless shows how the issue of religious exercises functioned in the operation of the district. As several witnesses explained, "the cause of the troubles are [*sic*] religious and political."[119]

Several parents signed a petition explaining Thomas's actions. Among them was a group from Bradman's own church:

> The teacher, Bradman, had (as we are informed by our children) every morning after school commenced, taken up some time to read

> a chapter from the Bible and in prayer commanded the children to attend revival meetings which were held for two weeks every evening at the Methodist church in this district. Your petitioners belong to different denominations and do not wish that a teacher impress upon our children with religious views in which we do not believe. [At] our earnest remonstrations the trustee appointed a [new teacher].
>
> [Bradman] and his fanatics accused in open church the trustee as forbidding him to serve the Lord and asking the congregation to stand by him. Bradman is a leading spirit and Sunday school teacher [at the church].[120]

After the trustee fired him, Bradman quickly assembled a private school at a nearby cheese factory where, initially, a large number of his students followed him. The partisan *Lowville Journal and Republican* reported, "Mr. F. K. Bradman, who was expelled from our school by the over-officious trustee," had consented to open the school "at the earnest solicitation of both patrons and scholars." The school lasted until Bradman won his appeal (based on the technicalities of his contract, not the exercises issue), and a new trustee rehired him to teach in the school. Appeals documents do not say what became of the religious exercises. Subsequent letters to the department of public instruction do, however, show continued animosity between trustee and teacher. Bradman spitefully reported to the Superintendent in an 1876 letter, "...such a scoundrel as Ed Thomas, he got beat by thirty-five (35) majority in school meeting and by 200 in town election for justice, he was on the Democratic ticket and the Democrats had, last election, about 200 majority."[121]

Conclusion

Despite their varied contexts and causes, the disputes in Cohocton, Dansville, and New Bremen shared a common theme. In each case, a trustee in the district had attempted to resolve the debate over religious instruction before offended parties appealed. District majorities behaved differently in each case—supporting the trustee in Cohocton but wavering in New Bremen and Dansville, where single religious congregations controlled significant voting blocks. Even in those cases, however, the majority acted through the trustee's principled mediation. Not surprisingly, failures at compromise at the local level had the same religious roots that the rhetoric of fear and crisis had at the national level. In almost every case, an appeal over religious instruction resulted when an overzealous teacher, trustee, or congregation rejected the interest of religious minorities out of hand.

Like the surveys of 1889 and 1898, these and other examples do not exhaustively settle the question of the extent of peaceable adjustments over religious exercises. They do suggest, however, a strong undertow of compromise beneath the waves of rhetoric and reform over religious education—a factor consistent with the remarkably low levels of letters and appeals concerning religious exercises. The movement to fuse religion with civil identity by offering "nonsectarian" religious exercises succeeded in many districts, probably because parents accepted the exercises—brief, rote, and without comment—as appropriately neutral or not worth bothering about. For those parents who rejected religious exercises as neutral (and given the great religious diversity of New York State and the large percentage of districts without exercises, there were probably many), the district system provided a reasonable means for voicing their concerns and making adjustments, without appealing to the state.

Part 3

Religion and Urban Schools

The previous chapters have explored religion in rural and small-town district schools in terms of process, using a patchwork quilt of evidence from appeals and letters to describe broad trends in New York's 11,000 district schools. This section on urban schools also examines process but does so in a different way. The relatively small number of incorporated cities in New York State (twenty-one in 1870) makes for a different narrative form—one that can examine policies in many, if not most, cities and can show direct influences of one city's policies on another. As we shall see, city boards of education closely observed changes in each other's schools, while a burgeoning newspaper industry not only fed its readers up-to-date statewide news but engaged in intracity editorial debates, linking cities as distant as Albany and Rochester in daily communication. Religious and political organizations—sometimes one and the same—played important roles in city school politics. All watched the legislature and the State Superintendent with increasing attention for decisions that they knew could affect their schools directly. And unlike most rural district school trustees, city school boards produced and published detailed records (city newspapers reported daily events as well), many of which survive today. In short, there *is* a story to tell within the broader historical processes at work.

Chapter 7 sets the context of this story, exploring the ways in which city school "systems" operated after the Civil War, both the features that they shared as urban systems (as distinct from district ones) and the points at which they differed. Although the chapter does not examine religion as an issue per se, it does set up a framework for subsequent chapters by exploring the politics of urban school districts. In particular, this chapter tests the tension between local control and centralization in urban schools—between school-level and ward-level control and central boards of education—and suggests the ways in which this tension played out over religion.

Chapter 8 offers a chronological account of the development of urban public school policy toward religious exercises from 1865 to 1900. Drawing on the experiences of the state's principal cities—Albany, Buffalo, Rochester, Brooklyn, and New York—as well as some smaller ones, the chapter develops a story that is as full of color and compromise as it is of discord. City by city, New Yorkers developed a variety of strategies for coping with the demands of a religiously diverse citizenry for and against religious instruction in their public schools. Not surprisingly, these policies reflected the great variety of contexts and relative autonomy of urban school boards. They also reflected the importance of site-level decision making in urban systems, what sociologists have called "loose coupling."[1] In terms of change over time, urban religious policy faced a major reform period in the 1870s but then remained relatively stable through the turn of the century—and relatively free from state-level interference.

Chapter 9 examines the second key aspect of religion in urban public schools: publicly funded parochial schools. From 1865 to 1880, at least four separate small cities—not to mention several villages that would soon be cities—negotiated plans with Catholic churches to operate parochial schools under the auspices of city boards of education. In Brooklyn and New York City, the state legislature provided brief periods of public funds for religious schools of different denominations. By the end of the 1870s, many of these arrangements had fizzled. Others survived, however, and in the 1890s, the issue resurfaced in state politics. This time state activism, not local circumstance, ended most city arrangements and in the process drove a wedge between the spheres of public and private education that would endure for well over a century. Despite their relatively short life, however, church-state deals were important and widespread expressions of decentralized, democratic control, and they reflected an unsung but vital phase of the common school system's growth in New York State in the context of religious pluralism.

Chapter 7

Local Control, Religion and Urban Schooling

VILLAGE TO URBAN SYSTEMS

"Probably no two cities or localities in the State conduct their schools on the same plan," observed the superintendent of Auburn schools in 1878. "Each locality determines its own methods, selects its own teachers, and textbooks, in fact, makes its own schools. More than this, teachers even in the same system of schools differ widely as to what shall be taught."[1] Unlike district schools, which operated under a blanket set of rules enforced (very loosely) by the state Department of Education, the laws governing the design of city school systems were approved on a case-by-case basis by the legislature.[2] As a result, there was much greater diversity in the structure of school governance among cities than between city and rural districts. Population differences exacerbated this diversity. In 1875, New York City was ninety times larger than the upstate city of Rome and fifty times the size of Elmira.[3]

Despite these differences, city central school boards generally shared a common feature: a strong tradition of school-level control. This point is key to understanding how religious policy worked in urban systems, because these diffuse, disorganized, and seemingly haphazard modes of governance in post-bellum cities left much room for variety and flexibility at individual schools. This flexibility did not manifest itself so much in the general curriculum, which was graded and standardized during the 1870s nearly universally, but in matters of identity and symbolism.[4] Citywide religious policies of one kind or another existed in most cities but were not necessarily practiced at every school, or were adapted to meet local needs. Often city governments showed reluctance to institute citywide policies that might offend local constituencies. In some cases, in fact, the tail seemed to wag the dog, so that school-level realities set the standard for centralized religious policy making.

By the 1870s, the process of growth from village to urban school had left much of the village aspect in place. Usually, newly formed city school systems officially conjoined formerly independent union free and district schools that sat within city boundaries into one single system. The city of Syracuse provides a typical example. In 1847, the state legislature granted a city charter to the three villages of Salina, Lodi, and Syracuse, creating the city of Syracuse and including land (and independent school districts) from the villages and their surrounding areas.[5] The new city comprised four wards, which corresponded roughly to the old village boundaries and grouped existing school districts within those wards. District trustees became "ward commissioners" and continued to maintain primary responsibility for the one or two schools in each ward. The city charter also created an elected central board of education to oversee these schools, comprising the two commissioners from each ward. In its first year of operation, this city "system" included ten schools.[6] Like an ice crystal expanding in freezing water, the city spread into its suburban and rural hinterland over the subsequent decades, adding more wards to the city government and more ward representatives to the board of education. In 1868, Syracuse had grown to eight wards, with one trustee from each on the board of education. In 1889, the board had grown to eleven members, and by 1894, it peaked at nineteen members from nineteen wards.[7] And, as he had from the beginning, each ward commissioner still served as the "special guardian of the interests of the schools in his ward."[8]

Syracuse's central board of ward representatives reflected the strength of the principle of local control in city schools, a principle that sometimes endured long after city schools ceased to represent individual districts. Most city systems maintained some form of the ward system in the 1870s, though the details varied greatly. In 1872, for example, eight of the eleven cities with accessible records reported central boards of education organized around ward, or, in a few cases, "district" representatives (see Table 7.1). This system emphasized local control by providing individual wards of a city (often relatively homogeneous by ethnicity and social class, especially in large cities) with direct representation in the central board of education. Brooklyn's system of management provided a "local committee" of three trustees, who were also members of the central board of education, for each of the city's sixty-three schools. (Board members sat on more than one local committee.[9]) New York City's school law organized the city into three layers of bureau-

TABLE 7.1 Organizational Patterns of Central School Boards for Select Cities, 1872

City	*Board of Education*	*Description*
Oswego	Ward system	8 wards, 2 reps from each
Rochester	Ward system	14 wards, 1 rep from each
Syracuse	Ward system	8 wards, 1 rep from each ward
Troy	Ward system	13 wards, 2 reps from each (replaced in 1873 by system of at-large elections)
Auburn	Hybrid ward/district	5 district trustees, 7 ward commissioners
Brooklyn	Hybrid ward/district	Central board of 45 (15 appointed by mayor), local committees of 3 for every school
Elmira	Hybrid ward/district	5 district reps and 4 at-large commissioners appointed by city aldermen
New York City	Hybrid ward/district	Central board of 12 district-level commissioners (elected and appointed), five trustees per ward
Yonkers	No board of ed.	School districts remained independent until 1881.
Buffalo	No board of ed.	Superintendent of Schools elected at large, Common Council has school committee
Albany	Dual party system	2 political parties alloted 6 seats each. Elected at large.

Source: Albany. *Annual Report of the Board of Education of the City of Albany*:1883, 149; Auburn. *Annual Report of the Board of Education of the City of Auburn*: 1872, 1; Brooklyn. *Annual Report of the Board of the Superintendent of Public Schools of the City of Brooklyn*: 1872; Buffalo. *Proceedings of the Buffalo Common Council*: 1872; Elmira. *Annual Report of the Board of Education of the City of Elmira*:1872, 1; New York City. *Manual of the Board of Public Instruction of the City of New York*:1871–72; Oswego. *Annual Report of the City of Oswego*:1873,1; Rochester. *Annual Report of the Board of Education of the City of Rochester:* 1872, 1; Syracuse. *Annual Report of the Board of Education of the City of Syracuse*: 1872, 1; Troy. Manual of the Board of Education of the City of Troy, 1873, 1–2; Yonkers. *Annual Report of the Board of Education of the City of Yonkers*, 1882, 1–2; Personal communication from Alvina Tyropolis, Records Management Officer, Yonkers Public Schools, dated June 28, 2001, in possession of author.

cracy: each ward of the city elected five trustees to oversee and maintain school property, to hire teachers and janitors, and to nominate principals and vice principals for approval by the central board. On top of wards sat the "district," one of seven sections of the city (each comprising two to seven wards) that elected commissioners to a central board of education and inspectors for the ward schools. Finally, atop the system sat a central board of education, made up of elected "district" commissioners and mayoral appointees.[10]

In some cases, localism proved strong enough that city schools resisted any central board at all. Yonkers, for example, became incorporated as a city in 1872, but its schools remained independent for nine years, until the legislature gave it a central board of education in 1882.[11] A Montgomery County commissioner complained in 1891 that the schools of the city of Amsterdam remained under the district system (and were thus *his* headache), despite the fact that the city had been incorporated six years earlier.[12] Such examples were exceptional, however, and none survived into the twentieth century.[13]

Even as it bloated city boards in the 1870s and 1880s to the size of an entire country school, ward-based representation in centralized city school boards fit the common school model of democratic control over one's local school. Made up of representatives of districts themselves, or of the local city wards in which the schools resided, ward-based boards of education were large and factious, owing everything to their constituents and little to the interest of the city as a whole.[14] Not surprisingly, many laypeople, especially religious and ethnic minorities, preferred them to professional or elite boards composed of members who owed them little, if any, political allegiance.[15] Although central boards of education (or superintendents) sometimes formally approved teacher hiring, such decisions were usually made at the school or ward level.[16]

Not all city school systems of governance operated on a system of ward representation in a central board of education. Even those exceptions, however, usually maintained a large degree of local (that is, school-level) autonomy or were very small themselves. The city of Buffalo had no board of education. From its incorporation in 1832 until 1838, the city had no authority at all over school districts, which continued to function independently. When the legislature passed a revised city charter in 1838, the common council formed a school committee and hired a superintendent to supervise city schools without a board of education.

While this arrangement would appear to be an extreme case of centralization, investing much power in the hands of an appointed official, the council later revised its policy to allow the biennial election of the superintendent at large beginning in 1853.[17] More importantly, the common council (elected at the ward level) still held most of the city's policy-making power.

When reformers in 1873 attempted to form a board of education for Buffalo along the lines of the one in Albany (organized around political parties), *The Catholic Union* blasted the proposal as "one of the most despotic measures that has ever been brought to the notice of this or any other community in the United States."[18] Individual districts within the city retained an unusual degree of financial autonomy. Until 1885, the Buffalo common council held individual school districts accountable for their own costs, up to a certain limit. Not surprisingly, this economic localism worked to the benefit of capitalists. Residential districts with many children paid disproportionately high property taxes for schools, while businesses located in downtown districts (where few children resided) paid next to nothing.[19] Although it did not have local committees, Buffalo invested the principals of individual schools with the power to set "any rules and regulations necessary and proper for the internal regulation of their respective schools" and to hire helpers to clean school rooms and light the fires in cold weather, holding some authority at the school level.[20]

Educational elites, nativists, and would-be reformers found the ward system nettlesome. A board of education member from Rochester explained in 1892, with dismay, the evolution of his own city's board of twenty ward representatives as follows:

> Years ago when the Board of Education was first established, the system then and since in vogue for the election of the Common Council was adopted for the election of commissioners of common schools, probably because at that time, that system was considered the best. The gradual growth of the educational system of the state has shown the necessity of a change in the manner of selecting school officers; until now it is perfectly apparent to every thinking person that the present method is unwieldy and unsatisfactory.[21]

A superintendent of schools of Rochester offered a more detailed critique: "School officers are elected annually, those of one section of the city for some specific purpose, those from another section for another purpose, such as that of ejecting or appointing a superintendent, or a teacher, or in some manner to aid self, or some friend, to a portion of said school fund."[22] As an alternative, school leaders advocated a strong, centralized, professional leadership in the hands of a superintendent or, at the least, of boards of education "taken out of politics."[23] Ward boards were also notoriously corrupt, creating vast opportunities for patronage and graft.[24]

As an alternative to the ward system, reformers advocated central boards made up of officials elected at large or appointed by various branches of city government. Over the course of the 1870s and 1880s, this movement picked up steam. The city of Albany typified a more common alternative to local control; it also highlighted the result: party rule. In 1866, the legislature approved a plan for Albany that replaced its ward-based "board of education" with a "board of public instruction," made up of twelve commissioners elected at large. Democrats and Republicans agreed to reserve an equal number of seats for each party.[25] In 1864, 1869, 1871, and 1873, New York's board of education (also renamed a "board of public instruction") suffered a string of reorganizations in a political tug of war between the Tammany Hall and Republican reformers that resulted in the appointment of (formerly elected) ward trustees and the decimation of its forty-four-member, ward-based central board.[26] In 1873, Troy's twenty-six-member board of ward commissioners fell to a twelve-person board chosen in a general election.[27] Elmira invented a creative hybrid of the two models—four at-large commissioners appointed by the board of aldermen and five representing the city's school districts.[28]

The transition from locally elected representatives to general elections or appointments did not hasten a renaissance in city governance, however. Even after the paroxysms of nine years' reform, New York City's ward trustees remained more powerful than the central board, having the power to hire teachers, select sites for new schools, and award contracts for supplies and fuel.[29] Brooklyn's hybrid system of combining appointees with locally elected board members proved little better than the old ward system. One board of education member described indignantly in 1869 that a local school committee had returned a questionnaire about extracurricular use of the schoolhouse with nothing but "none of your business" scrawled across it.[30] Thirty years later, little had changed. In 1894, the *Educational Review* wrote disapprovingly:

> The board of education cannot be held responsible for the deeds of its local committees, for it has become an unwritten law that whatever is done by one local committee should be approved by all other local committees, that is, by the board of education. Neither superintendent nor principals can be held responsible for the work of teachers in whose appointment they have no voice.[31]

The *Review* concluded that Brooklyn's dual system made it more like a village than a city. Size appeared to have mattered in the ability of central boards to run smoothly. The superintendent of the small city of Utica boasted in 1889, "Here there are no spasmodic jars, consequent upon violent changes of administration, no antagonisms between citizens and this Board, or those acting for them, this being in marked contrast with many of our sister cities and villages." This temptation to fate proved ill advised, however, as "politics" did indeed engulf the board a few years later.[32]

The politics of governance varied from city to city, but in general, political parties represented the concerns of competing ethnoreligious groups, with Irish Catholics voting solidly Democratic, and pietistic Protestants forming the backbone of the Republicans.[33] In New York City and Brooklyn, high proportions of Irish Catholics in the population strengthened the hand of Democratic politicians sensitive to local concerns—often by subverting the native establishment through political machines.[34] Thus even without a ward-based system, local groups could win concessions from central school boards, or even put members on them. Buffalo—a city without any board of education or local committees—provides a good example. One historian has found that although they constituted only 25 percent of the population, native-born Buffalonians made up most of the leadership of the city, including 50 percent of city clerks, 66 percent of retail merchants, wholesalers, and physicians, 80 percent of lawyers, and half of the presidents of the Buffalo Board of Trade from 1844 to 1881.[35] Yet despite this power in the hands of the native born, immigrants still held substantial political clout. When the superintendent of Buffalo and the common council "forgot" to pay several German teachers in 1873, the German populace held large meetings and organized investigating committees. In subsequent elections, every candidate connected to the discharge of the German teachers met defeat.[36] For those ethnic and religious minorities who opposed the policies of most native Protestants but lacked the numeric strength of Buffalo's Germans, the Democratic Party held as a general principle the devolution of authority to the local level, particularly on matters of cultural or religious difference.[37]

Another piece of the reform of ward systems—the superintendency—also failed to make significant headway against local control in cities. While often touted as generals in the urban educational army, superintendents usually did not enjoy the degree of autonomy or authority that their title suggested.[38] In Rochester and Elmira, the superintendent's primary responsibilities included serving as secretary for the board, working as librarian, and reporting statistics. Superintendents did not participate in setting district policy (having no voice in the proceedings of the board) except through formal reports and recommendations.[39] According to an 1873 *Daily Eagle* article, Brooklyn's board of education had all but ignored its superintendent—who was now involuntarily retiring after eighteen years of mediocrity. "There are [old] members of the board . . . who try in vain to remember ever having heard of any suggestion from the superintendent touching on public school management," the *Eagle* wrote acerbically. "Of the merits of school books, the construction of school buildings, the grading of school studies—on the thousand and one subjects which give rise to differences of opinion among those who take an especial interest in public education—the board never thought of consulting its superintendent, and the superintendent never hazarded his own peace by troubling the board on such matters."[40] And, of course, all superintendents were vulnerable to the same strong political winds as the boards of education who hired them. Between 1854 and 1882, only two Buffalo superintendents managed to win reelection.[41]

Whether oriented to the ward or political party, or some mix of the two, city school systems provided parents and pupils a large degree of autonomy in their neighborhood schools—either formally, through systems that placed wards in a clear position of power or that made political commitments to local interests, or informally, by their disorganization in the face of continuous expansion and change.

Neighborhood Schooling and Ethnic Diversity

The flip side of decentralized city governance, which endured into the 1890s, was local control. Showing their district system roots, urban schools grouped children into residential districts and generally required residents to attend their own district school (unless it proved too crowded). The only evidence to the contrary came from Elmira, where school boards maintained a church-affiliated school within the public system and opened it to children from all districts, and from Poughkeepsie, where the school board converted the city into a single school district for placement purposes, thus allowing children to attend two church-affiliated public schools there. Elmira scrapped its new districting plan after a brief trial, however, noting the "many evils resulting to the classification and discipline of the schools for the want of a regulation of this character."[42] Because city residential patterns created ethnic enclaves, neighborhood schools varied in their ethnic mixtures.[43] Most major cities had identifiable ethnic neighborhoods—grouped by social class, nativity, and race—well before the Civil War.[44] As the century progressed, this circumstance kept pace with urban growth, especially as new technologies, such as street railways and skyscrapers, allowed city dwellers to live farther from where they worked and shopped—opening new suburbs to settlement—and allowed them to live, work, and shop in greater numbers per square foot.[45] As one group moved outward to the suburbs, another moved into the central city to take its place.[46]

Most city school boards did not publish systematic records of the nationality and race of pupils in each school or each district, but Buffalo and Utica did. These records substantiate the idea of ethnically *flavored* schools (few schools were all one ethnicity)—but they also show substantial differences in how schools grouped ethnic groups that can be attributed to city size.[47] In Buffalo in 1874, there were thirty-six common schools for primary, elementary, and grammar grades. Substantial numbers of children of Irish,

German, and American parentage were enrolled at the majority of schools. In fact, only two schools in the city enrolled a majority of students with American-born parents. In school numbers 3 and 34, children of Irish parentage made up 60 percent and 65 percent of the student body, respectively. Children of German parentage formed a majority of the enrollment in six schools (over three-quarters of the enrollment at four of these).[48] In the small city of Utica, with only seven primary-through-grammar-level schools in 1874, children of "American" nationality (the board did not specify how it defined "nativity") constituted majorities in four of seven schools.[49] "Irish" children made up one-third of the enrollment in three of these and between 22 percent and 16 percent in the other four. "German" children also enrolled in every school, but their percentage of the whole ranged from 35 percent at one primary school to 3 percent at two other schools.

Neighborhood schools did not necessarily mean neighborhood-specific curricula adopted by ward trustees, or approved by the board of education. Graded schools, competition for spots in high schools, and outright regulation made city school curricula uniform from the 1870s to well into the twentieth century.[50] (The one exception, perhaps, was that most large cities in the 1870s provided German language instruction as an elective course in schools with large German populations.[51]) Neighborhood control of schooling meant presiding over the symbolic curriculum of a given school, including religious exercises. Even without teachers of the same ethnicity, having large cultural groups within a single school could work as a boon to the pride of children and their identification with school, particularly for those who could (and did) face fierce alienation in the larger culture, or at schools where they were a low-status minority.[52] As the superintendent of Auburn public schools noted at the beginning of this chapter, teachers could choose what to cover, and what to omit, within the official curriculum at the school level itself and take the children into consideration.[53] The children also could create their own special symbols of cultural pride and ownership. At Buffalo's Public School Number 2 in 1902, where over 90 percent of the children had Italian-born parents, boys set their own, distinctive clothing fashion. Eschewing shirts and coats, the "sweater brigade" donned knits of all stripes and hues—enough to "drive a French militiaman to shame," cheered the *Buffalo Times*.[54]

Neighborhood schools affected the attendance rates of children of various ethnic groups in different ways, though contemporary measurements of this process have produced somewhat enigmatic results. David W. Galenson, for example, has found that in 1860 in Chicago, being in an Irish neighborhood made Irish-American children more likely to attend public school, while in Boston the opposite was true. Galenson attributes this effect to the greater responsiveness of public school officials in Chicago to the needs of immigrant children, particularly in the face of fierce competition from the nation's most aggressive parochial school movement. In Boston on the other hand, school officials discriminated against immigrant neighborhoods with worse facilities and culturally insensitive regulations.[55] In the 1870s, neighborhood schools in New York State probably were much more receptive to children of immigrants than they had been in 1860: the Civil War had stifled nativism, and Catholics began winning major political victories, including the mayorship of New York City. As we have seen, parochial school strength varied in New York State cities, from nearly rivaling public school enrollments in Rochester and Buffalo to not offering much competition at all in New York City and Brooklyn. With the school or ward as the locus of power over such symbolic issues as teacher selection and types of religious exercises, however, the overall effects of neighborhood schools on attendance in the period 1865–1900 probably were quite positive for most immigrant groups.

African Americans demonstrated a complex and varied approach to the concept of neighborhood schools. At the end of the Civil War, most cities in the state maintained segregated school systems. In the following decade, black residents of New York State protested mandatory segregation into colored schools, winning the passage in 1873 of a state law forbidding the cities from blocking black students' admission into white district schools (but not forbidding *de facto* segregated district schools intended for black students). Some cities embraced the legislation, some grudgingly accepted it, and others, notably Brooklyn and New York City, ignored it. As African-American parents increasingly abandoned their colored schools, New York and other cities softened their "separate-schools" policies by the end of the 1870s. Yet factions pulled in the opposite direction as well—arguing that separate schools engendered cultural pride and shielded children from hostile white teachers and students. Separate schools also protected the jobs of black teachers, who rarely won jobs teaching white children.[56]

Teachers reflected the culture of the children in many neighborhood schools, particularly before the "new immigration" of the 1880s and 1890s, when new groups of immigrants entered the country in large numbers without a substantial generational base of American-educated, English-speaking countrymen to work as their teachers. Irish-Americans were the most successful non-native group at winning teaching positions in cities and could often be found in the schools of Irish neighborhoods. In New York City, one historian has found that in some wards, four out of five teachers were Irish, while in some schools—Grammar School 1, fourth ward, and Grammar School 24, sixth ward, for instance—Irish teachers and pupils accounted for nearly the entire school population.[57] Overall, Irish-born residents accounted for 19 percent of the city's population in 1875, and from 1870 through the twentieth century, approximately 20 percent of teachers in the city were of

Irish parentage.[58] In Grammar School 20 of Albany, six out of ten teachers were not only Irish but had graduated from Catholic high schools. The principal, Thomas O'Brien, had received his training at a normal school in his native Dublin, Ireland (a feat that new immigrants from non-English-speaking countries would have difficulty rivaling).[59]

Catholic gains in the teaching force did not come without resistance. In April 1881, a Methodist-Episcopal congregation in Brooklyn mobilized to block the proposed promotion of a Catholic woman to the position of principal in their new local School No. 41, a mixed Protestant and Catholic public school. The dissenting group proposed hiring a male Protestant instead and sent a petition to the board of education. When a ward trustee found the name of the church's minister on the group's petition, he challenged the man in writing and then presented the exchange as evidence at the city board of education meeting a few days later. In the face of direct confrontation, the minister dissembled. He claimed that he signed the petition against her only because he favored a new grammar school, while he understood that supporting her would lead to a new elementary school instead. "If the proposed Lady teacher can do the work, she should have it, so far as I'm concerned with pleasure. Brains, not sex, ought to determine this.... The question of denomination under your public school system has no place. Teachers are not there to spread churches, but secular knowledge."[60] The question of who should head the new school eclipsed whatever disagreement may have existed over a grammar versus an elementary school, however, and opposing board members refused even to debate the matter on record. For three consecutive meetings, opponents to hiring Ms. Lawrence blocked any action by the board. At a special meeting to resolve the issue, the chairman noted that seventeen members loitered in an adjacent room and refrained from answering to their names or attending the meeting in order to prevent a quorum. When the recalcitrant members did enter, they disrupted the proceedings to the point of driving the chairman from the chair. By August, the impending opening of school forced a decision. Seventeen to fifteen, the board approved Ms. Lawrence.[61]

In small cities, where schools were more mixed than in big cities, Catholic teachers may have faced similar opposition throughout the system. In 1880, the Lockport Board of Education heard the petition of Mr. Lawrence McFarlin on behalf of the city's Catholic population, which thought it reasonable to request that since Catholics "form a large proportion of the city's population and contribute toward the support of the schools, [they] were entitled to a share of the teachers' appointments."[62] Although the president of the board confessed that they gave preference to graduates of the union free high school (over graduates of Catholic high schools) because "they were more familiar with the workings of the public school system," he nonetheless promised that all qualified candidates would be given an equal chance. Over the next several years, the board faced increasing political pressure over the issue of teacher qualifications as Catholics pressed for their "right" of representation in the teaching force, eventually yielding by creating a single examination for qualification in 1885.[63]

Progressive Reform

Just before the end of the century, a new urban reform movement gripped cities large and small. Appalled by the horrific conditions of city life, alarmed by the growth of anarchism, communism, and political unrest, and motivated by an elitist, reformist ideology, progressive reformers sought to make major changes to the way city governments and institutions operated. The movement spurred the mother of all urban governance reforms: the consolidation of Long Island City, Brooklyn, and other satellite cities into one giant New York City in 1898. It also strengthened the hand of progressive educational reformers who had been decrying urban education for decades.

Progressive reform in public education pulled in several directions at once, from the child-centered pedagogy of John Dewey to penal reform to kindergartens, but it was those whom David Tyack has called "administrative progressives" who enjoyed the most success. This coalition of professional educators and businessmen sought to sweep away the "village" aspects of urban school administration, taking the school out of politics, and out of the hands of the ward, by replacing it with small, professional school boards with active, powerful superintendents.[64] Administrative progressive reform enjoyed remarkable success in altering the city school systems of New York State. By 1904, seven of the eleven cities noted earlier in Table 7.1 had uprooted and destroyed ward representation on central boards of education in favor of small, elite boards, either appointed or elected at large (see Table 7.2). In New York City, reformers led by Nicholas Murray Butler and a small coalition of wealthy do-gooders attacked the principle of local control in what they called a "school war," successfully abolishing ward-level boards of education in 1896.[65] Newly incorporated cities also reflected the administrative progressive agenda. Among the twelve cities incorporated by the state legislature after 1892, for example, not a single one had a ward-based board of education by 1904.[66]

Progressive reforms marked the end of some of the "village" elements of most urban school systems, particularly the significance of ward and district-level governance and the representation of local interests through lay representatives to the central school board. In New York City, it curtailed the ability of citizens to have direct influence over the hiring of their local teachers.

TABLE 7.2 Organizational Patterns of Central School Boards for Select Cities, 1904

City	*Board of Education*	*Description*
Albany	"reformed" board	3 members appointed by mayor
Auburn	"reformed" board	9 members elected at large
Oswego	"reformed" board	4 members appointed by mayor
Rochester	"reformed" board	5 members elected at large
Syracuse	"reformed" board	7 members elected at large
Troy	"reformed" board	3 members appointed by mayor
Yonkers	"reformed" board	15 appointed by mayor
Elmira	Hybrid ward/district	5 district reps and four at-large commissioners appointed by city aldermen
New York City	Hybrid ward/district	46 members appointed by mayor
Buffalo	No board of ed.	Superintendent of Schools elected at large, Common Council has school committee
Brooklyn	______	(Consolidated with New York in 1898)

Source: New York State. *First Annual Report of the Education Department of the State of New York*: (Albany: New York State Education Department, 1905), 46–47.

In other ways, however, the nascent movement had, by the early twentieth century, left some aspects of localism intact. First, no matter how well elite school board members and professional superintendents shielded themselves from the vagaries of local control, they still faced the winds of democracy, being either elected or appointed by elected officials. They also faced an increasingly active State Department of Public Instruction (and in the twentieth century, more active state and federal courts), which traditionally upheld religious appeals by minorities. And whatever the governance structures of cities, they still retained their geographic crazy quilts of ethnoreligious enclaves, which continued to produce ethnically flavored, if not homogeneous, neighborhood schools in the largest and, due to progressive reform, otherwise least democratic school systems in the state. The role that progressive reform played in the development of religious policy in public schools as the movement blossomed and faded in the twentieth century remains an unexamined, important question for future research.

Conclusion

The haphazard and varied character of city school governance of the late nineteenth century showed the enduring legacy of district schooling. Individual schools, districts, and wards sat uncomfortably within centralized bureaucracies intended to run them with smooth uniformity. City residents expected central board members to represent local concerns, but the tremendous growth of cities left these boards in especially awkward positions as central board memberships swelled beyond their reasonable capacity to govern effectively. As a result, much power remained at the school level, where local politicos, not to mention teachers in classrooms, mediated between district policy and the local polity. Despite modest reform measures during the 1870s, the strength of localism would remain formidable until the turn of the twentieth century.

Religious policy in the late nineteenth century reflected the variety and local focus of city governance. As we will see in the following chapters, compromises over religious exercises and deals between church authorities and school boards depended on several factors: small units of governance, schools situated in neighborhoods, school leaders who rejected one-size-fits-all approaches to religious education in public schools, and school boards at once relatively independent of state intervention, overwhelmed by growth, and permeable to the concerns of religious minorities.

Chapter 8

Religious Exercises in Urban Schools

The great ethnic and religious diversity of city school systems challenged the idea that common schools could be common at all, particularly when it came to religious exercises. How did a secular, civil system handle diversity of piety in city schools? First, urban school religious policy followed no single pattern but included a variety of approaches to the problem of offering common religious rituals in a pluralistic society. These rituals, where they existed, mirrored district school practice in their brevity and symbolic nature. More importantly, as city systems of governance developed after the Civil War, local control allowed religious minorities some power over school religious policies and resulted in a variety of approaches to religious exercises in school. As a result, despite their diversity, city public school systems shared a common denominator: they produced forms of compromise that belied the rhetoric of irreconcilable conflict.

During the last decades of the nineteenth century, city approaches to religious exercises fell into two general periods. During the late 1860s and 1870s, a number of cities reexamined and reformed previous policies, usually in favor of religious minorities. Some forbade exercises, one required them, and many maintained a laissez-faire policy that left the decision to conduct exercises, and their character, to school- and ward-level officials. In the 1880s and 1890s, these policies remained stable, with little change even in the face of agitation for public funding for church schools.

Before the Civil War, disputes over religious exercises had fanned the flames of already tense relations between Catholics and Protestants in major Eastern cities, particularly in New York and Philadelphia. During the 1840s, Catholic and Protestant leaders in New York City sparred over the overtly anti-Catholic content of textbooks, religious exercises, and teachers in schools run by the publicly funded, Protestant-controlled Public School Society. In Philadelphia, efforts to remove offensive Bible reading led to violence, death, and a three-day rampage by brutal mobs of Protestants burning down Catholic churches and homes. Over the next decade, as anti-Catholics rode a wave of "know-nothingism" that crashed over American politics, Catholic leaders hardened their resolve to build a separate system of education. In the aftermath of New York City's difficulties, the state legislature created a ward-based board of education that absorbed the Public School Society in 1853. The legislature also favored Protestant demands, however, by forbidding the board of education from outlawing Bible reading (it did not specify which version might be used, however, nor did it make the practice mandatory for every ward).[1]

New York was the only city where the legislature used such a heavy hand in school management, however, and the legislative requirement blocking the removal of religious exercises was one of a kind. The rest of the state's cities responded to the question of religious instruction on their own. In the transition from village to city system, boards of education encountered the problem of creating a one-size-fits-all set of regulations for schools that had been previously independent; opening exercises proved a particularly difficult topic. When Syracuse shifted from independent village schools to a centralized system in 1849, for example, the board of education attempted to require teacher-led Bible reading or prayer in all Syracuse schools. Objectors immediately petitioned the board, and after several months, the board backed down, somewhat. The compromise—which clearly favored proponents of the regulation—required "reading from the Sacred Scriptures provided that such reading be without note or comment; and provided also, that no pupil be required to be present during the exercises, whose parent or guardian shall object."[2] Brooklyn required opening exercises but made no specification as to the version of the Bible used.[3] After the Civil War, New York City continued to leave exercises up to ward boards. Elmira, Albany, and Buffalo made no explicit mention of Bible reading in the regulations, leaving it up to individual schools to decide. Lockport's intentionally vague rule stated that teachers "should endeavor on all proper occasions to inculcate principles of morality and virtue, and a sacred regard for the truth, neatness, order, sobriety, industry, and frugality. But no teacher shall exercise any sectarian influence in the schools."[4] And, beginning in 1875, some cities expressly forbade religious exercises altogether.[5]

Religious exercises took the same form in post-bellum city schools as they did in the country: mainly symbolic and not at all integrated into the regular, secular course of study. Most schools began at 9:00 A.M., and religious exercises (where they existed) were usually required to be over by 9:15 A.M.. City regulations, again where they existed, described exercises as a teacher's or principal's reading a portion of the Bible or Holy Scriptures—always with the stipulation, "without note or comment."[6] Often these exercises took place *ensemble*, with all classes sitting in a large hall with their teachers, while the principal led the exercises. Sometimes pupils themselves were required to recite pieces. Boards of education less often mentioned recitation of the Lord's Prayer and seldom prescribed anything as explicit as Jamestown's "Duties and Obligations" for teachers:

> The opening exercises of the morning session shall consist of the following duties: 1. The reading of a few verses of Scripture, without comment. 2. The repeating of the Lord's Prayer in concert by the pupils, the teacher leading. 3. The singing of one or two hymns. After opening exercises are concluded, the pupils shall be allowed ten minutes for study before the first recitation is called.[7]

Opponents observed that opening exercises were "perfunctory"—in Brooklyn they were limited officially to ten minutes—and some city superintendents suggested bravely that their educational value was "overestimated."[8]

Despite their pedagogical insignificance relative to the rest of the curriculum, religious exercises held great symbolic importance for parents with religious convictions. Not surprisingly, interpretations of this significance varied. Most active Protestants, what nineteenth-century pundits called "positive" Protestants, felt it an article of faith to "bring up their children in the practice of publicly thanking their Creator for his protection, and to invoke his blessing."[9] The *public* aspect of this worship was especially important to many native Protestant clergy, who argued that the national polity was founded on—and depended on—Protestant republicanism.[10] The Catholic Church officially supported the idea of winning public funds for its own schools (though some leaders objected) and, short of that, of protecting the minds of Catholic children from Protestant heresy, including reading from the Protestant Bible, being led in prayer by Protestant teachers, or singing Protestant hymns.[11] What was for Protestant clergy a symbolic affirmation of nationalism was for Catholic clergy a symbolic threat to much-cherished (and hard-won) spiritual liberty.[12]

On their face, these competing religious ideologies could not be reconciled. When, in 1869, the board of education of Cincinnati, Ohio, outlawed all Bible reading in the schools to accommodate a diverse student body of

Protestants, Catholics, Jews, and atheists, religious leaders and intellectuals nationwide published a large body of sermons, essays, and outright diatribes on the issue, many of these emanating from greater New York City.[13] But at the same time, the issue itself—Bible reading in schools—left no trace in the minutes of educational meetings of the leading cities of New York State.[14] Not until 1871, that is. Then the newly created board of education of Long Island City initiated an ill-fated policy of mandatory religious exercises. Over the course of that school year, the struggle between the board and the people who resisted it revealed more than the importance of Bible reading as a symbolic practice in public schools. It demonstrated the process by which religious minorities challenged the authority of the majority, the ways in which centralized school boards interacted with school-level administration, and the role that the appeals process to the State Superintendent could play in religious controversy.

Long Island City

In 1871, the state legislature approved the incorporation of a collection of villages at the northeastern tip of Long Island into Long Island City. The new city charter provided for a central board of education appointed solely by the mayor, while each school now within city limits also would have an elected board of ward-level trustees to oversee day-to-day management.[15] (This was a smaller version of the recently reformed Board of Public Instruction in New York City.) The system placed the board of education at the mercy of the mayor—whose concern was the majority of voters, not minorities. Moreover, for the first year of its operation, the board would consist entirely of members appointed by the same mayor at the same time. (In subsequent years, members' terms would expire in rotation.) Yet, unlike the Byzantine system of schools in New York City, which afforded schools a degree of autonomy by virtue of its unwieldy size, the system of schools in Long Island City was small (city population 16,000 by 1875),[16] and board of education members and their superintendent could, and did, regularly visit individual schools to check for compliance with board policies. As a result, the board displayed a strong disregard for the principle of local control embodied in the ward/trustee concept.[17]

Seizing on its new powers, the new board of education passed a bylaw requiring all of the schools of the city to conduct opening religious exercises, "reading, without note or comment, a portion of Holy Scripture, and the singing of secular airs."[18] A ward trustee of the predominantly Catholic Ward One protested the bylaw before its adoption, warning that a large portion of his ward would certainly oppose the provision. But the board considered this group but a small minority of residents of the city overall, while a majority of citizens favored the requirement.[19]

When city schools opened for the first school year under the new board, the regulation immediately brought protests from Catholic parents and pupils of Ward One to their trustees, who in turn protested to the board of education. Notably, the children did not refuse to participate in the exercises but waited until their local ward trustees acted. They soon did. Late in September, one of the trustees of Ward One, Joseph Fiesel, entered the school and read a protest in front of the teachers and pupils, demanding that it be written in the minute book of the school: "We admire the discipline acquired in this school, but protest and have protested this day publicly in this school in the presence of the above named gentlemen against the reading of the Bible or any rule of faith whatsoever in this public school."[20]

Fiesel's objection rested on standard Catholic Church law in the United States. Just five years prior, the 1866 Plenary Council of Baltimore had ruled that Catholic pastors should "diligently guard that the books and practices of [a Protestant nature] should not be introduced into public schools to endanger their [children's] faith and piety."[21] In later protests to the board of education and to the State Superintendent, Catholic parents of Long Island City wrote emphatically that teacher-led religious exercises—particularly from a Protestant Bible—violated their faith and imperiled the minds of their children. One parent objected to any religious worship in the presence of non-Catholics—regardless of the version of the Scriptures.[22] Several parents included copies of the Plenary Council's decrees in their letters of appeal.

The trustees' protest shocked the teachers and the principal, who described it as "violent and denounciatory [*sic*]" and "calculated to destroy the good order and discipline of said school." The children, too, were "greatly excited." Most importantly, for the trustees' purposes, however, the protest jolted the city board of education, which had thus far ignored the concerns of Catholics in Ward One. Three days later, the trustees of Ward One lodged a formal complaint at the board of education meeting. The board suspended the religious requirement one week later.[23]

The victory did not last, however. The board's decision appears to have been more of a litmus test of city politics than a capitulation to localism or the concerns of the minority. The board claimed:

> The suspension of the bylaws was granted, not at the demand, nor . . . any matter of merit, but [because] the Board of Education desired . . . an investigation of the merits of the question . . . and upon such investigation being had it did not then appear . . . to this board that general dissatisfaction, either as regards the city at large, or as to any particular Ward thereof, prevailed. . . . On the

> contrary . . . it was the movement of a faction at whose head stood [Trustee] Fiesel.[24]

Apparently feeling that the majority and the mayor were on its side, the board reinstated exercises at the end of October.[25]

Feeling betrayed by the city government, a number of Catholic parents and pupils, and other taxpayers of Ward One, organized and protested on several fronts. First, the children themselves bravely protested during the exercises themselves—first by blocking their ears as the principal read the Scriptures. The principal responded to this "blasphemy" by expelling them. A few tried sitting outside of the room during the exercises, but the principal compelled them either to enter or to go home for the day. Over the next week, some children continued to return to school to protest, covering their ears, and shouting "I don't believe in this," as the principal read passages from the Protestant Bible. At one point, the protests grew so fierce that the principal called the police, who arrested three young men for disturbing the peace. Other Catholic children did not protest—out of fear or lack of interest—and sat quietly through the exercises. Still others withdrew to attend a nearby parochial school, which enjoyed (not surprisingly) steady growth during these events. As the expulsions began, a few parents personally accompanied their children to school and angrily confronted the principal. Again, the principal called the police to remove those parents and pupils he found most threatening. The exercises, and the expulsions, continued.[26]

Edward McBennett took his son Frank (expelled from Ward One School) to seek admission at Ward Two School—and found the same situation. The principal refused to admit Frank unless he attended the religious exercises. Among his later appeal documents, McBennett included an account of the conversation he had had with the principal after school. (It should be noted that at this point McBennett's wife had been arrested for protesting her son's expulsion at the Ward One School, and the father was, by the time of the following conversation, *prepared*.)

> MCBENNETT: I am sorry that Frank cannot attend school.
> BARNES [principal]: There is no reason why he should not.
> MCBENNETT: Yes, Sir. I cannot allow my boy to be present at the religious exercises of this school.
> BARNES: I am obliged to open school with the reading of a portion of the Bible.
> MCBENNETT: Why not substitute some other exercise since some of the children object to the reading of the Bible?

BARNES: Sometimes children come running here to school and are unfit for study for some minutes after. The reading of the Bible prepares them well for the other exercises.
MCBENNETT: If they are unfit for any exercise, they certainly must be unfit for so difficult a subject as the Bible.
BARNES [changing the subject]: You knew that the Bible was read here before you sent your son.
MCBENNETT: I did not know it, nor was I ever at the school before, and knowing it to be a public school I knew that the Bible should not be read during school hours, and I do not think that where there are children of different creeds that any one creed should be taught in it.
BARNES: When I was a schoolboy the Bible was always read, but I never paid any attention to it. I do not think it makes any difference as the children pay no attention to it.
MCBENNETT: Since you admit that your party derive no benefit from it, why then do you read it to offend ours?
BARNES: It is customary, and I am obliged to read it by my superiors.[27]

The exchange cut to the heart of the matter for both sides. The principal simply could not understand Catholic reasons for objecting to religious exercises, particularly as the children tended to ignore them. His administrative instructions provided a much stronger motivation than the religious concerns of the parent. For the father, the symbolic value of the exercises was everything, even if it meant keeping his son out of school. His concern was not that his child would learn anything from the exercises (both he and the principal agreed on that point), but that the act of participating in the exercises held vital symbolic value for his religious identity. The board of education's lack of concern over the "Fiesel faction" was akin to that of the principal, and Long Island City's unique system of governance that made the board unaccountable to ward-level concerns made it all too easy to ignore principled Catholic objection.

As matters escalated, angry citizens organized a mass meeting to vent their frustrations (see Figure 8.1). At the meeting, they adopted a series of resolutions to express their sentiments and elected a committee to represent them. The resolution read:

Whereas: the civil authorities of this city have introduced into our Public Schools (which are supported at the expense of the citizens at large) a certain "rule of faith" called the sacred scriptures, acknowledged and professed by only a class of our fellow citizens; and
Whereas: the "rule of faith" of any other class is not admitted; and

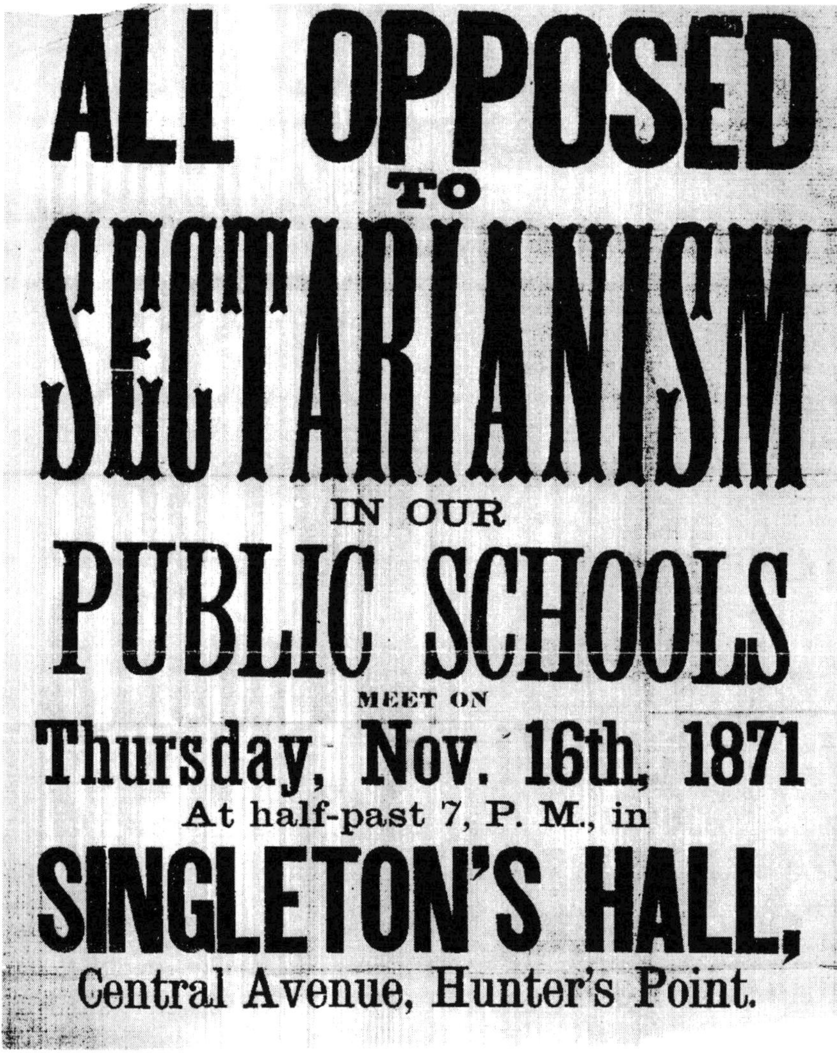

FIGURE 8.1 Poster advertising the meeting of outraged residents of Ward One, Long Island City. Catholics there charged that nominally "non-sectarian" Bible reading was still very much "sectarian." (Courtesy of the New York State Archives.)

> Whereas: many of our children have been expelled from the said public schools for refusing to listen to the reading of the said "rule of faith," believing it to be obnoxious and dangerous to the faith taught by their parents; and

Whereas: The parents themselves have been abused, arrested, and threatened with arrest, for remonstrating against the course pursued by the authorities; therefore
Resolved: that we, the citizens of Long Island City in mass meeting assembled declare against such action as being in open violation of every right of conscience and of religious liberty, sacredly guaranteed by the Constitution of this State and by the Constitution of the United States, and respectfully demand the repeal of said action by the Board of Education of said city."

The chairman of the committee then read the resolution to the ward board of trustees and the board of education. Adding insult to injury, the board of education not only ignored the request but announced an *expanded* religious exercises requirement that would include prayer in addition to Bible reading and singing.[28]

As the board of education made it clear that it would not respond to the usual channels of protest, the ward trustees scrambled to find a solution. While the city charter left some ambiguity as to the pecking order between ward trustees and the central board, the principal and teachers collected their paychecks from, and owed their allegiance to, the board of education. Nevertheless, the trustees tried to finesse their position by focusing on their control of the school building itself, which was the property of the ward, and which the trustees held in trust. In December, the ward trustees issued a statement that, they hoped, would strike a compromise between the wishes of the Protestant board of education and the Catholics of Ward One. Seizing on the body of law concerning the use of common school buildings for religious purposes (see chapter 5), the trustees wrote to the board of education and the principal of the Ward One School: "The public school premises buildings or property shall be no longer used or occupied by any person during school hours for the purpose of holding therein, religious exercises or practice, religious instruction, the reading of portions of the Holy Scripture or the recitation of religious prayers or hymns for or by the children attending the public school of this ward." As a token of their good faith, however, the trustees also declared that religious organizations were free to use the building outside of regular school hours for religious instruction—an arrangement long in use in many district schools, and in fact encouraged by past state superintendents.[29]

When the board of education ignored this final attempt at compromise, the ward trustees, the parents of one student, and a group of other parents filed three separate appeals to the State Superintendent of Public Instruction. They won. The Superintendent ruled that the action of the board of education in directing religious exercises and excluding those who demurred was "without warrant of law," and he ordered that all excluded pupils must be admitted and placed on "equal footing" with the rest of the students. The decision quoted a wide body of precedent for the decision and made no significant change to state policy. Nevertheless, the case marked a milestone in state legal history: it was the first time that the Department of Public Instruction had intervened in the religious exercises of a city public school system outside of New York City.[30] It would also be the last until well into the twentieth century.[31]

While the Long Island City incident demonstrated a long series of reasonable attempts at compromise on the part of Catholic parents and community leaders—in the face of an uncompromising board of education—readers of the popular magazine *Harper's Weekly* were told a very different version of the events. For months, *Harper's* writer Eugene Lawrence had teamed up with cartoonist Thomas Nast in an anti-Catholic Crusade against the Democratic Party in New York City. In December 1871, Lawrence reported the Long Island City incident thus:

> A teacher, directed by the law to read a portion of the Scriptures in his school, endeavored to perform his duty. The children of Romish parents, instructed by their elders, interrupt the exercise; the teacher still persists, and punishes one of the offenders. He is assailed by half-grown boys; denounced, it is stated, by the Romish priest, the keys to his schoolhouse are taken by him from one of the trustees; the schoolhouse is temporarily closed; the life of the brave teacher in threatened and in danger; and the peaceful citizens of a quiet town are overawed by the violence of the Romish faction.
> Hunters Point, Long Island City.[32]

Lawrence continued his rant by linking the events to "a long series of acts of violence occurring in various portions of our own country and in Europe" that pointed to a global conspiracy of Jesuit priests, who used Irish mobs as pawns in their game of global conquest. He appealed to intelligent Catholics to throw off their priestly shackles. He also concluded, in seemingly deliberate contradiction of fact, to chide the parents for their behavior. "Had those ignorant parents who excited their children to riot and disorder at Hunter's Point been early taught a proper knowledge of their duties as men and citizens, they would scarcely have encouraged acts of violence."

Thomas Nast drew an accompanying cartoon (see Figure 8.2) that highlighted the gist of the article: a scheming priest inciting anarchy in apelike Irish children, the portrait of a public school in danger.

"DON'T BELIEVE IN THAT."

WHAT THE IRISH ROMAN CATHOLIC CHILDREN WILL BE TOLD TO DO NEXT.

"Kick it out *Peaceably!*"

FIGURE 8.2 Thomas Nast ridiculed Catholic children of Long Island City who protested their teacher's mandatory (Protestant) religious exercises in their majority Catholic school. "Don't Believe in That," *Harper's Weekly*, November 18, 1871.

Over the months that followed, Nast and Lawrence teamed up for a series of articles and cartoons that periodically revisited the Hunter's Point controversy, focusing explicitly on the question of Bible reading in public schools.[33] These attacks moved from accusations of Irish mob rule to a more nativist accusation that the Irish Catholics were ungrateful for the blessings of America (see Figure 8.3).

ROMISH INGRATITUDE.—[Drawn by Thomas Nast.]

FIGURE 8.3 Uncle Sam swings the axe of Order at "ungrateful" Irish Catholic protestors against mandatory Bible reading in public schools. The accompanying article by Eugene Field identified Hunter's Point as the immediate subject. Thomas Nast, "Romish 'Ingratitude,'" *Harper's Weekly*, July 13, 1872.

When the State Superintendent of Public Instruction ruled in favor of the Irish protestors in Long Island City—abolishing Bible reading there—Nast and Lawrence turned their accusations of lawlessness and ungratefulness to sour grapes about the Democratic Party. (The State Superintendent was a Democrat.) A cartoon, "Romish Politics—Anything to Beat Grant," accused Horace Greely, presidential candidate against Nast's hero, Ulysses Grant, of pandering to irrational Catholic demands for the removal of the Bible (see Figure 8.4). The text of the cartoon read:

> IRISH CATHOLIC INVADER. "The YMCA want the Bible in the public school, assuming that this is a Christian country. We want the Priest, the Brother, and the Sister in our public schools, not assuming, but endeavoring to effect, that this is a Catholic country."—Saint Louis Western Watchman, July 13, 1872.[34]

Of course, those were not the demands of Catholic parents in Long Island City. They wanted, quite simply, for their children to not have to endure Protestant religious exercises at the start of the school day. Even the list of demands that parents themselves drafted at their citizen's meeting contained no mention of clerical presence in the school. Nast had to plumb his quote from a newspaper in Saint Louis.

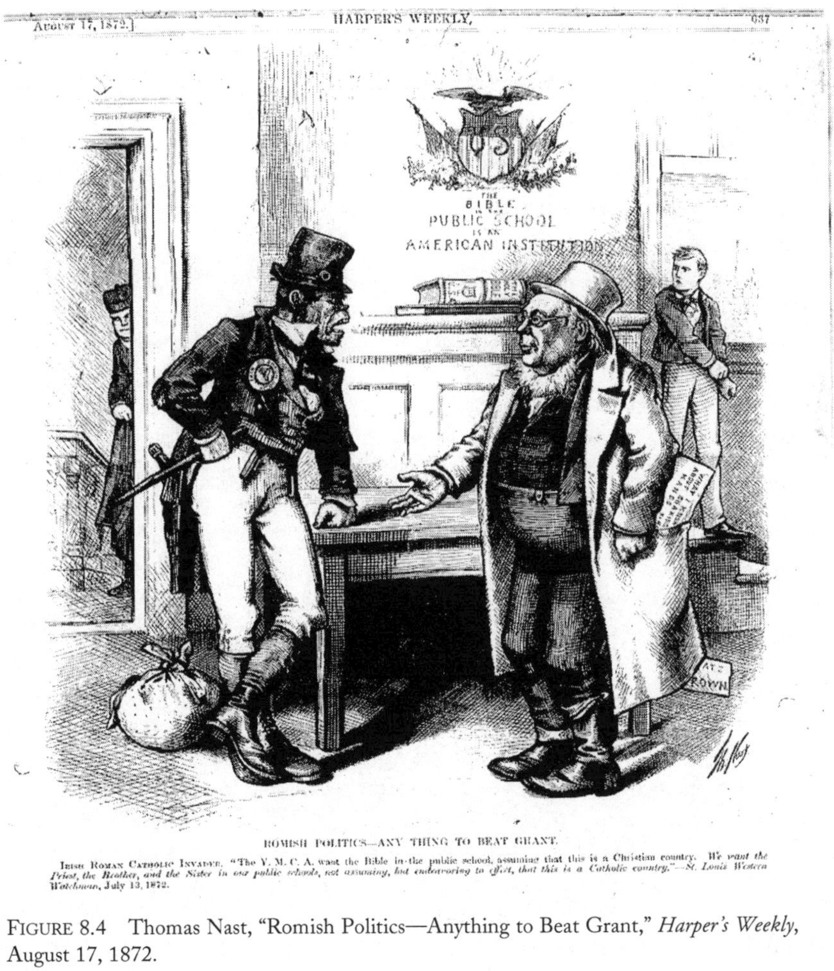

FIGURE 8.4 Thomas Nast, "Romish Politics—Anything to Beat Grant," *Harper's Weekly*, August 17, 1872.

Local Control

Despite *Harper's Weekly's* attempts at inciting animosity and conflict, outside of Long Island City no other urban resident appealed opening exercises requirements. In Brooklyn, African-American parents petitioned the board of education continually throughout the 1870s and 1880s over the issue of separate schools for their children. Jewish parents petitioned for money for their orphan school and to protest the punishment of their children for missing school on Jewish holy days (the board responded overwhelmingly favorably in both cases). Yet Jewish and Catholic parents did not petition the city board of education over mandatory religious exercises even once. In Auburn, the city superintendent noted in 1877 that "the Bible is openly recognized in our schools without apparent objection."[35]

Much of this calm was due to the neighborhood school's ability to mediate between policy dictates and practice. In cities that left the issue to local authority, teachers could conduct whatever exercises that they deemed appropriate for the pupils and that would preserve their jobs. I found no city records requiring Bible reading, for instance, that stipulated *which version* of the Bible was required. One writer explained in 1870, "What the Catholics require is not the exclusion of the Bible—for in all or nearly all the schools chiefly occupied by Catholic children and teachers, and under the control of Catholic trustees, the Douay edition of the Bible is regularly read without objection—but the permission to *teach the peculiar religious tenets of their sect as a part of the regular construction.*"[36] Even Bishop McQuaid's characterization of opening exercises as being inherently "Protestant" was somewhat misleading. At the time, no city required which version of the Bible be read, and all insisted on the teacher's providing no comment in any case.

The existence of separate nonpublic schools for Catholics also eased the burden of public schools and may have taken the steam out of the more ardent lay Catholic critics of public school policy. For German Lutherans and Catholics (and later for Poles), whose church schools offered the added attraction of nationalism, public schools failed on more counts than religious exercises, and nonpublic schools offered a popular alternative.[37] Polish historian Waclaw Kruszka described the cultural imperative for parochial schooling in 1908: "The Polish churches . . . are the citadels of patriotism; arks and vessels that protect the Polish people in exile from the flood . . . of denationalization and foreignness. But the foundations of these citadels, the hulls of these arks and vessels, are the Polish schools! Without them the Polish church would sink like a bottomless vessel in a sea of Anglo-Americanism."[38]

Since the ugly years of American nativism of the 1840s and 1850s, leading Catholics, particularly New York City's Archbishop John Hughes, had pushed for a separate system of schools, publicly funded or not. But the church's struggle to build an infrastructure of actual church buildings took top priority. After the Civil War, however, church policy shifted. McQuaid explained that

> for the past 30 years, since the first serious discussions of the right of religion to be in the schools, when we had very few Catholic schools in this state, we had been too busy providing church accommodations for our ever-increasing members to give that earnest attention to our schools which they merit. In the years to come, we shall be more occupied with school building and with the education of our children than in the erecting of churches, although this work will not be permitted to stand still.[39]

The Plenary Council of Baltimore had decreed in 1866 that parochial schools were a major priority, but church leaders differed in their enthusiasm for separate schools. Many, like Hughes, his successor Archbishop Michael Corrigan, and Rochester's Bernard McQuaid, saw parochial schooling as the only means to ensure truly appropriate religious education for Catholic children.[40] Others, like New York City's Father Edward McGlynn, urged Catholic parents to send their children to public schools and to avoid "the cruel injustice their parents, under the coercion of the Roman Catholic Church, would inflict upon them by depriving them of the magnificent advantages of a common school education."[41]

Despite these differences of opinion, however, the Church made very real gains in its institution-building efforts in the decades following the Civil War. Not all cities reported Catholic school enrollment (church schools frequently withheld statistics), but one sociologist has estimated from church and census sources that Catholic school enrollment in elementary school grew nationwide by 70 percent from 1870 to 1880.[42] In Auburn, all private schools (Catholic and others) grew from an estimated 500 to 1,000 pupils (from 19 percent to 30 percent of all school-aged students enrolled in school) over the same decade.[43] McQuaid estimated in 1872 that 40 percent of all children in school in Rochester attended parochial schools.[44] In New York City, on the other hand, Catholic school enrollment (primary and secondary) by 1880 amounted to less than 11 percent.[45] By 1881, in Elmira, Catholic school enrollment was less than 7 percent.[46] These differences bespoke a variety of local circumstances. Rochester would maintain high levels of parochial school attendance despite the removal of religious exercises in 1875. New York City continued to have low levels despite its mandatory exercises.[47] In either case, however, the very existence of an alternative system may have sapped militant Catholic objection to public school religious policy.

Finally, many Catholics, Jews, and nonbelievers may not have objected to religious exercises because they simply did not find them objectionable enough to protest. School itself, as I suggested in chapter 6, played a far more muted role in a child's social life than it does today, with low daily attendance rates and short terms, and many other social opportunities. During school, with few exceptions, religious exercises were required to be perfunctory, rote, and without comment. School officials off and on the record in Long Island City, Troy, and Rochester admitted that most children did not pay attention to the "listless" reading of the Bible.[48] The principal of Long Island City's School Number Two expressed surprise that a parent would even think to object to such meaningless exercises. When conducted to emphasize the dominance of one group (as in Long Island city), religious exercises could indeed evoke a response. But exercises without much perceived meaning, or intended to bring children together, may not have. A listless tone could, in a roundabout way, be perceived as a gesture of compromise.

The specific exercises themselves were a bare-bones attempt at religious rituals that could be conducted in a Pan-Christian sense. Teachers and principals required to conduct exercises could find passages of Scripture that were close to identical in the Douay and King James versions, from whichever they might choose to read. By the 1890s, in fact, several authors published religious textbooks for public schools that did just that.[49] Differences in the Lord's Prayer were more difficult, as congregations varied the words. But even these were not insurmountable, particularly when children were not required to repeat them.[50] Where time permitted hymns, these too could be Pan-Christian, as we saw in the compromise between Catholics and Protestants in Wayland (see chapter 5). The *Catholic Review* confessed in 1889, "Without a doubt there are many Catholics who look upon the public school as safe enough for Christian children, just as many Protestants of a religious tone think."[51]

Many Catholics, in fact, supported their neighborhood public schools. In his 1975 book, *Irish-American and Italian-American Educational Views and Activities,* Howard Ralph Weisz found that Irish Catholics had complex feelings about parochial schooling—some staunchly defending it but others demurring in preference for public schools. In New York City and Brooklyn, where Irish control of neighborhood public schools was strong, conservative priests had to resort to denying the sacrament (which meant damnation) to children and parents who refused to attend church schools in order to take children away from their neighborhood public schools. Some liberal priests, on the other hand, refused to open parochial schools and encouraged attendance at public ones. Leaders of both sides admitted that their schools were often academically inferior to public schools. (They also usually charged a small tuition, which added a disincentive to parents.[52]) Though every bit as Catholic as other nationalities, Italians in Brooklyn and New York City showed little enthusiasm for parochial schooling, balking at the nationalistic education that attracted Germans and opting for the chance at assimilation that the public school offered.[53] In the early 1890s, most Polish children in Buffalo attended parochial school. When the city built a new public school in the Polish district (where there had been none), however, half of all Polish children switched to public school over the next ten years. Some parents kept children in parochial schools until their first communion, then they switched to public schools afterward.[54]

Jews largely embraced public schools and set up after-school religious programs to complement them.[55] Yet this embrace was not whole or unconditional. Though small in number, Jews did play a major role in shaping the religious policy of several cities, including Troy, Albany, and Rochester. Because of their strongly pro-public school posture, their objections did not attract the same venom that some Protestants issued toward Catholics in discussions of the school question of the 1870s. Jews, however, had the strongest argument against Pan-Protestant or Pan-Christian religious exercises. They could reasonably object to the Christian tone of most of the hymns and the New Testament. And Jews, unlike atheists, could not be written off as amoral or irreligious infidels.

Jews were not entirely alienated by Bible reading. They recognized the Old Testament portion of the Bible and the Judeo-Christian God (though *sans* the multiple personalities of Son and Holy Spirit). This left wiggle room for compromise, as teachers could select Old Testament readings from any version of the Bible. And, indeed, Jews made no formal appeals to the State Superintendent at all over the issue. Local behavior varied. Recall that Jewish parents in Brooklyn petitioned the city board on separate occasions for support of a Jewish orphan asylum (which they were legally entitled to) and asked that their children not be penalized for missing school on religious holidays. Both were granted.[56] But they did not protest the board's mandatory religious exercises. Nor did New York City Jews, who found the Bible reading without proselytizing to be relatively innocuous compared to what they had experienced back in Europe, and whose children felt safe in schools where nearly all of the children were Jewish.[57] For Jews outside of New York City and Brooklyn, whose small numbers could not guarantee the degree of representation in pupils or teachers that Catholics enjoyed, religious exercises rankled. By 1875, Jewish leaders in Albany and Rochester had weighed in publicly against religious exercises in public schools.[58]

Outlawing the Bible in Rochester and Troy

The Long Island City case raised the dander of pro-Bible enthusiasts, but it did not have an immediate impact on the policies of other cities in New York

State. It proved that city policies could be brought to heel by state case law, but such cases would still require someone to file an appeal. No one else did. In his famous argument for publicly funded parochial schools, for example, Rochester's Bishop Bernard McQuaid attacked public schools that had religious exercises as being "to all intents and purposes . . . Protestant schools," and those that did not as being "godless and un-American." McQuaid claimed to prefer Bible reading without comment to none at all, but he objected to both options. Just three weeks before the Superintendent handed down his decision in the Long Island City case, McQuaid issued an indirect but a clear challenge to the lay opponents of "Protestant" religious exercises in the public schools of Rochester: they could appeal to the State Superintendent of Public Instruction over opening exercises and win. "The time is not far distant," he said, "when, if no Catholic calls for the observance of the law, there will be found others who will demand the complete secularization of the schools as the law directs."[59] Over the next three years, not a single resident of Rochester filed an appeal, and the boards of education of Rochester and Troy abandoned the practice without organized protests from Catholics.[60]

In the 1874–1875 school year, the school context statewide was ripe for reform. During the 1874 campaign, state Republicans had played up the "Catholic menace" to public schools in an effort to win nativist votes. Newspapers across the state periodically ran stories about the "school question" of public funds to parochial schools, and, alongside these, discussions of the propriety of religious exercises in public schools. After the election, the issue continued in the religious press, in part, to encourage action. After several months of public debate, the Buffalo Common Council heard and rejected a proposal to give parochial schools a share of the school fund (discussed in chapter 9). Newspapers across the state discussed the decision, but the question of religious exercises per se did not come up.[61] On May 4, 1875, *Harper's* reissued Nast's "The Priests and the Schools," with Tweed's image erased.

At the same time, in May 1875, the question of religious exercises came before the board of education of Albany. Rabbi Schlessinger, a Jewish community leader, presented a petition to the board on behalf of the Jewish citizens of the city. The petition complained that though city policy left religious exercises to the discretion of school principals and teachers, the practice was universal, and it asked that such exercises be discontinued. The board appointed a special committee to investigate the matter (and to stall for time). At the July meeting of the board, the committee reported back that, yes, indeed, all schools of the city, save for two departments in one school, were opened with "prayer of a denominational character, and that the reading of the Bible and singing of religious hymns are part of the school exercises." The committee then recited state case law on religious exercises and agreed with the petition that the exercises should cease when parents objected. At the same time, however, the fact that religious exercises were left to local discretion presented the committee with a politically brilliant opportunity. To satisfy the petitioners but to avoid angering Protestant enthusiasts, the board simply blamed the teachers for the error. "It is the opinion of your committee," it declared, "that the teachers of our public schools have acted in this matter entirely on their judgment and with the best intentions, but without authority and contrary to the spirit of the laws regulating public instruction in this state." The full board of education adopted the report and let the matter drop without further action.[62] The Albany board made it clear that teachers must respect religious dissenters, but it did nothing to stop future exercises in districts where no one complained. This policy of laissez-faire mirrored state policy.

Yet while the Albany board hedged, two other cities took on the issue squarely. There was no advance indication in the summer of 1875 that Troy would be the decisive city for the movement banning religious exercises. After the November 1874 election ousted incumbent Republican Governor Dix, the biggest news in Troy during the spring and early summer of 1875 concerned the salacious details of a drawn-out courtroom sex scandal involving the nation's most prominent Protestant minister, Henry Ward Beecher. In politics, the Democratically inclined *Troy Daily Press* mused on the propriety of term limits should President Grant seek reelection. In religious news, ministers of various denominations ruminated over physicist John Tyndall's scientific analysis of religion. Monthly board of education meetings plowed through routine matters—finding space for students and repairing damaged buildings.[63]

Five days before the final board meeting of the year, the printing committee of the Troy Board of Education met to discuss changes to the *Manual of the Board of Education*, which included citywide regulations for schools. These regulations included specifications for opening religious exercises, which included "reading a portion of the Scripture, and by audibly repeating the Lord's Prayer, in which all may unite."[64] Revealing that it too had been affected by the media hype over religion in public schools, the committee voted unanimously to include a provision prohibiting these, and indeed *all* religious exercises, and it vowed that the resolution would be "strictly enforced."[65] When the full board met the following week, the printing committee's report came last in the order of business. The committee announced its resolution: that the citywide requirement for religious exercises should be omitted and, further, that all religious exercises be explicitly prohibited.[66]

No one objected to the removal of the Bible. One commissioner, Bainbridge, did move to keep the Lord's Prayer, saying that he had "read all of the scientific lore of the period, but that he had not forgotten the Lord's

Prayer taught him by his mother." He urged the Catholic members of the board to agree that the prayer was acceptably nonsectarian for all faiths. Another commissioner, Browne, replied that the law gave parents the right to object to religious instruction of any sort. After all, "It was Mr. Bainbridge's mother who taught him the Lord's Prayer, not a hired schoolteacher." Like the principal of Ward Two School in Long Island City, Browne also noted that "a majority of the pupils listen to a listless reading of the Bible, or recitation of the prayer, and it has no effect on [them]." A Catholic commissioner declared that the version of the prayer currently in use was not acceptable to Catholics, and that the Catholic alternative would not be acceptable to Protestants. The board voted unanimously to forbid the Bible. Bainbridge's motion to spare the prayer lost 10 to 2.[67] In what was probably a political gesture to protect the board from charges of Catholic conspiracy, an Irish commissioner punctuated the vote with a lame-duck proposal that the salaries of the teachers in the Catholic orphan asylums be raised by $100. The board obligingly shot it down.

Four days after the board meeting, the *Troy Daily Press* reported that the action of the board had "caused a good deal of comment throughout the land." The paper claimed, "It is generally admitted that Troy has done a very wise thing in taking the lead in the settlement of this vexatious controversy. Only bigots and those people who want to shirk their duty of religiously instructing their children at home will find fault with it."[68] The *Albany Express* and the *Rochester Daily Union and Advertiser* applauded the decision.[69] The board's action also caught the particular attention of Commissioner Michaels, a Jewish member of the Rochester Board of Education. At the penultimate meeting of the Rochester School Board for the 1874–1875 school year, and only six days after the Troy board had met, Michaels made an unexpected proposal: that Rochester too officially forbid religious exercises. The move caught the board off guard. One commissioner immediately proposed that it be referred to a committee. Michaels said he hoped the matter would be settled in open board and not "smothered in a committee." Another commissioner attempted to table the motion, but Michaels insisted. "The time has come for this question to be fairly met," he repeated.[70]

The board then discussed the matter. One commissioner supported the measure but pointed out that there was no official requirement in the schools at the moment. (Rather, it was left to schools to decide—and most did in favor of exercises.) Two commissioners debated whether the policy would attract more Catholic children to public schools. Another confessed that he had no objection to religious exercises—after all, Congress had them. Like the Troy board three weeks earlier, the Rochester Board of Education showed strong support for the removal of the Bible. The resolution carried,

14 to 2, that "all religious exercises of any nature be prohibited from the public schools."[71]

The *Rochester Union* had claimed, before the vote, that most of the city's clergy were probably in favor of the Troy resolution. A group of twenty-two evangelicals, half of whom were Presbyterian, tried to refute this claim in a petition to the board of education. "We regard [the action of the board] hastily taken, and at once impolitic and unjust. We regard it as a mistake to propose that the action taken will conciliate the enemies of the public school system; and we utter on behalf of the religious people of this city, who are outraged by this procedure, our distinct and solemn protest against it."[72] Baptists, on the other hand, united to support the decision.[73] Bishop McQuaid did not join in the petition, but he also expressed disappointment. He had predicted in 1872 that the public schools of Rochester would eventually become secular. What he had not predicted, however, was that the city would reach the decision internally, in a moderate fashion. (He had predicted an appeal to the State Superintendent.) Even as he admonished priests in parishes outside of Rochester to push for the abolition of religious exercises in public schools, McQuaid privately lamented the fact that the board had removed the Bible in his own city—and thus made schools more palatable to Catholics—just when he had prepared hundreds of new spaces for Catholic children in his parochial schools.[74]

At the following school board meeting, the last of the school year, the president of the board attempted to reverse its decision, bowing to the pressure exerted by activist clergy. "From many pulpits, and the almost, if not entirely, unanimous religious press of the country," he implored, "we hear deprecation of the action taken by this board, especially with the apparent haste with which the subject was brought up and pressed to final action." Instead, he resolved that the board change the meaning of the prohibition to forbid *sectarian* reading of the Bible but to allow Bible reading without note or comment. His resolution offered an out for those board members who wished to save face and change their votes from the previous meeting. Those in favor of the original prohibition conceded that their action had been hasty, but they rejected any recantation. Instead, they offered the following set of preambles to explain their previous decision:

> Whereas the following are among the reasons which actuated the board and its vote at the last meeting in the common schools:
>
> Whereas the principles of religious liberty in which our Government is founded forbids the retention of religious exercises that are a matter of conscientious objection to any portion in schools for the support of which the entire committee is taxed,

> Whereas the religious exercises hitherto permitted in the public schools are (while not essential to the inculcation of sound morality) a matter of conscientious objection by many taxpayers,
>
> Whereas the spirit of true religion requires that we should show that regard for the conscientious scruples of others which we would have them, in this similar circumstances, show to us,
>
> Whereas due regard for the welfare of the state demands that all reasonable grounds for objection to the public school be removed, in order that children of all class's [*sic*] may share in that education essential to good citizenship, which has wisely been provided by the state, therefore resolved [that all religious exercises of any nature be prohibited from the public schools].[75]

The president of the board rejected this list on a technicality, but those in favor then proposed it as a set of resolutions. The resulting vote sustained the prohibition of religious exercises—adopting the resolutions and rejecting the president's attempted reform—11 votes to 5.[76]

Over the summer vacation, the board of education prepared for the first fall meeting, when the issue of religious exercises would doubtless return in full bloom. The superintendent of the Rochester public schools in particular prepared an eloquent, heartfelt report for the board as a part of his annual report for the previous school year. As it turned out, the board did not vote on the issue again. (Probably the results were predictable, given the strong backing given to the abolition of religious exercises at the last two board meetings.) Nevertheless the superintendent's preparation for a *redux* of the previous June produced a major document in the history of religion in public schools.[77]

In his report, the superintendent described how his opinion on the subject had changed in recent years, as he had researched the issue in preparation for such a situation. In fact, he confessed that as a teacher himself he had once conducted religious exercises without a second thought. Now, however, he could not longer endorse such practice in good conscience. He listed six reasons for his opinion, but these could be grouped into three, each of which echoed the experiences of other cities: First, the practice had been ruled illegal during school hours by the State Superintendent—doubtless a reference to the Long Island City case. Second, the claims of Unitarians, Catholics, Jews, and others that religious exercises violated their conscience were legitimate, and if the state forbade funds to church schools, then it had to provide a religiously palatable alternative. Third, religious exercises were not necessary for sound moral instruction, and were largely overrated.[78]

The arguments of the superintendent appear to be genuine expressions of his and the majority of the board's sentiments—and not the work of enemies of religion. (The superintendent claimed that it cost him many friends.) The exclusion of the Bible was certainly not the direct result of Catholic Church influence in Rochester politics. The superintendent himself derided such a claim as "frivolous," adding that, "In the first place, no such demand, of late, has been made by that church; and in the second place, if parents of that communion who are patrons of our schools had made the request in a formal way, I know of no good reason that this board should not have paid respectful heed to it." As we have seen, Bishop McQuaid had mixed feelings about the provision.

The superintendent and the majority of the board defended the action—publicly, at least—in terms of the need for a civil system of mass education to respect the consciences of all citizens.[79] In fact, later in the 1875–1876 school year, the same board of education cracked down on the independent Catholic orphan asylum, which received city funds but enjoyed freedom from regulation by the board. First, members of the board questioned whether the school was entitled to funds at all. The city attorney assured them that while the city did not have to share state funds, the law did require the city to provide a share of city funds. One year later, the majority of the board then voted that since it had to give public funds to church orphan asylums, then it also would subject the orphan asylums to as strict regulation as regular common schools.[80]

Nor was the elimination of religious exercises anti-Protestant or purely secular in reasoning. Both the board resolutions of June 1875 and the superintendent's report of September argued in *Christian* terms for the exclusion of the Bible. The board wrote that "the spirit of true religion requires that we should show that regard for the conscientious scruples of others which we would have them, in this similar circumstances, show to us." The superintendent claimed, "I would respect the conscience of another, as I would ask for respect for my own." Both referred to the Golden Rule, "do unto others as you would have them do unto you," a staple of mainstream Protestant thought.

In 1879, a group of Protestant ministers again petitioned the Rochester board to change the prohibition of Bible reading. The ministers still assumed that the action had been made simply to mollify Catholics—seeing the issue as a black-and-white struggle between Protestant and Catholic—and did not even acknowledge the other arguments that the board had put forth, including the concept of the Golden Rule. They wrote, "We believe that such act was hastily passed, and that it did not meet the approbation of the best friends of our school system, and, as is well known, it has utterly failed in the design of bringing back to our schools the children of Roman Catholic parents." Instead, they insisted that the public schools were their turf and demanded that "matters be placed precisely where they were before, and that in our schools and elsewhere we may be protected in our constitutional rights—the freedom to worship God." The petition failed to impress a majority of the board, however, and the Rochester schools would remain Bible free for the rest of the century.[81]

After 1875, the question of religious exercises in public schools receded from newspapers and boards of education minutes though New Rochelle formally outlawed Bible reading in 1879 after several years of debate. As if to punctuate its exceptionalism, the board of education of New York City capped a successful Protestant countermovement to require religious exercises in 1877, by slipping Article XXVI, Section 134, into the bylaws of the city schools, which stipulated, for the first time since the "Bible Wars" of the 1840s, "All the schools of this city under the jurisdiction of the Board of Education shall be opened with reading a portion of the Holy Scriptures, without note or comment."[82] The move merely formalized what was already general practice in New York City public schools.[83]

Religious Exercises in the 1880s and 1890s

After the 1870s, the issue of religious exercises faded from the agendas of city school boards. And, in general, city policies of the 1890s reflected those of the late 1870s. In 1884, residents of a suburban district of Orangetown, Staten Island, appealed a policy similar to that of Long Island City, requiring children to be present and behave "with decorum" during religious exercises.[84] The State Superintendent sustained the plaintiffs. With the exception of that case, however, religious exercises all but disappeared from the popular press and state politics. In 1885, the superintendent noted in his annual report that the subject caused only occasional contention in school districts.[85] Not until the legislature consolidated New York City in 1898 did any major change in city policy take place. The consolidation of New York City joined a number of cities and towns, including Brooklyn and Long Island City, to the New York City Board of Education. The Bible-reading requirement from 1877 stood and now went into effect in Long Island City schools, where exercises had been banned by the State Superintendent in 1872. No one appealed this time, however, although the special status of New York City versus the increasingly powerful State Superintendent would have sparked a spectacular legal battle.

City boards of education did not collect or report statistics on religious exercises, and there is little evidence to give an overall picture of them in city schools. The best available information comes from *Religion and Public Education*, the 1889 survey by the New York Synod of the Presbyterian Church (introduced in chapter 6). To conduct the survey, a special committee mailed a questionnaire to city superintendents and county commissioners throughout the state. Of the twenty-five cities in the state, twenty-two sent replies. Table 8.1 has distilled its often confusing questions and reporting to three types of exercises: Bible reading, prayer, and Christian hymn singing. Sadly, the Synod Committee did not share the results for individual cities. Fourteen of twenty-five cities (56 percent) reported daily religious exercises. Seven (28 percent) reported having occasional or no religious exercises. And another four (16 percent) made no response to the question, and it seems likely that those superintendents who did not respond to the Synod's repeated queries lacked enthusiasm for the project. City schools reported conducting opening prayers less frequently than Bible reading, and only one-quarter of cities reported regular singing of Christian hymns.

TABLE 8.1 Frequency of Various Types of Religious Exercises in Urban Schools Reported by the New York Presbyterian Synod's Survey, *Religion and Public Education*, 1889

Type of Exercises	*Number and Percent of City Superintendents Describing the Frequency of Religious Instruction in Twenty-Five City Schools*									
	Daily		*Occasionally*		*Never/Forbidden*		*No Resonse*		*Total*	
	n	*%*	*n*	*%*	*n*	*%*	*n*	*%*	*n*	*%*
Bible reading	*14*	*56*	*2*	*8*	*5*	*20*	*4*	*16*	*25*	*100*
Prayer	*10*	*40*	*2*	*8*	*9*	*36*	*4*	*16*	*25*	*100*
Christian hymns	*6*	*24*	*3*	*12*	*11*	*44*	*5*	*20*	*25*	*100*

Source: Religion and Public Education: Reports of the Committee on Religion and Public Education, Presented to the Synod of New York of the Presbyterian Church in the United States of America, at Its Meetings in Auburn, 1887 and in Poughkeepsie, 1889, 26–30.
Note: City superintendents from Buffalo, Ogdensburg, and Oswego did not reply to the survey. The Synod did not differentiate among versions of the Bible, nor whether the practice was universal in each city or left to local discretion.

The authors of the study did not comment on any individual statistics in particular but expressed disappointment throughout the document. They were particularly saddened by the fact that most of the religious education in city public schools did not extend beyond the perfunctory morning exercises. Although poor questioning led to garbled data, the committee found that most city school leaders believed that religious exercises, where they existed, were as nonsectarian and inoffensive as possible. As for any religious instruction beyond that, the superintendent of schools from the city of Schenectady summed up the responses of many of his colleagues: "The difficulty of distinguishing between genuine religious instruction and sectarian teaching is so great that on the whole it is better to let the churches attend to the matter. . . . Our manuals and rules are for good reasons entirely silent on the subject except as they direct the opening of schools by reading the Scriptures and Prayer." In short, fear of offending any particular religious sect ran deep in the rhetoric of even those city superintendents who condoned religious exercises.[86]

In response to the decidedly secular nature of public schools, the majority of the survey committee recommended that the Presbyterian Church model itself on the Women's Christian Temperance Union (WCTU), which had recently won passage of mandatory temperance education in public schools and used a far-flung network of members to monitor compliance. The majority report urged Presbyterians to organize a social protest movement to put religious instruction in schools by exerting pressure at the local level, as well as the state and national levels.[87] A vocal minority of the committee, though, recommended that the Presbyterian Synod *not* take action and maintain the separation of religion and public schooling that currently existed.[88] Their position—leave well enough alone—better captured the spirit of the times in New York State.

As part of its report, the Presbyterian Committee on Religion and Public Education included a section on the legal standing of religious exercises in the state of New York. The committee broke its analysis down into a discussion of the three bodies of law that affected school practice: the decisions of the State Superintendent (deferred to by regular courts in religion in public schools matters), laws passed by the legislature, and the state constitution. Four different legal authorities—three Manhattan lawyers and a law professor from Cornell—offered their opinions, and all four were virtually the same. First, state superintendents had ruled consistently against any religious instruction during school hours, but these decisions were not binding for schools other than those in consideration. The legislature had not passed any law regarding religious instruction in common schools, nor had it mentioned the issue in the incorporating acts of any city or village, except New York City. Finally, the state constitution made no mention of religious or moral training in public schools. Professor Charles Collin, of Cornell, concluded that, "It would appear that any school commissioner may, under present statutes, recommend to the trustees and teachers the inclusion of religion and morality in the course of study. If the trustees and teachers adopt, or refuse to adopt, such recommendation, an appeal may be taken to the [State] Superintendent." Unless the legislature enacted a special law, however, or unless the people amended the constitution, all four experts agreed that the superintendent's predictable decision would be final.[89]

Three of the four attorneys repeated an injunction that though it had no force of law as a statute or constitutional provision the legal principle had become nearly universally understood. Any religious instruction that the

Presbyterians did add to the common school curriculum could not be "sectarian." As we have seen, the meaning of "sectarian instruction" varied from situation to situation, and even from person to person. In Long Island City, Catholics had challenged opening exercises as being sectarian. In other cities, they did not protest, and in still others, Catholic teachers conducted opening exercises from a Douay Bible to classes full of Catholic children. Jews in New York City did not protest opening exercises in predominantly Jewish schools, but Jews in Rochester and Albany did. In this light, "sectarianism" itself was relative to local circumstance. In the context of democratic control of schools, cries of sectarianism rose most shrilly in those places where majorities used religious exercises as a symbol of cultural dominance.

In 1902, State Superintendent Skinner conducted his own statewide survey of Bible reading in public schools—for two reasons. In general, the turn of the century saw a growing, organized movement to include Bible reading in public schools. The National Education Association, for example, resolved in 1902 that the Bible be read in public schools for its literary and moral merits.[90] The Superintendent's survey immediately followed a set of surveys on the question conducted by the Chicago Women's Educational Union in 1898, then reprinted in the *Annual Report* of the U.S. Commissioner of Education (see chapter 6). More importantly, however, Superintendent Skinner conducted his survey to further his own political agenda: ending the state's tradition of defending religious minorities from religious exercises. Rather than try to ascertain the numbers of districts that conducted (or did not) various types of religious exercises, Skinner asked for the *opinions* of normal school principals, county commissioners, and city superintendents. It appears from the accompanying report that Skinner intended to demonstrate a universal opinion in favor of Bible reading. And, indeed, reports from other states suggested that Bible reading was quite common in the New England and Middle Atlantic states. It also was common in New York State itself—nearly, if not wholly, universal in New York City—and (in Skinner's estimation) common practice in a "large majority" of the state's remaining public schools.[91]

The opinions on which Skinner reported regarding the Bible in public schools ranged from strong support for expanding religious study (even beyond Bible reading without comment) to opposition to any religious instruction at all. Most, however, fell somewhere in the middle—endorsing nonsectarian Bible exercises but expressing concern that they be made to not offend parents and pupils. The majority of normal school principals opposed mandatory religious exercises for all students; the majority of city and village superintendents favored them. County commissioners emphasized the need for local districts and teachers to decide based on whether any minorities objected, but generally they supported Bible reading. Some respondents urged that such use of the Bible should focus on it as great literature, not as a religious exercise per se. Many of the answers were so terse that they did not provide clues as to how advocacy for Bible reading might translate into actual policy. Even those who advocated mandatory religious exercises often expressed the hope that exercises *could* be made inoffensive to all, while others maintained that they already were.[92]

The Beginning of the End: Superintendent Skinner's New Democracy

Until 1903, state superintendents had ruled consistently in favor of religious minorities in appeals cases against exercises during school hours, and this consistency had probably exerted much influence at the local level by offering minorities a legal trump card for their complaints. State legislatures refused to handle the issue at all from 1865 to 1900. Social protest groups, on the other hand, swarmed to the issue. Some, such as the CWEU, adopted a "big tent" approach, attempting to form an all-inclusive religious alliance in its attack against the "secular atheism" of public education.[93] The Presbyterian Synod—with its own internal divisions on the issue—proved mild next to such aggressive nativists as the National Reform Association, the American Protective Association, and New York's own National League for the Protection of American Institutions, each of which targeted Catholics as enemies of American public education. Their efforts came to a head in the state constitutional convention of 1894. As part of a larger movement to prohibit public funds to church schools, the convention passed an amendment (later ratified by the state) that prohibited public funds to any school "in which any denominational tenet or doctrine is taught."[94]

Yet these groups did not manage to win any decisive victory. The constitutional amendment did little to resolve the issue of what, exactly, defined "sectarian" or "denominational" instruction. The amendment strengthened the hand of the State Superintendent but did not guide it (acting more as a punctuation mark than a predicate). Now state superintendents could, and did, buttress their arguments with the state constitution; but by the same token, they were open to define sectarian instruction for themselves. As we have seen, throughout the late nineteenth century, superintendents consistently deemed any religious instruction during school hours inappropriate.

Increasing agitation of anti-Catholic organizations nationwide and growing interest in Bible reading generally (as suggested by the number of surveys from 1889 to 1902) put renewed pressure on local school boards in the 1890s and 1900s to include religious exercises. In the context of progressive reform of school governance, however, this pressure now had fewer release valves. Administrative reform swept aside ward-based control in favor of centralized administration in most of the cities in New York State during the 1890s. Incorporated villages probably felt similar effects, particularly the emphasis on increasing the authority of school superintendents. Fewer systems in place at the local level to ameliorate religious differences meant a greater need for complaints to higher levels of authority. One county commissioner noted in 1903 that he had been "called upon five times to settle the matter of reading the Bible in the public schools" for his county alone.[95] Superintendent Skinner noted a "great increase in the number of protests received at this department against the reading of the Bible as a part of the opening exercises in the public schools."[96]

Using this increasing agitation at the local level as a pretext, Skinner announced a new departure for the State Department of Public Instruction, buttressed (in his mind) by his religious survey results, in his annual report to the legislature in 1903. Rather than protect minorities against "majority rules," he would now affirm the majority. Skinner reasoned that because the legislature had never forbidden religious exercises, it had therefore affirmed the right of local majorities to conduct them, and even to compel all students to attend them. If public school authorities conducted sectarian or inappropriate exercises, then citizens could appeal. "But where the scriptures are read, as the statute provides they shall be in the city of New York, without note or comment, in the presence of the pupils thereof, as part of the opening exercises, I shall deem it my duty to rule that such practice is not in violation of the constitution or statutes of this state."[97]

In essence, Skinner argued that religious exercises were not sectarian, nor did they violate the religious freedom of children who objected. He rested this assertion on the fact that the majority of states, as well as (he claimed) the majority of Americans, believed that such exercises were nonsectarian. He also cited a pan-denominational tract developed under the auspices of the CWEU along with various Protestant, Catholic, and Jewish clergy. "If the reading of the Bible in the public school, therefore, is a cause of contention in any locality, I would respectfully suggest that either the work referred to herein be used, or another be prepared by representatives of all interests locally affected, containing selections from the Bible to be used in the public schools."[98]

The new policy repudiated a legal tradition that had from 1865 to 1900 played a major role in the settlement of religious controversies at the local level. For as long as Skinner remained in office (until 1904), he would not hear appeals from objectors to mandatory religious exercises. At the local level, this meant that religious majorities in districts would have less incentive to make peaceable adjustments and forge compromises. Skinner's departure signaled a move toward democratic governance as a form of majority rule without the protection of minority rights. The majority itself, in his conception, would define what it meant to be religiously neutral.

Skinner's policy also created a new role for religious authorities. For decades, religious leaders had used the pulpit, the press, and the polls as their means of influencing public school policy. Now Skinner opened the side door: those religious leaders who were willing to support Pan-Christian, or Pan-Judeo-Christian exercises in public schools could have a direct say in determining the character of those exercises. Individual conscience no longer mattered in this view. Religious views mattered only as legitimated through religious leadership. And even then, the state gave no truck to those leaders who refused to sign on to its vision of "non-sectarian" religious exercises. Skinner's policy also repudiated the state's former tradition of allowing for diverse religious policies reflecting group diversity in distinct wards and districts—the Douay Bible in Catholic districts, for example. (Though Skinner's words made no impact on actual practice in this area.) Instead, all were expected to share the same general view of religion, wedded to citizenship and wearing the clothes of approved churches. In other words, religious exercises, like public education more broadly, had now become a matter for the experts.

Conclusion

Skinner left office in 1904, when the legislature reorganized the Department of Public Instruction into the state Department of Education. His replacement, Andrew Sloan Draper (a former state superintendent), returned the department to its previous position of defending objectors to religious exercises, but the writing was on the wall. Skinner's vision better fit the progressive revolution in administration that was underway statewide—emphasizing the authority of central school boards and city superintendents and delegitimizing localism and dissent. Not until 1962, in the U.S. Supreme Court decision in *Engel v. Vitale,* did a New Yorker successfully mount a legal challenge against a city's religious exercises policy.

In 1906, officials at Christ Lutheran Church in New York City inaugurated a program that would come to reflect a new compromise between Skinner's vision of religious neutrality in public schools and the reality of a diverse population—a peaceable adjustment for a progressive age. Officials at the church teamed up with local school officials to offer weekday religious instruction under the auspices of the public school, during the regular school schedule. "Released time" programs for religious instruction caught on in the next few decades, especially after gaining notoriety in the Gary, Indiana, schools in 1914. By 1920, over fifty towns and cities in New York State would adopt some form of released time programs.[99] This new approach to religious diversity, using the public school as a clearinghouse for religious experts, fit well with a new Progressive emphasis on centralized authority and social control. The unique set of legal and practical conditions that had characterized public school religious policy in the late nineteenth century had ended.

Chapter 9

Public Funds for Religious Schools

INTRODUCTION

The strongest post-bellum challenge to the common school system came in cities, and came over the issue of public funding for church schools. Since Catholic and Protestant confrontations over the Free School Society's control of public funds in New York City in the 1840s, most Catholic Church leaders demanded public funding for separate, denominational schools. (They still do.) In the decades following the Civil War, Democratic Party strength and localism in city school systems across New York State made such funding possible. Driven by overcrowding, and facilitated by a fluid understanding of "public" education, cities large and small began channeling public resources into church-run schools after the Civil War. Funding for city common schools came from two sources: state funds, under the auspices of the legislature, and local tax, under the control of city government. Proponents of public aid to religious schools used both with varying degrees of success. From large metropolises such as New York and Buffalo to small cities such as Elmira, Utica, and Ogdensburg, state residents and lawmakers considered, and often created, publicly funded church schools.[1]

The success or failure of these ventures depended on their relationship to the needs of their city school systems and their "fit" with the principle of democratic control of schools. In New York City, proponents of state aid—led by Boss Tweed—exploited Tweed's influence in the state legislature to sneak such funding into state appropriations bills. In a more above-board mode, several cities and incorporated villages created such plans in the late

1860s and 1870s in the absence of coherent state policy toward city governance in general and toward religious issues in particular. Other cities voted on such plans but failed to adopt them. Even though they failed more often than they succeeded, however, plans providing public funds to church schools marked an important phase in the development of urban public schooling in religiously pluralistic cities.

In the late 1880s, the tide turned. Beginning with a landmark decision in 1886, state government played an increasingly active role in regulating local agreements over public funding for church-related schools. This activism reflected more general trends in state educational policy and culminated in a constitutional amendment in 1894 banning state funding of "sectarian schools." It also led to a string of appeals decisions that effectively ended local arrangements in most, if not all, cities. By the turn of the century, legal distinctions between "public" and "private" education sharpened on the stone of religion and set firm patterns of control and funding that would endure into the twenty-first century.

"The School Steal": Funding for Parochial Schools in New York City, 1869–1871

Church-state cooperation was not new to New York State education. Since the inception of state support in the late eighteenth century, the State Board of Regents had provided funds for private academies of all denominations to provide elite education—and teacher training—for a small percentage of children. The Regents also provided funds to colleges and universities, many of which were denominationally affiliated. The Department of Public Instruction, which "oversaw" common schools, also provided funding for church-run charities targeting specific "problem" populations: orphan asylums, which offered instruction as well as room and board, and Indian schools.[2]

As long as they remained outside of the common school system—and thus could not threaten the premise of civil control—measures to assist orphanages earned the support of all but the most ardent protagonists in the church-state drama (and taxpayer protectionists). The state traditionally supported denominational academies as well, but when these began to compete with the public high school movement, cries of "sectarianism" grew apace, resulting in an 1873 law that forbade (albeit loosely) state aid to "any religious or denominational academy of this state."[3] Church-run orphanages also weathered much criticism in the 1860s and 1870s for violating the separation of church and state and even lost all state funding in 1872 as part of a major realignment of state funding for private charity. Nevertheless, by 1875, the legislature had returned, and even expanded, its support of educational charity institutions, regardless of their religious affiliation. Urban social reformers hailed the return of support, arguing that private orphanages provided a public good that could not be accomplished by existing public institutions.[4]

The same could not be said of mass education, however, and aid to church-run schools challenged the fundamental principle of civil control by creating a rival system of schools. But at the same time, such support was not entirely inconceivable or unprecedented. At the end of the Civil War, New York City's school system, finally freed from the Free School Society, was little more than a decade old. Although most cities maintained free public schools, mainly to target poor children, the state itself did not embrace the concept until 1867. In short, the common school system was still young. And in city systems, where religious leaders, particularly Catholics, demanded separate schools, the meaning of public vis-à-vis private schooling was not always clear.

Although the state legislature passed the Free School Act in 1867, the body was by no means united in its view of the common school system. The legislature represented diverse constituencies, including those in favor of loosening the common school system's grip on state appropriations. In 1869, one assemblyman proposed a resolution in the Democrat-controlled House condemning the public school and demanding its immediate removal.[5] More moderate opponents of the status quo proposed sharing the wealth. New York State Senator Boss William Tweed, head of Tammany Hall, New York's corrupt Democratic Party political machine, introduced a bill to provide state funds to parochial schools in New York City. The Republican-controlled Senate defeated the bill, but Tweed found another route to passage. Tammany men in the House slipped similar provisions in the annual tax levy bill for the city, and, using a combination of bribery and secrecy, they managed to pass the bill through the legislature without attracting notice. The bill provided that 20 percent of the excise funds of the city go to "schools, educating children gratuitously in said city who are not provided for in the common schools thereof."[6]

Two days later, the *New York Times* broke the news. Republican leaders and Protestant ministers rushed to start a crusade for the bill's repeal. A Methodist paper charged that it was the result of a "Papal conspiracy," while the Republican Union League Club of New York City circulated petitions upstate to drum up support statewide. Protestant ministers and Republican leaders together organized a State Council of Political Reform in Albany to investigate and report findings and recommendations.[7] The council reported the incident as part of the long historical "attack" on the public school by the Catholic Church in New York City. "The enormity of this legislation led us to investigate, and to our astonishment we found that, aided by this statute and a city government controlled by one religious sect, more than half a million dollars annually of the public money of the City of New York is . . . given to certain Churches, and Church and Sectarian Schools." The council resolved to protest the action vigorously to the legislature.[8]

Tweed did not have the votes to resist the tide of reform, but he did manage to extend the appropriations for a second, final year. The legislature also managed in 1871 to provide funds to several parochial schools in Brooklyn, listed as "charitable institutions."[9] After that, the legislature made no more of such appropriations and briefly cut off aid to "sectarian" orphan asylums as part of the same reform effort, only to reinstate it in 1875.[10] Despite the opportunistic diatribes of anti-Catholics, several Protestant and Hebrew parochial schools also benefited from the bill, although Catholic schools did win the lion's share of the money.[11]

The manner of the bill's passage alone probably doomed it to long-term defeat, particularly as it stoked the flames of anti-Catholic conspiracy theories. Even without Tweed's tricks, however, the trajectory of state education—the death of privatized school management in New York City in 1854, the embrace of free common schooling by the legislature in 1867, and the growth and consolidation of public school infrastructure and enrollment—made statewide repudiation of the common school system highly unlikely. The school steal did beg an important question, however. Could church-related schools exist within the common school system? Even as Boss Tweed's political pyrotechnics burned and then faded away in the Albany sky, smaller cities and towns quietly answered this question for themselves.

Church Schools within the Public System: Permutations of the "Poughkeepsie Plan"

The second, as well as more common, form of public support for church schools was to incorporate parochial schools within the general public system, leaving church officials varying degrees of discretion. These policies answered the demands of many church officials for public funds, but they also grew out of the greatest practical challenge to post-bellum public schools: overcrowding. For rapidly growing cities, particularly those with anti-tax Democrats at the helm, deals with church schools killed two birds with one stone.

The growth of city populations, combined with redoubled efforts at providing truly mass education, strained the capacity of urban school systems of all sizes, from the village of Saratoga Springs to the city of New York. Rapid growth challenged city boards to find enough space for pupils not only by overfilling old school buildings but by creating the need for new ones as dense settlement pushed outward. Nearly every city, large and small, experienced overcrowding and insufficient facilities in the decades following the Civil War.[12] Some cities conducted school in buildings that were unsafe, foul, and even condemned. A Brooklyn parents' committee found in 1877 that in its district

> more than 400 of their primary children are confined in a basement, where the ventilation is so inadequate, as that when the doors communicating with other parts of the building were opened, the foul odor of the vitiated air was so offensive as to render their being instantly closed in the necessity to the comfort of those on the upper floors, but which was very often tolerated while in mitigating the evil effects on its occupants.
>
> A large number of our children are detained at home on account of the inadequacy of accommodation in the schoolrooms proper, and because of the unfit condition of the basement rooms.... We have not less than 800 children at the present time, part of whom are either wholly deprived of a means of Education, or are detained at home rather than have their health destroyed and their lives endangered by confinement in rooms unfit for occupation.[13]

In other cases, school boards actually turned children away, denying them the public education for which their parents paid taxes. Overcrowding could push parents of means into private or parochial schools by failing to provide tolerable conditions for their children; other parents had no choice.[14]

School boards tried to keep up with enrollment with varying degrees of zeal but often blanched at the specter of raising taxes to construct new buildings or found their funds choked off by penurious city councils. Members of the board of education of Elmira wondered in 1877 whether they could sue the city's common council for refusing to raise enough money to provide adequate space for students. (The city could provide seats for only 644 of the city's 1,600 school-age children.[15]) Oftentimes areas with the newest immigrants had the worst schools, or none at all.[16] A popular solution to the overcrowding problem was to rent classroom space, which offered a cheaper alternative to building new schoolhouses. Many boards rented public space wherever they could find it, especially from churches, which had suitable rooms that were usually available during school hours.[17]

Renting space from Catholic churches served both city and church interests. For cities, these arrangements—sometimes costing only a nominal fee—provided a far cheaper alternative than building new schools. Moreover, board of education members may have found it the political equivalent of killing two birds with one stone—not only saving money but also showing at least mild sympathy with the religious demands of parents and prelates by making the church the literal focus of a neighborhood's schooling. In other cases, the threat of parochial schools' closing—adding hundreds of children to the public school enrollment—may have strengthened this inducement[18]

For churches, these arrangements provided income, but more importantly they also kept the church in focus in children's lives. For Catholics in particular, renting space for a public school for neighborhood children could be construed as keeping within the spirit of the Plenary Council's admonition for parish schools. Once children came to the church for public school, it was certainly easy to keep them before or after school for additional religious instruction outside of school hours. After all, such was fairly common practice in village schools, and was also encouraged by the state.

In the late 1860s, several small towns and cities began making agreements with existing Catholic schools, with no formal objection from residents. In 1868, the village of Corning subsumed St. Mary's School under the auspices of a rental agreement, where three teachers taught half-day classes to 400 pupils. (As a condition, the sisters were all certified common school teachers.) The sisters taught religion outside of school hours and were forced to be in session on holy days, including Good Friday. Despite concessions by both parties, however, the school continued to the general satisfaction of all and survived Corning's transition to an incorporated city in 1890. (The State Superintendent would later order it closed on appeal in 1898.[19]) The cities of Elmira and Utica made similar rental agreements in 1867 and 1869, respectively. Two decades later, the city of Ogdensburg reached an accord with St. Mary's Academy in 1893, and an indepentent union free school district in West Troy (subsequently moved to Watervliet) rented St. Bridget's Parochial School for one dollar in 1895.[20]

Elmira

The Elmira story in particular is worth examining closely, because it shows the three factors of local governance, neighborhood schooling, and overcrowding at work together in the rise and fall of a church-state agreement. In 1864, Elmira became the first of a string of cities to spring up along the Pennsylvania border between the Civil War and the turn of the century. Already a rail and canal transportation center by the 1850s, Elmira enjoyed rapid growth during the Civil War as an official rendezvous for Union soldiers and later as the location of an infamous prisoner of war (POW) camp for captured Confederate soldiers.[21] The city population grew from 13,000 to 20,000 from 1865 to 1875.[22] The educational system grew even faster, with expenditures alone increasing tenfold from 1865 to 1870[23] Not surprisingly, the board of education welcomed an offer in 1867 from the pastor of Saint Peter and Paul's School to place it within the city's system of public schools.[24] As a result, the board found more space for children without the cost of a new building, reduced competition with a parochial school rival, and catered to the interests of a large number of Catholic parents. The parochial school, in return, got rent and public school salaries for its teachers.

Over time, however, the parish school showed itself to be too small to accommodate the continuing growth of the city, and in 1873, the board of education completed several large buildings to replace old schools, including the parish school. This did not, however, mean the end of the arrangements. The following year, the city and church again forged a compromise, this time making the parish school an auxiliary primary school for district one, and again employing the sisters of Saint Mary. Officially, the board explained the agreement in terms of a larger plan to accommodate growth by creating small, inexpensive primary schools located in various neighborhoods within a district, one larger grammar school to attract older children in each district, and one central public high school (a recently converted academy) to serve the whole city.[25]

The decision to start the new Catholic primary school had as much to do with ethnocultural politics as it did with overcrowding. In an unusual move, the board of education permitted Catholic children from other districts inside the city to attend the school—much to the delight of their parents. In the same vein, the board of education rented a second auxiliary space from the German School Society for another primary school, although in this case there is no evidence of bending district boundaries.[26]

The lease agreement between the parish and the board of education meticulously positioned the school as a regular school within the public system. As a board member described in a committee report in 1875:

> It gave to this board control of the premises from half past 8:00 A.M., until a quarter past 4:00 P.M., during all the school days of the year, and imposed upon the board the duty of keeping during the year a primary school subject to all the rules and regulations of the other schools under its charge; (thus placing it within the operation of the general laws of the state); to pay all the expense of keeping the teachers employed by the board in keeping said schools; to pay for fuel and necessary and ordinary repairs, and all other expenses necessary and usually incident thereto. They reserve the right to use the premises at any time, other than in the allotted hours granted, for any purposes which will not interfere with the keeping of the school.[27]

The board also was expected to approve the selections for teacher that the parish pastor recommended, which it did, annually, when it approved the lease. What the sisters of Saint Mary taught to children who wished to stay before or after school was their business.

Not all on the board of education were happy with the arrangements. In March 1875, the board voted unanimously to require children to attend schools in their own districts again, though the High Street School would remain open for the (primarily) Catholic children of that district. When the board took up the matter of renewing the lease in June, two board members consistently voted to end the arrangement, making motions to hire alternative teachers for the school and even suggesting that the problem of overcrowding in district one be solved by redrawing district boundaries and ending the lease agreement. They charged that maintaining the High Street School saved the city nothing—in fact, that it cost more than the alternative.[28]

In the ensuing political maneuvers over the plan, parents and politicos showed their stripes. Fifty-eight Catholic parents living outside of district one petitioned the city's common council to rescind its new strict districting policy and let their children continue at the school. "We are well pleased with the unprecedented progress made by our children in the branches of study there taught," they wrote, "as well as in general decorum and morality, and are now exceedingly desirous that we may be permitted to have them attend during the coming school year the said High Street auxiliary school." They also claimed that their children "took great pleasure in attending said school." The mayor and a majority of the common council members endorsed the petition and forwarded it to the board of education.[29]

Despite such political pressure, however, the board rejected the petition and defied the common council in September, directing the teachers of the High Street School to dismiss out-of-district children and send them back to their district schools. (Twenty percent of the school's children came from outside of the district.) The reason, they insisted, was purely practical: the loose districting system caused confusion and poor discipline, presumably because of unpredictable registration and attendance from long distance. The committee to whom the petition had been referred argued that the school, as a public school, was subject to the same rules and regulations as other schools in the city.[30] Implicit in this argument was the idea that public schools must conform to a uniform standard. A second reason given by foes of the plan was that it actually cost the city extra money to pay for the separate school, when redistricting could obviate the need for more space. When they lost the privilege of allowing pupils of all districts to attend the school, church officials decided not to renew the lease with the city at the end of the 1875–1876 school year—intensifying the city's chronic overcrowding and further straining the relationship between the board of education and the common council.[31]

Poughkeepsie

While the Elmira Board of Education was inaugurating its revised primary school plan with the sisters of Saint Mary in 1873, the board of education of Poughkeepsie settled the details of the best-known church-state agreement of the nineteenth century, the so-called "Poughkeepsie plan." In reality, the plan did not differ substantially from those already begun in other cities, nor was it the longest lasting. It was, however, the best publicized and has subsequently been the most studied.

Like the Elmira plan, the Poughkeepsie plan emerged in a school system overwhelmed by growth. Historically, the city of Poughkeepsie made particularly poor provisions to house its students. Since 1843, the village and later the city of Poughkeepsie operated its public schools at minimum expense, renting many—and at times all—of the spaces used for public schools. (A State Superintendent would later charge that Poughkeepsie had the worst educational facilities of any city in the state. By 1896, the list of spaces rented for classrooms would include several churches, a theater, and even a coach factory.[32]) Growing enrollments continued to overcrowd school facilities, and in June 1873, the pastor of Saint Peter's Catholic Parochial School formally approached the board of education with an offer it could not refuse: the use of two recently outfitted parochial school buildings for the token rent of one dollar each per annum.[33]

Over the summer, the board of education and the pastor, Reverend McSweeny, ironed out the details. The board of education would select, pay, and have power to dismiss the teachers, though, as in Elmira, it tacitly agreed to hire the church's selections. The board would also pay for expenses and repairs. Reverend McSweeny agreed to forbid all religious teaching during public school hours and to open the school to children of all denominations. The two schools were to remain single sex, and children from other districts could attend them, but in other respects they functioned as regular public schools.[34] In practice, the arrangement gave more to each party than the plans of other cities. The nominal rent allowed the city to save hundreds of dollars annually (leading McSweeny to boast that he could educate children for half the cost that the state could).[35] For the church's benefit, the city used a generous definition of "school hours" (9 to 12 A.M. and 1:30 to 4 P.M.), which allowed the schools to have the following daily schedule:

8:45 A.M.—Morning prayers
9 A.M. to 12 P.M.—Regular secular course as in other schools
12 P.M.—Short prayer, then recess.
1 P.M.—Religious instruction
1:30 P.M.—Regular secular course
4 P.M.—Closing religious exercises[36]

McSweeny promised that no child would be compelled to participate in the religious exercises unless authorized by a parent.

As religious journals began publishing accounts of the plan in the 1870s and 1880s, polemicists seized the opportunity. One Protestant minister warned McSweeny, "What we need is peace between Catholics and Protestants. Your plan would produce war, where the bad passions of both sides would have it all their own way.[37] A well-known anti-Catholic Presbyterian minister actually inspected the schools personally but reported that the only evidence of Catholic influence during public school hours was the presence of a small decorated statue of the Virgin Mary at the side of each teacher's desk. The militant Catholic *New York Freedman* did not defend the compromise plan but condemned it for watering down true religious education. After all, Schools 11 and 12 did have to accommodate the common school system's secular curriculum during school hours, and the city board of education, not the church, ultimately called the shots.[38]

At the same time, however, neither the board of education nor the Catholic Church in Poughkeepsie reported any *local* objection to the plan. No one appealed to the Superintendent of Common Instruction, and no one appealed to the Poughkeepsie Board of Education. In fact, only one person from Poughkeepsie mentioned the plan to the State Superintendent by mail from 1873 to 1874—a city attorney who asked for a copy of the Long Island City decision of 1872 (see chapter 8). Most Catholics in Poughkeepsie endorsed the plan by enrolling their children. McSweeny estimated in 1887 that four-fifths of Catholic children in the city attended Schools 11 and 12. For those who attended public schools, he offered the following explanations:

> First of all, parents are often acquainted with teachers in the public schools, many of whom are Catholics, and they send their children to them from motives of friendship, especially as, according to the system, it is of importance to the teacher that she should have a full class. Then there is the true or false belief in the special ability of a certain teacher. Then, very often the unjust judgment is made that, in secular training, the parish school is not equal to the state school. . . . There is a class of people who never seem to find their home dinner taste as well as the one they eat with the stranger. Again, there is the oft-repeated reason, that the building may be more roomy and airy, more convenient to the home, etc., etc.[39]

But he did not report any outright Catholic opposition to the plan per se. Local Protestants did not mount any serious challenge, whatever their opinions. A Lutheran minister actually approached the board of education with a similar proposition, but the board balked at the condition of compulsory German language instruction at the school.[40]

The Poughkeepsie plan endured until 1898, no doubt due to the generous concessions made on the part of both parties. The plan outlasted those in the similarly sized cities of Utica and Elmira, both of which had much narrower windows for religious instruction outside of school hours and cost districts substantial rental fees. Eventually an appeal to the state closed down the arrangement, but the significance of the Poughkeepsie plan, and others like it, was not that it was permanent (few reforms are) but that it existed at the very time political and religious dialogue suggested that it could not.

No Compromise in Buffalo and Yonkers

Obviously not every city that faced the question of public support for religious schools solved the problem with the same apparent ease as Elmira and Poughkeepsie. Local control—even in heavily Catholic neighborhoods, or with Democrat-controlled city governments—did not always translate into Poughkeepsie-like plans. In the cities of Buffalo and Yonkers, advocates of state aid failed to win concessions from school boards, despite the numeric strength of Catholics and Democrats in both. The efforts in these two cities highlight the strength of the principle of democratic control as a core of the public school system—even among those who would seem to gain the most from a sectarian solution.

Buffalo

From 1874 to 1875, Buffalo's Bishop Ryan and a large number of lay Catholics organized a movement to win public funding for that city's parochial schools. The time and place were ripe for the action. Since the late 1860s, a number of smaller cities had made such arrangements, as we have seen, and some of these lay within the diocese of Buffalo itself.[41] By 1874, the question of public funds for church schools, referred to by newspaper editors as "The School Question," had won a prominent and regular place in the city's religious press: the city's militant Catholic newspaper, *The Catholic Union*, frequently exchanged barbs in 1873 and 1874 with the equally biased Protestant evangelical rag, *The Buffalo Commercial*.[42] As we have seen, the concern reflected the broader political movement on the part of the Republican Party to ignite anti-Catholicism in state and national politics.[43]

But the movement also reflected the unique situation in Buffalo. Unlike New York and Albany, with their large Irish populations, Buffalo's principal immigrant group was German. German Catholics and Protestants alike enjoyed a strong sense of ethnic identity and an equally skeptical attitude toward public schools. In 1874, the *Union* reported that Germans of all denominations patronized church schools over public schools, 7,000 to 6,000.[44] Among school-age Catholic children of all ethnicities, approximately 4,400 attended public schools, while 6,000 attended Catholic schools.[45] The Catholic Church leadership of Buffalo, though Irish, reflected this strong separatism in its unyielding call for separate schools for Catholics of all ethnicities. Bishop Ryan, less widely quoted than Rochester's McQuaid, preached the same message: Catholic children did not belong in public schools, and simple justice demanded that public funds pay for the Catholic education of Catholic children.[46] (In fact, since his installation in 1869, Ryan had ordered parish priests to refuse the sacraments to children whose parents sent them to public schools when parochial ones were available.[47]) In 1873, German-American politics within Buffalo bestirred the movement to win public funds for church schools—but the original issue was language, not religion.

Like many major cities in New York State and elsewhere, Buffalo offered limited German language instruction in its public schools, having begun the practice in 1866.[48] A historian of Saint Louis public schools in the period has argued that this policy usually stemmed from wanting to appease German voters (whose culture was generally more valued by the population at large than that of the Irish or other groups) and to compete with ethnic denominational schools.[49] These reasons appear to have guided the decision in Buffalo as well, though Buffalonians did not unite in support of the policy, particularly when faced with the expense of paying for extra teachers.[50]

In April 1873, the superintendent of schools sabotaged the plan by "forgetting" to pay teachers of German. Angry German-Americans reacted strongly at the polls at the subsequent election, voting out every member of the city council connected to the debacle.[51] Mobilized and motivated by the event, German-Americans continued to actively petition in the board in early 1874 to reform the existing system of German instruction. They did not all ask for the same things, however. First a "committee of 35" petitioned the board on behalf of German-American patrons of public schools. It urged the common council to expand its program, citing the fact that the German-American children accounted for half of all children enrolled in public schools. It also argued that the expansion of German would woo children away from denominational schools and benefit non-Germans as well by giving them a useful language for business transactions in the city.[52] Two weeks later, a second group petitioned the board on behalf of German-American parents who did *not* patronize public schools. This group argued that Germans preferred denominational schools for religious reasons, not linguistic ones. Further, it argued that since German-Catholic children could not conscientiously attend public schools where German was taught, parochial schools should receive money from the city to defray the cost of German instruction.[53] *The Catholic Union* hailed the request and urged its passage.

The school committee recommended to the common council that the petition of the "committee of 35" to expand public German instruction be granted. As for the second petition, it stated, "Your committee does not deem it necessary to enter into a discussion of the question" of providing public funds for parochial German instruction. "Even if the justice of such an appropriation is conceded, the Common Council have no power to appropriate money to defray the whole or any part of the expense of maintaining schools which are not under their control."[54] In other words, they understood the public schools to be, at heart, a system of democratic control. Several council members played for time, asking that the decision be deferred, while others wanted it settled immediately. Increased funds for public school German passed, while the question of aid to parochial schools was tabled indefinitely. *The Catholic Union* applauded the delay. "Let them take time to consider it in all its bearings. The step they are asked to take is a new one."[55]

While the school committee took its time, Bishop Ryan himself took charge of the effort, organizing a major campaign on behalf of all Catholics. As Bishop McQuaid had done in Rochester, Ryan launched a public relations campaign in the pulpit and press to unify the Catholic vote and to generate sympathy among non-Catholics. It began with a rhetorical *imbroglio* with the main evangelical newspaper of Buffalo, *The Buffalo Commercial.* In a series of letters to his own unofficial organ, *The Catholic Union*, Ryan tangled repeatedly with the *Commercial* over the question of Catholic hostility toward public schools and the justice of their demands.[56] "We are not opposed to the present system of public schools for the children of the non-Catholic parents who are satisfied with them . . . [But] we hold and teach that parents are bound to educate their children; that they cannot in conscience allow their children to grow up in ignorance." He warned that readers should "not be startled by what sensational preachers . . . may inadvertently say about foreigners attempting to destroy our public schools."[57] *The Caholic Union* attempted to close ranks by publishing a bitter screed against the president of the common council, a Catholic who opposed aid to church schools.[58] Together, Ryan and *The Catholic Union* provided upsetting stories of recent Catholic persecution in public schools.[59]

Ryan then delivered a lecture at St. James Hall entitled "A Plea for Christian Schools." In it he reiterated much of McQuaid's argument three years earlier: Catholics could not attend the "godless" public school, were opposed to "Protestant" opening exercises such as Bible reading and prayer, and deserved public funds for their necessarily separate schools. He also attacked the Catholics who chose to attend public schools whom he had "exhorted, entreated, and implored" (not to mention threatened) to attend parochial schools. "We do know of two classes of Catholic parents who may send their children to the public schools: those who are only Catholics in name and do not believe in the necessity of faith, who do not practice their religion or obey their pastors; and secondly, poor parents with very small children . . . who are afraid to trust their children to go far from home."[60] *The Catholic Union* hailed the lecture as a rousing success, "red hot shot, thrown into the enemy's camp."[61]

In March 1875, the common council announced its readiness to consider the school question and scheduled a special meeting of the school committee to hear petitions on the issue. Ryan had a brainstorm. To win legitimacy for the crusade, he directed each parish to democratically elect representatives to deliver a petition to the common council. Because they had engaged in a form of the democratic process, the representatives then claimed to be speaking on behalf of all Catholics, "variously estimated as one-third, one-half and three-fifths of our entire population."[62] Moreover, allowing congregations to elect their own representatives parried the attacks of anti-Catholic Protestants who complained of "scheming priestcraft" and "Popish plots."

At the special meeting of the school committee, the memorialists asked that the Roman Catholic schools of the city be subsumed under the general common school system of the city. "We seek only the adoption of a system which, in other lands, and in sections of our own beloved country, has proven itself eminently benign and satisfactory." Along the lines of the Elmira and Poughkeepsie plans, church schools would reserve the right to maintain their own teachers—paid public salaries—and offer additional religious instruction outside of school hours, while the city would reserve the right to supervise and inspect such schools. "Such supervision the public would have a right to demand, and we would freely accord." Further, the petition suggested that such an arrangement was in fact a major concession on the part of Catholics, and "less in justice than we might claim."[63]

A large majority of the common council did not see it that way, however. By a vote of 20 to 4, members rejected the petition. In their report, they cited the main obstacle to the plan as legal, insisting that they as a body had no authority to add schools to the public system that did not conform to the *uniform* features of a public system of schools, as cited by state law "to inquire into matters relating to the management, course of study, text-books, etc., and to recommend to trustees and teachers proper studies, discipline, and management of schools." Catholic schools were not common schools, the report argued, according to state case law. Unless they ceased to be

Catholic altogether, and became regular city institutions, the Catholic schools in question had no right to receive public funds, and the common council had no right to grant them.[64]

Whether this was the council's only motivation is unclear, and probably unlikely. Nevertheless, for large city school systems and for professional educational leaders, uniformity was an increasingly powerful mantra in the 1870s. It was reflected in state policy toward schools as well, especially as the state department took a more active role in school regulation beginning in the mid-1880s. Uniformity meant treating all pupils the same—giving them the same textbooks, for example, and ushering them through large, graded schools in a factory-like production model.[65] For small cities such as Elmira and Poughkeepsie, with a handful of schools and small, overwhelmed budgets, uniformity may not have played an important role in the understanding of what made a school "public," particularly when church-state arrangements could save the city money. In large cities such as Buffalo and New York, it did—especially when their very size exposed them more directly to attention from the state.[66] And, by the same token, small cities had an advantage over larger ones: school board members had more direct personal contact with individual schools and thus had less to worry about in terms of using formal, legalistic methods of monitoring church-state arrangements.

The rout of the Buffalo measure showed that Catholic opposition to the current alignment of public and parochial schools was not as strong as church leaders had hoped. In the wake of their overwhelming defeat in common council, Bishop Ryan and *The Catholic Union* responded bitterly to the lack of support from within the Catholic community. *The Catholic Union* wrote: "We are sadly puzzled and bewildered as to the cause of the seeming apathy of many good and saintly Bishops in entering actively on the campaign" and vowed "The question will never be solved until the Catholics of every State are led by their Bishops, even on poll-day, and until the great and persuasive authority of the episcopacy be brought to bear on educating the people as to their duties." *The Louisville Catholic Advocate* wrote a sympathetic letter to the Catholics of Buffalo, urging them to redouble their efforts:

> A few defeats are very wholesome training. The Buffalonians have not yet got stung or roused enough. Let them have mass demonstrations again and again. . . . But above all let them look to their ward politicians and aid good men into office who will thwart and hamper and hinder the pet schemes of the Know-nothing element in the Council.[67]

Both responses demonstrated a powerful faith in the democratic process. As head of his church, Bishop Ryan was more autocratic. In September, he issued a stinging pastoral to be read in all churches in the diocese, both a rebuke and a threat to parents who chose public schools over parochial ones in the new school year:

> No vague notions of Christianity, or superficial acquaintance with Bible history, scriptural axioms, or gospel narrative will suffice to instruct and dispose the child for the greatest and most holy and solemn act of his life, his First Communion, on which so much in time and eternity depends.
>
> Catholics will, then, understand though others may not, that when we tell our Rev. clergy, that children, wherever there are Catholic schools, must attend such schools and spend at least one year under Christian training and competent teachers, previous to their First Communion, that we are requiring the minimum with which any good Catholic pastor or parent can be satisfied.[68]

The bishop's strong language bespoke frustration as well as resolve. Threats would not be necessary were his flock in agreement on the question.

A few Catholics had actually expressed their opposition to the plan openly. The *Albany Argus*, the state's premier Democratic newspaper and one sympathetic to Catholic concerns, hailed the decision of the Buffalo Common Council and endorsed a recommendation by the *Buffalo Commercial* (arch enemy of *The Catholic Union*) that the common council go a step farther and forbid all religious exercises in the schools.[69] Several months later, New York State Senator Francis Kernan, a Catholic and a Democrat, also defended the council's decision in a speech in Buffalo, much to the chagrin of *The Catholic Union.* An anonymous letter in that paper followed up Kernan's remarks, explaining how one could be both Catholic and a supporter of the current public school system. "Rest assured, Mr. Editor," it said, "that if a vote were to be taken on the question of the common schools at the ensuing election, the Roman Catholic vote would be given for their maintenance." It was signed, "an Irish Catholic."[70]

Yonkers

Soon after the Buffalo attempt, Catholics in New York City petitioned the board of education in that city to the same effect, and with the same result. In fact, no large city in New York State ever managed to inaugurate a Poughkeepsie-like plan to support parochial schools. Church-state deals that bent the public school system emerged in small cities only. But being a small city, even one with a large Catholic population, was not a guarantee of success. In 1880, a proposed church-state union in the small city of Yonkers failed as well.

The Yonkers story deserves attention because of the city's unusual configuration of school governance. Recall that since its incorporation in 1872, the city had no central board of education. Schools within the city remained independent, each operating on the union free school model. Beginning in 1874, a few Catholic leaders made public calls for a Poughkeepsie-like plan, but not until 1879 did the issue come to a head, when swelling enrollments in district six, a mixed Catholic and Protestant area, filled the school building to, overflowing. The pastor of Saint Joseph's Church offered to allow a new branch school in the church's existing parish school, with religious exercises limited to time outside of regular school hours. In a familiar fashion, the city's newspapers, the *Yonkers Gazette* (Democratic) and *The Statesman* (Republican), squared off over the issue with purple prose and mudslinging. Despite accusations to the contrary, advocates of the plan anchored their proposal to key notions of democratic governance and separation of church and state. Thomas Cornell, the editor of the *Yonkers Gazette* and a member of the school board, averred that, "we are opposed to sectarian common schools as earnestly as any of the opponents of the bill." A proponent calling himself "Toleration" explained the rationale to Republican opponents in an Oct 31, 1878 letter to *The Statesman:*

> Not a penny of the state money, under the plan proposed, goes to any sectarian teaching. On the contrary, the State procures the secular education which [*sic*] it undertakes to furnish, at less cost that it can procure anywhere else. And this secular education is given wholly by such boards, held in school houses controlled by such boards, and by teachers whom the board approves, employs, pays, and controls.

Instead, Toleration argued, any religious influence would occur outside of regular school hours and only at the private discretion of parents. Proponents tried several approaches to winning approval. First, they wrote a letter to State Superintendent Neil Gilmour asking whether a history book in the school library could be removed for being offensive to Catholics, presumably trying to make the case that the current school district six was not suitable for Catholic children. (Gilmour wrote back saying, "I do not know of any law or regulation of this department which would exclude from your library "D'Ambigui's *History of the Reformation.*") Second, in an unusual move, they requested that their state representative send a bill to the state legislature that would authorize the creation of a new school district. The school board agreed to this move unanimously, and the mayor and town council also agreed to offer no opposition. In Albany, the Assembly Committee on Schools conducted a hearing on the question. Leaders of both sides attended and took the opportunity to lay out their arguments. Neither side challenged the notion that schools receiving public funds should be under public control, however. Rather, they disagreed over whether the details of the plan would create a *de* facto form of sectarian control. In good, political form, the Assembly Committee on Schools tabled the bill, thereby killing it without an actual vote. (71)

Back in Yonkers, the majority-Catholic school board did not vote to create the school at Saint Joseph's. Instead, the board agreed to hold a special meeting of the district and allow the voters to determine the question for themselves. In the weeks leading up to the vote, *The Statesman* continued to hammer away at the notion of sectarian encroachment while the *Yonkers Gazette* assumed a moderate stance. *The Statesman's* most damning argument came from a reprinted letter from Patrick McSweeney, the architect of the Poughkeepsie Plan, to A. A. Lings, the parish priest at Saint Joseph's. In the letter McSweeney advised Lings about the official details of the Poughkeepsie plan, but also included the *private* agreements that he had made with the Poughkeepsie school board. The most important of these, McSweeney said, was that he would secretly select the teachers for the school, and the board would rubber stamp its approval. McSweeney explained,

> It would not be well to show this letter to your Board, as they may not understand it. Tell them that we have no privilege here except what the other public schools have. The parents of the children who frequent them are supposed to be of no particular faith, still actually they are all Protestants without exception. Whether this happens by accident or design we dare not to dispute. All we want is that the same coincidence may happen, whether by accident or design we care not, in our schools, so that all the teachers may be Catholics, since the parents are Catholics. The only way to bring about the happy "coincidence" is to consult the Catholic pastor, who is legally nothing but a private citizen, but actually the chosen representative of his flock.

For *The Statesman,* McSweeney's secret deal smacked of conspiracy. How could a private citizen usurp the powers of the elected school board? The distinction between a pastor as a representative chosen within a church hierarchy and a representative chosen democratically was everything. "Voter, what think you of it?" the editor asked. "Let your ballot answer on Tuesday evening." Thomas Cornell of the *Gazette* denied that the plan for Yonkers would require the board to cede control of teacher selection to the parish priest, and instead scolded the Statesman for being divisive: "I do not doubt but the Catholics will believe that the majority of their Protestant neighbors mean to be just, and will not hold them responsible for the un-neighborly spirit of the few who speak as does *The Statesman.*" (72)

Over a thousand people packed into the hall on a hot summer evening as the voting began. Both the *Gazette* and *Statesman* agreed that the voting went smoothly and calmly, and after three hours, all the ballots had been cast: 337 in favor of the branch school, 430 against. The losers later appealed the vote to the state superintendent on the grounds of illegal voting, but lost. The Statesman claimed that some Catholics, as well as Protestants, had voted against the measure because they thought the public school offered a superior education to the parochial one. It gave children of lower classes a chance to mix with those of upper classes and provided them with better teachers (many of whom were also Catholic). For two years afterward, the parish school at Saint Joseph's remained closed, and enrollment continued to swell at the district six school, reaching 99 children in some classrooms. At the same time, the city prepared for a new system of school governance: a central board of education that would put an end to independent districts like number six. In September 1881, the public school opened as usual, but school officials were soon embarrassed by the departure of a large number of students for a newly opened Saint Joseph's Parochial School. The new central board of education scrambled to control damage but nevertheless had to fire six public school teachers: Cora Mackrell, Hannah Murphy, Emma Fawcett, Mary Casey, Emma Simpson, and Martha Shaughnessy. (73)

The experience of the city of Yonkers provides a good counterexample to the seeming ease of the arrangements in Elmira, Poughkeepsie, and elsewhere. It also serves as a coda to the 1870s, a decade that began with the "school steal" in New York and a number of quiet agreements between boards of education and Catholic parish schools. Although a few other small cities and incorporated villages would make agreements between church and state, they would never again do so in the context of so strong a tradition of local control of city governance, or with the absence of any state-level interference. Beginning in the 1880s, these factors would change the fundamentals of state aid to church schools.

The State in Charge, 1887-1905

In 1876, State Superintendent Neil Gilmour issued a stern warning to the people of New York State. "Already in some sections of the State warning is given that there is danger to our system of public education, and it is an absolute necessity that any attempt to destroy it be guarded against at once." The cause of this threat? Public aid to parochial schools. Gilmour revealed:

> There are reports that propositions have already been made, and in some cases accepted, that certain parochial schools, not under the control of the state, should be used by the trustees or boards of education of the districts in which they are located, on condition that the teachers be appointed by those having the control of such schools, or that the course of instruction be subject to their approval. The adoption of such a policy would be a step towards the destruction of our system of public instruction.[74]

Gilmour's warning echoed the Republican Party line toward "sectarian appropriations" that had formed a central plank in the party's anti-Catholic platform. It showed that the state government was well aware of the developments in Elmira, Poughkeepsie, and Buffalo, but it also showed the limits of state policy toward such aid in the 1860s and 1870s: Gilmour issued a clarion call, but a majority of the state legislature and, indeed, most of the populace as a whole failed to follow. Until the late 1880s, the state Department of Education did not actually engage the question of state aid at the local level. Even after that point, it would not be until the end of the century that the legislature, the courts, and the state Department of Education would reach a common accord.

In the wake of the "school steal" of 1869, when Boss Tweed's allies snuck appropriations to parochial schools through the state legislature, opponents of state aid to church-affiliated institutions gained considerable strength—temporarily. In 1872, a Republican-controlled state legislature blocked all state funds to private charitable institutions. Both Houses also called for a state amendment banning state or local funding of "sectarian institutions." In 1874, the state as a whole adopted a constitution that addressed the issue for the first time, though it did not provide a blanket banning of public funds to parochial schools, and through various technicalities appeared to condone it at the local level. When the Democratic Party won a major victory in the 1874 election, however, the tide turned. A Children's Law of 1875 not only resuscitated but even expanded state aid to church-affiliated charities, including orphan asylums. One historian found that the number of such institutions, most of them church affiliated, doubled by 1885, as did the number of pupils they served and the budgets they commanded.[75]

The state Department of Education played virtually no role in the question of state aid to church schools in the late 1860s and 1870s. True, annual reports included a few statements about state aid to sectarian institutions in the 1870s (though none as strong as Gilmour's, quoted earlier).[76] But the state Department of Education remained reactive, not proactive, and it could intervene only in cities where residents appealed. From 1867 to 1886, not a single resident of Elmira, Poughkeepsie, Utica, Corning, or any other city challenged Poughkeepsie-like plans. In fact, it was by no means certain that such arrangements were illegal. The state courts remained silent on the issue as well.

In 1887, however, the tradition of laissez-faire changed for good. The case came from the village of Suspension Bridge, a small town just north of Niagara Falls. For twenty years, Saint Raphael's Church of Suspension Bridge had maintained a parochial school, but in 1885, the trustees of the church petitioned the board of education to absorb the school into the public system, along the lines of other plans in the 1870s. The terms were generous: "The board leased from the trustees of the church the premises known as 'St. Raphael's school lot,' together with the schoolhouse, furniture, fixtures, stoves and pipe and all school appliances, for the term of one year, at the nominal rent of one dollar per year." The church held to one condition though: the school board must employ the sisters currently teaching the school, as long as they passed examinations, and pay them as it would any other teachers in the district. The board accepted the conditions, particularly in light of the fact that it was desperate to accommodate all of the children of that overcrowded district, and Saint Raphael's Parochial School opened in October 1885 as a regular public school in district seven.[77]

Regular, but not regular enough. Leander Colt, a resident of the district, immediately appealed the board's action, and in February 1886, Acting State Superintendent James Morrison issued a decision vacating the contract on the grounds that the school of education could not abrogate its authority to select teachers. The board did not give up without a fight, though. It immediately negotiated a new contract, virtually the same as the old one, with the exception that the church did not explicitly reserve the right to appoint the teachers. In a nominal act of good faith, two of the sisters resigned at the end of the school year, and the board of education hired two replacements—both sisters of the same order. Colt appealed again in the fall of 1866.

In the intervening months, the state assembly elected a new, and formidable, State Superintendent, and his decision would set state policy into direct confrontation with "Poughkeepsie plans." A successful lawyer, author, and rising star of the Republican Party, Andrew Sloane Draper would remain in office until 1892 and would return as the state's chief educational officer in 1905.[78] In deciding the St. Raphael's case, Draper defined the meaning of public education more specifically than any superintendent had done before. First, he conceded that the board of education had acted lawfully in renting space to alleviate overcrowding, even if the fee was nominal. "But," he went on, "the school that the board maintains in this building must be, in all regards, a *public* school." For Draper, "public" meant more than receiving public funds or being connected to the board of education. It meant:

> [A school] must be absolutely free from all things not essential to the purpose for which it is maintained, namely, the general education of its pupils. All must have common and equal rights in it. These must be no discrimination in favor of or against any one. Nothing must be done in it or about it to which any interested person can reasonably or properly object, and most surely must this be so concerning matters which the people hold so sacred as their religious faith and opinions.[79]

In this articulation, even democratic, local control did not define a public school in itself. Instead, a public school was understood to be an institution that reflected the common values of all, or at least, that could not infringe on the conscience of any. *Public* schools in this vision were not defined by what the majority wanted but by what the minority would willingly accept.

This vision required a certain degree of uniformity among schools, and that uniformity included rules governing the selection and behavior of teachers. Leander Colt, the appellant in the case, objected to the fact that the teachers in the school wore distinctive clothing (the habits of nuns), and that they were addressed as Sister Martha, Sister Mary, and so on, and not as other teachers were in other schools. The board of education defended its actions, arguing that the teachers had passed examinations and were duly qualified to teach as any other teachers were. As we have seen, large cities had particular schools where the teachers reflected the ethnicity—and religion—of the students. Draper agreed with the board, insofar as he conceded that "the purpose to discriminate [in favor of a single religious creed] would not be so manifest if these teachers had all held a common religious faith and nothing more. That would be found to be true in many other schools, I apprehend." But the fact that they all belonged to the same organization and were not treated like other teachers but dressed as members of a religious organization and addressed by their religious titles could not stand. "The conclusion is irresistible," declared Draper, "that these things may constitute a much stronger sectarian or denominational influence over the minds of children than the repetition of the Lord's Prayer or the reading of the Scriptures at the opening of the schools, and yet these things have been prohibited, whenever objection has been offered."[80]

Draper ordered that the teachers of the St. Raphael's school adopt regular dress and be addressed as "Miss," followed by their family names. While this order did not vacate the agreement itself, it nevertheless forced the church to abandon the plan. Nuns could not discard the sacred trappings of their order, and having regular lay teachers would effectively end any special religious character that the school had.[81]

Draper's objections to the St. Raphael's plan did not differ substantially from those voiced in the majority report of the School Committee of the Buffalo Common Council. Public schools could (and did) reflect the religious differences among local constituencies, but these differences could be reflected in only the barest of ways—the social backgrounds of teachers, minor differences in opening exercises, or none at all. What could never pass as public, however, was the presence of ecclesiastic authority within a school. The Buffalo Common Council would have welcomed the use of Catholic Church buildings for school space but not the implicit authority of the church itself—either in the selection of teachers or in their persons. Draper conceded the acceptability of nuns out of their habits and thus divested of their religious identities, but he could not accept them in their regalia. Protestant ministers had long been accepted as schoolmasters in country schools, but with a similar caveat: their official church capacity ended as they entered the classroom. Like case law regarding religious exercises, Draper's decision affirmed the necessity of secular schooling as a component of civil control. Unlike religious exercises, however, which often were left to school-level discretion in large cities such as Albany and Buffalo, or open to adaptation in New York and Brooklyn, church and board of education arrangements required formal leases and thus made more likely targets for appeal.

The St. Raphael's case heralded a decade of major reforms to public education in New York State. As we saw in chapter 7, Progressive reformers in the 1890s overhauled urban school governance and mounted a full-scale assault on localism. State Superintendents marched in the vanguard of this movement and by the turn of the century issued several decisions that effectively ended local power to fashion church-state deals. The principle of state authority over schooling found popularity among reformers who sought to professionalize school leadership and close off school policy from democratic interference and manifested itself in a movement to regulate religion in public schools more directly.

In the aftermath of the St. Raphael's case, the school question resurfaced as a major issue in the religious and secular press. Catholic clergy and their foes sparred over the question of state aid to religious schools, issuing predictable jeremiads. Within the Catholic Church, liberals and conservatives debated over whether to embrace or reject the public school system through compromise plans such as that in Poughkeepsie. Moderate Catholics, Protestants, and secularists confronted the issue as well, but hotheads attracted the most attention. Anti-Catholics in New York State formed the National League for the Protection of American Institutions (NLPAI), which pledged to win "constitutional safeguards" at the state and national levels for the common school system against Catholic encroachments such as the Poughkeepsie plan. The NLPAI also encouraged the revival of the American Protective Association, a reactionary, nativist organization. Together, they targeted the 1894 New York State Constitutional Convention as a ripe opportunity to curb the "Catholic menace."[82]

At the convention, the vigor of the anti-Catholics collided with the tradition of laissez-faire policy toward religious issues in education and the interests of those in favor of continuing state support for Poughkeepsie plans for public schools and state aid to church-affiliated charities. The result was only a partial victory for the NLPAI. The state constitution, adopted in 1894, included an amendment that prohibited any state or local governmental agency from giving funds to "any school or institution of learning wholly or in part under the control or direction of any religious denomination or in which any denominational tenet or doctrine is taught." On the other hand, the constitution protected the right of church charities to continue to collect public funds.[83]

The constitutional amendment gave the New York State Department of Education and the state courts a clear mandate to continue to rule against church-state agreements—as long as "partial control" by church officials could be shown. After its adoption, residents of several cities and towns with Poughkeepsie plans appealed to the State Superintendent. The first and most strongly contested of these came from West Troy in 1896. There, the board of education had fashioned an agreement with St. Bridget's Roman Catholic Church, in 1895, along the lines of the St. Raphael's and Poughkeepsie agreements. Also, as in other instances, the board of education defended its actions in terms of ameliorating overcrowding in the regular public schools. The Superintendent of Public Instruction ruled against the plan, citing the language of the St. Raphael's case and also citing the recently passed amendment to the state constitution. "This amendment to the organic law of the State has but recently been adopted by an overwhelming majority. It indicates very clearly an unmistakable and earnest desire on the part of our citizens to permanently establish and maintain a public school system that shall be entirely nonsectarian." He also applied a new principle to the issue: public schools were to be held in buildings owned by the public, except in cases of emergency. This point expanded on the decision in the St. Raphael's case that a public school embodied a set of uniform characteristics. As a result, the Superintendent ruled that while the teachers could not be fired, as they were duly qualified, regular teachers, they were henceforth required to wear regular clothes; the board of education would end its lease of the church building for the coming year.[84]

Proponents of the plan did not give up; at stake was a key component of local control: the power of local school boards to fashion their own religious compromises. During the proceedings of the case, the district in question had been absorbed as part of the new city of Watervliet, which nullified the old district board of education and rendered the Superintendent's decision invalid. Superintendent Skinner had hoped that a new trial would not be necessary, but he underestimated the strength of the principle of local control. On January 1, 1897, the West Troy district became part of the new city of Watervliet; the board of education continued to use St. Bridget's, and the teachers there continued to wear religious garb. In February, under threat of appeal, the mayor of the city sat in the school board meeting and urged the board to obey the previous appeals decision. In a 2 to 2 tie vote, it failed to do so. (The four-member board of education represented the progressive movement toward small, elite school boards "above politics.") Residents of Watervliet then filed an appeal to the State Superintendent.[85]

Incensed, Superintendent Skinner issued a stinging rebuke of the Watervliet school board. He reiterated his previous order to end the rental agreement and require the nuns to abandon their habits or be fired. Furthermore, he ordered the state treasurer to withhold all state school funds from the city until they complied with the order. Finally, he set a firm date of compliance.[86] Two of the four members of the board of education, James McLeese and John McKeever, did not back down. They stood on the argument that the city had a right to determine its own affairs, including hiring duly qualified teachers and renting space for schools. The Superintendent's deadline passed, and still the deadlocked board could not act. On the first day of school in the fall of 1897, Watervliet schools remained closed for lack of funds. The remaining two members of the board of education, William Flewwellin and Isaac Braman, then appealed to the Superintendent to have the others removed from office.[87]

Superintendent Skinner acted with a vengeance. Declaring that "the common school system of the state is a *State* and not a *local* system," he proceeded to take over the Watervliet school system. First, he summarily ordered the school board to open schools. When it declined, he appointed A. M. Wright educational czar of the city (his official designation was "temporary superintendent of schools"), and he ordered Wright to hire teachers and other school personnel and to open the schools directly, without the board. On uncertain territory, Superintendent Skinner did not formally dissolve the board. He did, however, fire the nuns of Saint Bridget's.[88]

With Albany's resolution of the Watervliet crisis, the position of other Poughkeepsie-style plans looked bleak. Corning, the city with the longest-running church-state plan, lost on appeal in March 1898. Poughkeepsie itself followed suit in December. In these cases, the Superintendent cited the same reasons he had given in Watervliet: public schools were to be conducted in public buildings, and teachers needed to be uniformly treated and viewed by pupils, parents, and public school officials alike. Furthermore, the Superintendent had found that Poughkeepsie had been grossly negligent in providing adequate accommodations for public schools and had the worst facilities in the state. In 1902, the village of Lima lost on appeal. The town then held an election, and though a majority of the voters were not Catholic, they resolved to keep the arrangement and challenge the State Superintendent's decision in regular state courts.[89] In 1906, the court of appeals affirmed Skinner's decision unanimously, citing the state constitution of 1894.[90]

The movement against public funding of church schools created a stronger legal definition of *public*, as opposed to private, schooling than had ever existed in New York State. According to case law, now fortified with the constitution of 1894, schools needed to be held in public buildings and taught by lay teachers (at least in terms of their official capacity) and could not be under the influence of any organization save the civil body in charge of their operation. Ecclesiastical control of mass education, the primary form of school governance at the beginning of the nineteenth century, had died a legal death by its end. Furthermore, the Watervliet crisis in particular had forced the State Superintendent to declare that state power superseded local authority: local bodies could act as custodians, enforcers, and managers, but they were not, in the state's opinion, in charge.

Like any set of laws, however, these new policies did not necessarily translate into actual practice, nor did they mean that support for church-state deals had ended completely. Following the decision against them in 1898, the board of education in Poughkeepsie entered a new rental agreement with Saint Peter's Church for one year at $1,000, although the teachers were regular lay teachers. As long as no one appealed, these arrangements could have endured well into the twentieth century.[91] The other method of providing public funds to church schools—legislative subterfuge—had not died either. In 1901, the state legislature snuck a provision into a revised charter for New York City that provided public school apportionment to several "private schools." Unlike Tweed's infamous 1869 "school steal," however, this attempt died in the cradle—vetoed by the mayor and hastily revised by the legislature.[92] Legally speaking, public aid to parochial schools would continue to cycle in and out of New York State politics, but the pattern set

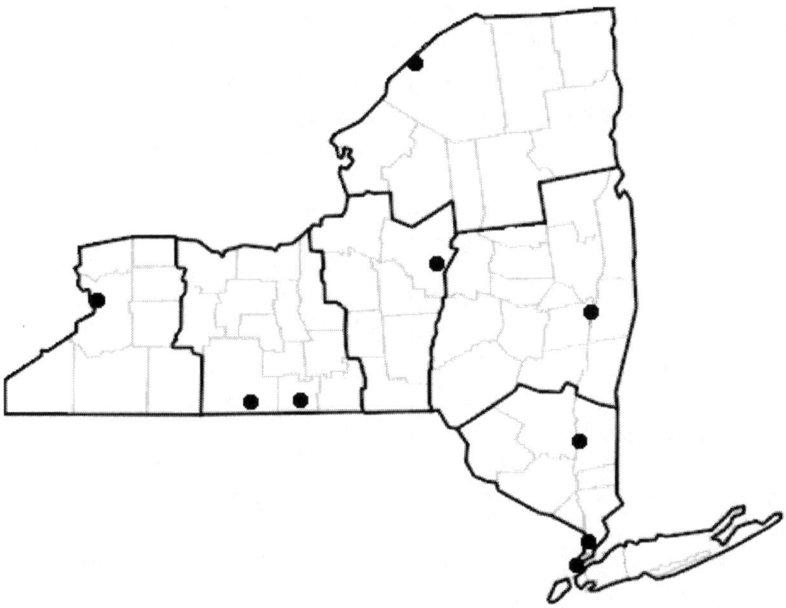

FIGURE 9.1 Location of Cities Considering or Adopting Poughkeepsie-Style Plans, 1865–1900, and Catholic Dioceses of New York State as of 1900.

at the end of the nineteenth century faced no serious challenge over the course of the twentieth.[93]

CONCLUSION: THE CHANGING MEANING OF *PUBLIC* SCHOOLS

How do we explain the rise and fall of public funding for church schools? Church-state deals thrived in an era when state and local leaders alike widely accepted the principle of local control, particularly over the question of religious diversity. The state Department of Education had long provided safeguards to religious minorities that objected to mandatory religious exercises, as long as they spoke up. Aid to church schools proved a more difficult problem to resolve. Escapades such as the school steal revealed the strength of a substantial minority in New York politics that approved of aid to church schools, whatever the consequences. (Indeed, some Catholic leaders, such as Bishop McQuaid, attacked public schools without mercy.) Nevertheless, the response to the legislation showed proponents of unregulated state aid to be a minority. Regulated local aid, on the other hand, fell under the purview of local school boards, not distant state legislatures. Love of local control proved stronger than fear of local aid to church schools in the 1870s and mid-1880s as the legislature, the state Department of Education, and the constitutional convention of 1874 all left public support of church schools alone.

As a local issue, public support of church schools hinged on three competing factors: practical matters (particularly taxes and teachers' jobs), church matters (the opinions of church leaders and laymen), and political ideology. Practically speaking, those cities that adopted Poughkeepsie-like plans also were renowned for their stinginess toward funding public schools. The Elmira School Board, which showed lukewarm enthusiasm for its deal with Saint Peter's and Saint Paul's School, considered suing the city council a few years later for failing to provide enough funds for public schools. In 1891, a group of irate citizens actually did sue when the school board failed to open schools in the fall for lack of funds.[94] Practical matters cut both ways. In Yonkers, protecting Irish women's jobs probably influenced a vote against a deal with Saint Joseph's. And in Buffalo, Bishop Ryan's proposal for paying teachers in existing parochial schools (which showed no signs of ever closing their doors and sending their children to public schools) would have cost taxpayers tens of thousands of dollars had the city council adopted it.

Church leaders such as Ryan played an important role in forging compromises. Catholic clergy expressed a variety of opinions on the question of state aid. Conservatives viewed any capitulation with public authorities as an implicit failure and urged an uncompromisingly separate system, with or without state aid. McQuaid and Ryan spoke in similar terms, but in fact worked in a greater spirit of compromise. Most of the bishops in the state approved of such agreements, to some degree, judging by the location of such deals in cities with so many different dioceses (see Figure 9.1), not to mention the villages of Suspension Bridge, Lima, and others.[95] In other words, though nationally many New York State bishops opposed church-state compromises, parish priests tried to make such arrangements in all but one of New York State's dioceses.

A few Protestant ministers, including the leadership of the Protestant Episcopal Diocese of Long Island, also joined in the call for state-funded church schools.[96] Most self-proclaimed Protestant writers opposed these propositions. A few Catholic priests in the New York City area spoke against parochial schools altogether, but they were in the minority.[97] There is little evidence showing that extremists from any religion had much direct influence on school boards' decisions.

Laypeople, even lay Catholics, showed mixed support for public aid, and Catholic votes were not a strong predictor of a plan's success. In the village of Lima, with its Catholic minority, a majority of voters resolved to fight for its church-state compromise in court. But in Buffalo, with its Catholic near majority, the common council roundly rejected a compromise, 20 to 4. Leading Catholic politicians such as Senator Kernan did not endorse such plans, nor did the Democratic Party generally.

The size of a city was a better predictor of a plan's success or failure, and that size related to the third major factor in public funding of church schools: political ideology. Throughout the period of this study, the idea of common schools requiring civil, democratic control remained dominant and ubiquitous. Local agreements such as the Poughkeepsie plan were accepted by school boards only with the caveat that the schools remain under civil, not ecclesiastic, authority. Even the school steal of 1869 and the attempted repeat in 1901 couched their appropriations in terms of charity schools and did not overtly threaten to make any church school a dollar-for-dollar rival with actual public schools. Within the principle of democratic control, however, coiled two competing ideas. One emphasized localism and insisted that school boards had the right to settle religious disputes and make compromises. The other emphasized uniformity. The former envisioned the public school system as a political system—a method—that allowed local constituents to operate their own schools at public expense. The latter envisioned the public school system as an interconnected whole, an institutional organism. Both visions rejected the idea of ecclesiastic control as anti-democratic or uncivil, but only the former allowed for creative responses to diversity, for compromise. Uniformity necessarily regarded any other system of schools, such as Catholic schools, as foreign—a virus in need of an immune response.

In small cities, imbued with the village mind-set and virtually free from state interference, local control was a more cherished principle than uniformity, particularly in the 1860s and 1870s. Tempted by the practical advantages that church leaders offered, the trustees of Elmira, Poughkeepsie, and other small cities and villages felt that as long as a school remained under the authority of the board of education, it was part of the system. Distinctive garb, or even distinctive appellations, meant little in these contexts, because the schools responded to local, individual need. Moreover, as we saw in Long Island City in chapter 7, school boards of small systems could exert a large degree of direct control over schools, making frequent personal visitations and inspections to monitor conditions and conflict.

In large cities such as Buffalo, placing a church school under the general authority of the board but allowing for individual differences was not enough. First, as we have seen, central boards did not—could not—enjoy the same degree of control over their local schools as did boards in small cities. In Buffalo, the common council and superintendent left much power in the hands of principals. In New York City and Brooklyn, ward trustees oversaw the operation of schools. In both cases, central school authorities could not guarantee that they would truly be in charge of a single school. By the same token, and perhaps as a way to compensate, large city boards insisted much more on uniformity and regulation. The hardbound *Manual of the Board of Education of New York City* for 1878, for example, filled 400 pages, including 209 pages of bylaws, rules, and regulations. (Elmira's "By-Laws, Rules and Regulations" from 1874 numbered twenty-two pages and appeared in the annual report of the board of education as an appendix.) When the Buffalo Common Council rejected the proposal for compromise with parochial schools, members cited uniformity as the key impediment to the plan. As appeals from Poughkeepsie plans trickled into the State Superintendent's office in the 1880s and 1890s, uniformity became the state's key legal argument against them—even before the amendment to the state constitution in 1894.

Allegiance to the concept of uniformity did not eclipse local control in all areas of religion in public schools. As we saw in chapter 8, the state's laissez-faire policy toward religious exercises continued into the twentieth century. This difference in attitude—tolerance for religious exercises but rejection of aid to schools—demonstrated a qualitative difference in the perception of the two issues, a difference that hinged on the idea of the public system as a civil system, not an organizational one.

Recent historians of the period have generally picked up on and echoed what contemporary religious leaders such as McQuaid would have argued. The examples of blocked aid to Catholic schools but tolerance of religious exercises both show the failure of the common school system to be anything more than rule by the (Protestant) majority. The reality of local control of public schools as permeable institutions suggests an alternate thesis. School-level discretion over religious exercises, in cities where they were allowed, posed no threat to the civil system of governance. Indeed, the ability to accommodate local variation was one of the greatest strengths of the system. Public aid to church schools, on the other hand, threatened the system on a fundamental level by blurring the distinction between democratic and theocratic control of education. The question at stake was not about religion *in* public schools. The question was about ownership. The answer—at least until progressive reforms in the 1890s—was democratic local control.

Chapter 10

Conclusion

Explanations and Implications

By the early twentieth century, the relationship between the state of New York and its public school districts had changed dramatically. The State Superintendent spoke openly against the use of the schoolhouse by religious organizations, refused the state's traditional protection to parents opposed to religious exercises, and actively rooted out local church-state compromises over school funding. The change in the state's policies mirrored a broader movement against localism and democratic control. As we have seen, Progressive reform in the 1890s and early 1900s brought sweeping changes to the common school system of governance in New York State. These changes touched city, village, and rural districts in varying degrees and at varying times but left an unmistakable stamp on all. The unique context of laissez-faire state policy and strong localism in city and district schools that had once characterized religion in public school policy had ended.

This did not, of course, spell the end of all peaceable adjustments. While trying to eliminate policies friendly to particular religions, especially minority religions, the state Department of Education balked at disavowing all religion. Instead, Superintendent Skinner cast his lot with Pan-Protestantists and liberal religionists who were willing to compromise on one-size-fits-all, "neutral" religious exercises at the start of the school day. When the drive to win the statewide mandatory religious exercises failed in the legislature, new kinds of compromises, such as released time for weekday religious instruction, sprang up as older reforms wilted. Even when city after city abolished ward control, nondemocratic localism continued to play a significant role in the ethnic identity of individual schools, and the Douay Bible continued to be an acceptable alternative to the King James version for decades.

But democratically determined, locally generated agreements now faced severe curtailment from the state, and local boards had far less room in which to operate. At the same time, the main objector to the public school system, the Roman Catholic Church, continued to build educational capacity of its own and squashed internal debate in favor of the conservatives. With early-twentieth-century distinctions between religious and public schools sharpened, it is not surprising that school historians throughout the twentieth century were equally divided—writing house histories that defended either public or parochial schools while assailing the other. Nor should it be surprising that these historians, living in a time when people upset over public school policies had to fight the educational system itself (as opposed to working within it), have looked to the past and found warfare and bitterness there.

The Historical Significance of Peaceable Adjustments

I have argued that the bitter rhetoric of polemicists and state and national politicians over religion in public education did not reflect local reality. This argument pushes against the standard "warfare thesis" that shapes, implicitly and explicitly, most historical accounts of the subject. In the field of religion and public education, the past has always played a role in the present. Church-state intellectuals of all stripes still debate the intentions of the religious founding generation, for example, with religious conservatives and originalists clinging to the proposition that the United States was and is a Christian nation.[1] And there is no end in sight. Would-be policy makers seem to have an implicit stake in explaining how things ought to be based on how they might once have been.

I have addressed a few historical issues in particular that still play a large role in contemporary rhetoric about religion in public schools: the religious roots of public schools in the United States, the role of "liberalism" and liberals in driving religion from public school curricula, and the allegedly liberal Protestant character of public schools (and thus offensiveness to non-liberal Protestants and non-Protestants alike).

What Are the Religious Origins of Public Schools?

Since the late nineteenth century, advocates of religious instruction have claimed that Bible reading was once universal in common/public schools. In

1903, for example, a normal school principal from Cortland lamented, "It seems to me it was a distinct loss to the young people of our country when the Bible was excluded [from the public schools.]" Even today, those on both sides of the debate on religion in public schools commonly assume that Pan-Protestant religious practice was synonymous with nineteenth-century public schooling.[2]

Looking at nineteenth-century schools in terms of democratic localism, though, I have shown significant evidence to suggest that in New York State, at least, Bible use was a minority practice in common schools as early as 1830, and it actually declined precipitously by 1840. By the time semi-reliable sources reappeared in the 1880s and 1890s, Bible use had climbed to roughly half of all school districts, and if we consider New York City's massive population, probably close to three-quarters of the total state school enrollment. At no time, though, does evidence support the claim that Bible reading was a universal practice, or anywhere near it. Likewise, the flexibility of New York and other city boards of education about the version of the Bible that could be used and the practice of optional exercises before school hours give the charge of Pan-Protestant tyranny a hollow ring. Bible reading is only one measure of religiosity in schools, of course—leadership, textbooks, and student culture would be other factors—but it was a practice that district residents specifically chose for its distinctly religious content.

Did Liberals and Liberalism Drive Religion from the Public School?

Contemporary popular belief attributes the lack of formal religious worship in public education to the efforts of a liberal elite. In the landmark Supreme Court decisions *Schempp* and *Engle*, wisdom has it, an over-zealous court capped the twentieth-century assault on religion by secularizing public education. Did liberals kick religion out of the schools? Was the very idea of nonsectarian schooling a liberal Protestant *coup*, as one historian has claimed?[3]

As we have seen, the actual content of most late-nineteenth-century common schools was overwhelmingly secular: day-long study of the 3 Rs, tempered by fifteen minutes, at the most, of religion. Protestant leaders may have controlled common school propaganda, urging districts to engage voluntarily in nonsectarian Bible reading, but did they made headway in actual policy? In the 1830s, the vast majority of New York State districts chose to exclude the Bible on their own, well before major Catholic immigration in the 1840s and later. As long as Yankee clergy held the monopoly on textbook production, academic textbooks contained many religious references, but as professional educators entered the market after the Civil War, this religious tone largely disappeared. The Bible slowly crept into

New York State common schools over the nineteenth century but never occupied them fully.

What kept religious exercises out of common schools in the early nineteenth century and what kept them out of the schools of many cities and towns in the late nineteenth century was not liberalism or atheism but locally determined compromises. Even firm Protestants sometimes defended the exorcism of religion from public schools in religious terms. "It would be poor policy and poorer Christianity," observed a county commissioner in 1903, "for those in authority to force their opinions on a district one way or another."[4] Local voters drove religious organizations from the schoolhouse after hours not because they burned with Christian fervor, but because they burned the schoolhouse wood. Where religious exercises existed during the school day, they did so legally (perhaps with the exception of New York City) only as a result of the tolerance of religious minorities, not despite it.

In this book I have suggested a number of ways, some of them paradoxical, in which democracy, localism, and the state managed to minimize dissent over religion. The state legislature maintained a broad legal framework for public school policy in the 1860s and 1870s but left much room for school districts to fashion a variety of approaches to diversity, including homogeneous districting, ethnoreligious theme schools, teacher recruitment, the banning of religious exercises, the absorption of parochial schools within public systems (and under public supervision), the development of compromise religious exercises, the accommodation of religious groups' use of the schoolhouse after hours, and the strategy of requiring religious exercises but leaving the specifics to teachers and school administrators. According to appeals and letters to the state, district trustees and other leaders frequently demonstrated a commitment to keeping the schoolhouse out of controversy, just as textbook publishers sought to avoid controversy within the curriculum itself. Moreover, appeals and letters suggest that many New Yorkers endorsed and supported the process of local democratic decision making, seeing it as a legitimate form of decision making and abiding by its results even if they disagreed with them.

Compromise did not always stem from altruism, however, nor did it necessarily flow from peaceable relations among religious and ethnic groups in American society. By establishing the clear possibility for state intervention (and thus a potential financial and emotional drain on a school district), the appeals system itself encouraged local majorities to avoid violating the legal rights of minorities—rights that included not having to hear objectionable religious exercises. Penurious city school boards cut deals with church officials to meet increasing enrollments without raising taxes. Moreover, common schools provided employment to janitors, teachers, and principals, not to mention contractors for various goods and services, creating a vested interest in the success of common schools among those religious and ethnic groups that could win such jobs.

By decentralizing decision making, democratic localism sometimes put questions of the relationship between religion and public schools within the hands of religiously or ethnically homogeneous districts, or into city boards sympathetic to their interests. In other words, the "local" part of democratic localism may have been as important as the "democratic" part, as homogeneous districting made compromise unnecessary, as long as the state stayed out of the way. Even in New York City, the central board of education had little direct control over the religious tone of individual teachers, scholars, and schools. New York City public schools belonged first to their neighborhoods, then to their wards, then to their districts, and only then to the city at large.

How a given school used religious exercises had much to do with how religious minorities responded to them. Minorities often seemed to tolerate the practice because the exercises themselves were already a form of compromise—rote, brief, unannotated, and often ignored. Many parents may have found these exercises unpleasant but did not consider them worth protesting formally. In a number of cities and towns, parents did not object until someone gunning for conflict fired them up. As we have seen, in Long Island City, an obnoxious Protestant school board deliberately used religious exercises to alienate Catholics. Not surprisingly, Catholics responded angrily and demanded that the exercises cease. In Lockport in 1903, Catholic Church officials may have been the emotional arsonists. The superintendent of schools reported:

> We have endeavored to be careful not to provoke opposition [to the city religious exercise] and have never had a protest until last year, when, after a visit from one of their officials, the Catholic priesthood began to speak against it and to demand of parents that they decline to permit their children to attend such exercises in our public schools. Quite a little excitement grew up over it, many requests to excuse children from the devotional exercises were received and granted, those children remaining in some other room during the devotional part of the exercises and them coming back in to participate in other things. That has allayed all feeling so far as I can learn and has satisfied all people fairly well, though there are some Protestants who would have urged that no heed be paid to the Catholic protests and requests.[5]

But in other cases, school officials noted years of accord and respect for diversity within the school, even as ethnoreligious and class differences rent the fabric of American social life outside. "Even in districts where the Roman Catholic element is strong," wrote the Yates County commissioner in 1903, "there seems to be no objection to [Bible use], provided the teacher wishes to follow this custom." The superintendent of Jamestown schools noted, "Experience shows that where those who favor the use of the Bible are moderate in their demands and considerate in their attitude, a satisfactory adjustment can usually be made."[6]

How Protestant Were New York State Public Schools?

Before the Civil War, many Catholics in New York City had cause for complaint against the public schools, where the curriculum often reflected explicitly anti-Catholic bias and where Protestants controlled the teaching force and school administration. It is important to note, however, that when Catholics pointed to objectionable passages in the school textbooks in the 1830s, and again in 1840, the School Society offered to work with Catholic authorities to expunge them. Both Bishop Dubois and his successor John Hughes declined the offers, preferring to press for their own program of Church-controlled schools. After the Civil War, democratic localism in district schools and ward-based control in cities gave ethnoreligious groups, including Catholics, a powerful voice in the management of their own public schools. Some problems persisted, as we have seen, but public school districts responded to these concerns in a variety of ways—from banning religion, to insisting exercises take place before school, to forging compromise exercises, to allowing the Douay Bible, to hiring Catholic teachers, to incorporating explicitly parochial schools within the public system—and only rarely did a district's failure to compromise necessitate an appeal to a higher authority. Some Catholics did, out of a sense of fear of excommunication, pious duty, or disgust with public schools, attend the parochial schools that their church built for them. More, though, remained in public schools despite the exhortations of leading New York State bishops. Parish priests themselves often came out on both sides of the issue. There is much evidence that Church leaders, especially at the level of bishop and higher, favored the official church policy of building a separate, church-run system of schools; there is much less evidence that the laity attended them out of a sense of strong dissatisfaction with the "Protestant" public schools.[7]

Considering the common school "system" as a method of governance treats Catholics as active participants, as opposed to passive victims, in nineteenth-century public schools.[8] My intention has not been to ignore the very real differences in power between many religious minorities and the primarily Protestant middle class but, rather, to understand how those differences actually mattered in a system of governance built upon district- and school-level control. The Catholic Church's official opposition to public schooling did not represent the views or interests of all Catholics, who acted, spoke, and voted for a variety of reasons, not all of them religious. More importantly, religious minorities of all stripes often had the opportunity to participate actively and powerfully in the politics of their school districts. Irish-Americans provide the best example. In 1894, a Protestant observer penned a lament over the Irish-American "genius for municipal government—at least for getting municipal office." During the post-bellum era, Catholics won election to the mayorships of most major Northern cities in the East and Midwest, including New York City. A state public school system designed around democratic participation, while perhaps not fully countering the forces of anti-Catholic discrimination and economic oppression, nevertheless provided Catholics and other religious minorities with opportunities to flex their political muscles in school district politics.[9]

National Politics and National Policy

What happened as a result of all of the political bluster over religion and common schools in other states and at the national level? The movement *against* local control over religious matters in public schools enjoyed major success in state- and national-level legislation. In state debates, the question of prohibiting public funds to parochial schools often appeared cut and dried—Democrats and Republicans alike barely debated the point—in favor of prohibition. The question of religious exercises, on the other hand, attracted serious and sustained discussion.[10] As we saw in chapter 9, special interest groups had a hand in pushing religious policy in the New York State Constitutional Convention of 1894, winning a strict separation of church schools and state funds (although they failed to get wording specific enough to make their victory certain). Across the North and West, states passed laws and revised their constitutions—sometimes to prohibit public funds to parochial schools, but less often to mandate religious exercises. Seventeen states modified their constitutions in this period to include such provisions. Many of these also contained provisions against "sectarian instruction" in schools, but they did not clarify the phrase, leaving the door open for nondenominational exercises.[11]

In Congress, radical Republicans sponsored a constitutional amendment banning public money to church-controlled schools, or sectarian instruction in public schools. The amendment rocketed through the House (180 yeas, 7 nays, and 98 abstentions), later falling short in the Senate.[12] Republicans had more success in shaping the constitutions of incoming states. Exploiting the power of Congress to ensure that new states had "republican forms of government," congressional Republicans insisted that this definition required states to forbid public funding of "sectarian" schools in their state constitutions. As a result, all new states admitted to the union between 1870 and 1900 had constitutions either forbidding public funding of sectarian schools or forbidding sectarian instruction within public schools.[13] (The role of the Republican-controlled Congress in this process has not been extensively researched.[14]) The legislative and political trajectory was clear: from 1870 to 1900, the school question worked its way into national politics and state law. How much these provisions mattered in practice depended on each state's configuration of state *versus* local control. New York State's period of peaceable adjustments may or may not have been replicated elsewhere. But the existence of widespread compromise in the North's most influential and politically dominant state is vitally important in its own right and calls for more research into religion in public school policy and practice at the local level of other state "systems" of public schooling.

Implications

The major paradigm for religion in American public education today is the secular public school. In this vision, which guides most (but not all) public education in the United States, schools receiving public funds for providing mass education must be public institutions, linked to the political process through boards of education and local and state government. Because they are agents of the state, the argument goes, these schools must be secular—observing a "high wall of separation" (in the words of Thomas Jefferson) between religion and the state. The reason for this separation is to protect the rights of religious minorities, including atheists and humanists, Mormons and Muslims. Some states and individual schools play political games with this legal paradigm—in 1999, the Kansas State Board of Education flirted with fundamentalism by dropping evolution from state science standards, reinstating it two years later.[15] Nevertheless, the core idea of a religiously neutral school, with neutrality determined by courts or state governments, continues to dominate the policy scene. Democracy, in this sense, provides for government-controlled schools for mass education and handles religious diversity by providing a one-size-fits-all policy that protects the rights of objectors to religious instruction of any sort.

Religious conservatives, particularly Roman Catholic leaders, push for an alternative paradigm. In 1967, M. Raymond McLaughlan wrote *Religious Education and the State: Democracy Finds a Way*, which argued that among its Western democratic peers—Great Britain, Italy, France, and so on—the United States stood alone in its strict separation of religion and public education.[16] In so many other nations, McLaughlan wrote, democracy had "found a way" to give public funds to religiously controlled schools. Why could democracy not do so here as well? The argument put a new twist on the century-old Catholic Church policy toward public education: namely, that religious organizations ought to be allowed to participate in the mass education of American youth and be given public money to do so. The Catholic Church is not a democratic institution. (In the 1860s and 1870s, the Vatican was strongly, explicitly anti-democratic.) But McLaughlan's thesis, she argues, is consistent with a democratic vision of the United States: Whether schools are organized by state or church, the important thing is that the students learn values consistent with the democratic needs of the nation as a whole.

Much of the contemporary rhetoric around "choice" programs, such as vouchers and charter schools, makes a similar claim. In a free nation, why not let parents choose the organization that will educate their children? As Bishop McQuaid argued over a century ago, why not let the state set minimum requirements for instruction and pay a per-pupil allotment to any organization that meets those standards? As long as the schools churn out citizens, who cares who is turning the wheel? Following this line of reasoning, religion in public education ceases to be a problem, since parents can choose a school based on its policies and opt out if they are unhappy.

The paradigm offered by late-nineteenth-century New York State differed fundamentally from both the secular school system currently in place and the growing movement toward a voucher system. In the context of a society far less dependent on educational credentials and extended enrollment, the common school system of post-bellum New York State left decisions about religion in the public school to local districts. State law insisted on a certain set of rules: institutions that provided mass education had to be controlled democratically, such schools must be open to all religions, and they could not be explicitly sectarian during school hours. The state provided one more crucial component: the objections of religious minorities would be protected through a process of legal appeals.

The system attracted abuse on many levels, and New York State residents often acted out of self-interest, prejudice, and ethnic defensiveness. Yet New York State public schools did not suffer widespread, irreconcilable conflict over religious matters. Instead, schools generated a variety of approaches toward religious diversity, some of which resembled the major paradigms today, and some of which did not. But nineteenth-century democratic localism embodied a fundamentally different *process* of decision making. The common school system of New York State provided enough flexibility and stability to allow the massive expansion and consolidation of public schooling, despite dramatic social cleavages among religious groups and despite the best efforts of its opponents. Thus the most historically significant feature of our story was not the war of words over church and state policy but the myriad ways in which the locals kept the peace.

Notes

CHAPTER ONE

1. Paul Kleppner, *Who Voted? The Dynamics of Electoral Turnout, 1870–1980* (New York: Praeger, 1982), 32–38.

2. Michael Schudson, *The Good Citizen: A History of American Civic Life* (New York: The Free Press, 1998), 155–168.

3. Historian Paul Kleppner has argued, "Engaging in the act [of voting] inculcates or strengthens citizens' feelings of subjective competence, the sense of their own potential significance in the governing process." See Kleppner, *Who Voted?*, 4.

4. The works on this subject are too numerous to cite completely. See Paul Kleppner, *The Third Electoral System: 1853–1892: Parties, Voters, and Political Cultures* (Chapel Hill: University of North Carolina Press, 1979); Samuel P. Hays, *American Political History As Social Analysis* (Knoxville: University of Tennessee Press, 1980).

5. David Grimstead, *American Mobbing, 1828–1861: Toward Civil War* (New York: Oxford University Press, 1998), 229–44; Lloyd Jorgenson, *The State and the Non-Public School, 1825–1925* (Columbia: University of Missouri Press, 1987), 76–78.

6. See, for example, Robert Cross, *The Emergence of Liberal Catholicism in America* (Cambridge: Harvard University Press, 1958), 22–25.

7. Jerome Mushkat, *The Reconstruction of New York Democracy, 1861–1874* (Rutherford, N.J.: Farleigh Dickenson University Press, 1981), 177; John Higham, *Strangers in the Land: Patterns of American Nativism, 1860–1925* (New Brunswick: Rutgers University Press, 1998 [1955]), 28.

8. Ward M. McAfee, *Religion, Race, and Reconstruction: The Public School in the Politics of the 1870s* (Albany: State University of New York Press, 1998), 27–40; *The Bible in the Public Schools: The Opinion and the Decision of the Supreme Court of Ohio in the Case of John D. Minor versus the Board of Education, City of Cincinnati. Extracted from Volume 23, Ohio State Reports* (Cincinnati: Robert Clarke and Company, 1873), as cited in *12 Pamphlets on Education*, Department of Special Collections, Milbank Memorial Library, Teachers College, Columbia University.

9. See chapter 9 for a full discussion.

10. This is McAfee's central argument.

11. David B. Tyack, "Onward Christian Soldiers: Religion in the American Common School," in *History and Education*, ed. Paul Nash (New York: Random House, 1970), 212–55, 235.

12. Ibid., 236.

13. James C. Mohr, "New York: The Depoliticization of Reform," in *Radical Republicans in the North: State Politics during Reconstruction*, ed. James C. Mohr (Baltimore: Johns Hopkins University Press, 1976), 66–81; Mushkat, *The Reconstruction of New York Democracy.*

14. Emphasis in original. "The Democratic Party and Its Public Schools. Gov. Tildon Favors Appropriations for the Support of Roman Catholic Parochial Schools" and "Politics and the School Question. Attitudes of the Republican and Democratic Parties in 1876," from *25 Pamphlets on Education*, Department of Special Collections, Milbank Memorial Library, Teachers College, Columbia University.

15. Jorgenson, *The State and the Non-Public School*, 146–204.

16. Ibid.

17. S. V. Ryan, " 'A Plea for Christian Schools': Lecture by Rt. Rev. S. V. Ryan, D. D., Bishop of Buffalo, Delivered at St. James Hall, Thursday Evening, February 25, 1875." Printed in full in *The Catholic Union*, Buffalo: Wednesday, March 3, 1875, pp. 4–8; Bernard McQuaid, "Christian Free Schools: The Matter Discussed," reprinted by the *Rochester Union and Advertiser*, December 9, 1871.

18. See the Buffalo *Catholic Union*, 1872–1875, and *Catholic World*. The stream of articles in the former was virtually unending.

19. Daniel Flavian Reilly, *The School Controversy (1891–1893)* (Washington, D.C.: Catholic University Press, 1943); Cross, *The Emergence of Liberal Catholicism*; Thomas T. McAvoy, *The Americanist Heresy in American Catholicism, 1895–1900* (Notre Dame: University of Notre Dame Press, 1963).

20. Notable calls for research have gone beyond the politics. See Robert D. Cross, "Origins of the Catholic Parochial Schools in America," *The American Benedictine Review* (June 16, 1965): 194-209. Neil G. McCluskey was overly optimistic, though, when he wrote in *Catholic Education in America* (New York: Bureau of Publications, Teachers College, 1964), "As the Catholic-Protestant polemic fades farther and farther away, the chances increase that more historians and fewer apologists will turn their attention to the dreadfully neglected field of American education" (p. 15).

21. Grimstead, *American Mobbing*, 244.

22. The best scholarship on the ideas of the various antagonists in this warfare can be found in Robert S. Michaelson, *Piety and the Public School: Trends and Issues in the Relationship between Religion and the Public School in the United States* (New York: Macmillan, 1970).

23. Elwood Patterson Cubberley, *Public Education in the United States: A Study and Interpretation of American Educational History* (San Francisco: Houghton Mifflin, 1934); Bernard Bailyn, *Education in the Forming of American Society* (New York: W.W. Norton and Co., 1960); Lawrence A. Cremin, *The Wonderful World of Elwood P. Cubberley: An Essay on the Historiography of American Education* (New York: Teachers College Bureau of Publications, Columbia University, 1965). For more on Progressive-era anti-private-school activity, see Jorgenson, *The State and the Non-Public School*, chap. 9, 10. See, for example, Robert Danforth Cole, *Private Secondary Education for Boys in the United States* (Philadelphia: Westbrook, 1928).

24. Leonard V. Koos, *Private and Public Secondary Education: A Comparative Study* (Chicago: University of Chicago Press, 1932), 208–17.

25. Vincent P. Lannie, "Church and School Triumphant," *History of Education Quarterly* 16 (Summer 1976): 131–45; Marvin Lazerson, "Understanding American Catholic Educational History," *History of Education Quarterly* 17 (1977): 297–317, quoted from p. 298; James A. Burns, *The Growth and Development of the Catholic School System in the United States* (New York: Arno Press, 1969), 16.

26. David B. Tyack, "The Kingdom of God and the Common School," *Harvard Educational Review* 36:4 (1966): 447–69; Timothy L. Smith, "Protestant Schooling and American Nationality, 1800–1850," *The Journal of American History* 53:4 (March 1967): 679–95, 695.

27. Cross, "Origins of the Catholic Parochial Schools"; McCluskey, *Catholic Education in America*; Jay P. Dolan, *The Immigrant Church: New York's Irish and German Catholics, 1815–1865* (Baltimore: Johns Hopkins University Press, 1975); James W. Sanders, *The Education of an Urban Minority: Catholics in Chicago, 1833–1965* (New York: Oxford University Press, 1977).

28. James W. Sanders, "Roman Catholics and the School Question in New York City: Some Suggestions for Research," in *Educating an Urban People: The New York City Experience*, ed. Diane Ravitch and Ronals Goodenow (New York: Teachers College Press, 1981), 116–40.

29. F. Michael Perko, "Religious Schooling in America: An Historiographic Reflection," *History of Education Quarterly* 40: 3 (Fall 2000).

30. Diane Ravitch, *The Great School Wars* (New York: Basic Books, 1974).

31. Jorgenson, *The State and the Non-Public School.*

32. Warren A. Nord, *Religion and American Education: Rethinking a National Dilemma* (Chapel Hill: University of North Carolina Press, 1995); James W. Fraser, *Between Church and State: Religion and Public Education in a Multicultural America* (New York: St. Martin's Press, 1999); Timothy Walch, *Parish School: American Catholic Parochial Education from Colonial Times to the Present* (New York: Crossroad, 1996): Stephen Macedo, *Diversity and Distrust: Civic Education in a Multicultural Democracy* (Cambridge: Harvard University Press, 2000).

33. Fraser, *Between Church and State*, 3, 64.

34. Kleppner, *The Third Electoral System*, 144, 220, 221–26. I cite Kleppner here with due respect, as I admire his scholarship and use his idea of pietism versus ritualism in later chapters. I do disagree with him, however, as his interpretation strays from voter attributes to assumptions about school politics. The very idea of a study of partisanship and parties, by definition, will inevitably result in the description of irreconcilable differences of some sort. At the same time that worldviews of ethnocultural ideology led to conflicting ideas, though, they also offered a means to compromise. Moderate pietists, including Henry Ward Beecher, for example, used the language of Christianity to urge their fellows to compromise on school issues, as did liberal Catholic priests and bishops. In other cases, localism in schooling also meant that many children attended relatively homogeneous schools, which would make ethnocultural conflict somewhat irrelevant.

35. Jean H. Baker, *Affairs of Party: The Political Culture of Northern Democrats in the Mid-Nineteenth Century* (Cornell University Press, 1983), offers a more skeptical approach to interpreting voter data and makes the important observation that schools were traditionally held to be off limits to partisanship and sectarianism. Furthermore, Baker argues that Republicans and Democrats alike tapped into a common body of ideas about American government and thus acted as unifying forces as much as divisive ones. Baker does not, however, make the link between what happened in schools and how they were run. Michael F. Holt argues that economic and social change, and issues themselves, may have played larger roles than Kleppner gives them credit for. See Holt, *Political Parties and American Political Development from the Age of Jackson to the Age of Lincoln* (Baton Rouge: Louisiana State University Press, 1992), 18–23. Holt also focuses on conflict, which may be more appropriate for his time period—the nativist 1850s. In his study of Pittsburgh from 1848 to 1860, for example, Holt argues persuasively that Protestant/Catholic clashes over public school religious policy and aid to parochial schools swelled the roles of the virulently anti-Catholic American Party and led to extreme politics in that city. Yet, by 1887, a Catholic priest of that same city managed to forge a peaceable adjustment by getting hired as principal of a public school and operating it as a *public* parochial school, remaining religiously neutral during school hours but asking Catholic children to come a half hour early for extra instruction. The plan failed after a year—*not* because of nativist attacks, bitter conflict, or any state legal challenge, but because the children soon stopped showing up to the early session. The priest cancelled the arrangement and reopened his parochial school. See Michael Holt, *Forging a Majority: The Formation of the Republican Party in Pittsburgh, Pennsylvania, 1848–1860* (Ph.D. diss, Johns Hopkins University, 1967); *The Independent*, vol. XLII, no. 2179 (September 4, 1890).

36. Thomas Bender and others have noted the disparity between local culture and politics and state and national politics. See *Community and Social Change in America* (New Brunswick: Rutgers University Press, 1978).

37. As a rule, historians should not be held accountable for the summaries that appear on jacket covers of their books. Nevertheless, Jorgenson's plainly describes the essence of his project, which runs through the whole work: the "excesses" of religious

leaders drove common school policy toward religion. McAfee's argument about local reality can be found on pp. 6–7, 181, 188–92.

38. Timothy Walch, *Parish School: American Catholic Parochial Education from Colonial Times to the Present* (New York: Crossroad Publishing Co., 1996), 168.

39. David B. Tyack, "The Spread of Public Schooling in Victorian America: In Search of a Reinterpretation," *History of Education* 7:3 (1978): 173–82: 174–75.

40. There is a significant body of literature on the disconnection (or, at best, loose connection) between rhetoric in the national media and in state party politics and community-level experience. For a review, see Bender, *Community and Social Change.* On the tendency of the press to emphasize the worst-case scenarios, see Charles W. Calhoun, "The Political Culture: Public Life and the Conduct of Politics," in *The Guilded Age: Essays on the Origins of Modern America*, ed. Charles W. Calhoun (Wilmington, Del.: Scholarly Press, 1996), 185–213, 187.

41. Samuel Hays discusses similar goals for scholarship, which he referred to as "social analysis" in his 1964 lecture, "New Possibilities for American Political History: The Social Analysis of Political Life," reprinted in Samuel P. Hays, *American Political History and Social Analysis* (Knoxville: University of Tennessee Press, 1980), 88-132, see 96–110. Schools do not fit Hays's paradigm well, however, as this book hopes to show.

42. See Burns, *Growth and Development of the Catholic School System*, 268. We saw a similar disaster in the "Cincinnati Bible War" of 1869.

43. A further omission, which offers a promising opportunity for future research, is the temperance movement and its potential as a form of "religion" in public school governance and curriculum. Hays and others argue that temperance was a vital issue in state and local politics in the North in this period *(American Political History,* 54–55). See also Jonathan Zimmerman, *Distilling Democracy: Alcohol Education in America's Public Schools, 1880–1925* (Lawrence: University Press of Kansas, 1999). Comparing alcohol education to Bible reading in schools raises important questions about the strength of the principle of separation of church and state in the face of ethnoreligious politics.

44. Thanks to Eamonn Callan for this turn of phrase.

Part 1

1. Organizational theorists and sociologists differ in their assessment of just how tight this interconnectedness is, but they largely accept the paradigm of a system in the sense I describe.

2. See "system" in the *Oxford English Dictionary Online* (www.dictionary.oed.com: Oxford University Press, 2000).

CHAPTER 2

1. Richard D. Brown, *The Strength of a People: The Idea of an Informed Citizenry in America, 1650–1870* (Chapel Hill: University of North Carolina Press, 1996), chap. 2–4, especially chap. 4.

2. Ibid., 94, 99. On a general discussion of the various educational proposals of that generation, see pp. 103–109.

3. As we saw in chapter 1, this view dominated Progressive histories of common schools in the first half of the twentieth century. See Elwood Patterson Cubberley, *Public Education in the United States: A Study and Interpretation of American Educational History*. Rev. ed. (San Francisco: Houghton Mifflin, 1934). On Cubberley, see Bernard Bailyn, *Education in the Forming of American Society* (New York: W.W. Norton and Co., 1960). and Lawrence A. Cremin, *The Wonderful World of Elwood P. Cubberley: An Essay on the Historiography of American Education* (New York: Teachers College Bureau of Publications, Columbia University, 1965).

4. David B. Tyack, "Monuments between Covers: The Politics of Textbooks," *American Behavioral Scientist* 42:6 (March 1999): 922–32; R. M. Elson, *Guardians of Tradition: American Schoolbooks of the Nineteenth Century* (Lincoln: University of Nebraska Press, 1964); John Westerhoff, *McGuffey and His Readers: Piety, Morality, and Education in 19th Century America* (Nashville: Abington Press, 1978); Dolores P. Sullivan, *William Holmes McGuffey: Schoolmaster to the Nation* (Rutherford, N.J.: Farleigh Dickenson University Press, 1994); Thomas J. Davis, "Images of Intolerance: John Calvin in Nineteenth-Century History Textbooks," *Church History* 65: 2 (1996): 234. It is important to note that I do not include textbooks in my overall argument for two reasons. First, it is difficult to tease out exactly what people of the 1820s and 1830s understood as religion and what they accepted implicitly as truth, or tradition, or never thought to question at all. Second, however polarized politics and religion were in American life, textbooks from the mid- and late-nineteenth century eschewed controversy of any kind, promising to be free of sectarian or secular matters. After the Civil War, professional educators broke what had been a Yankee Protestant ministers' monopoly on textbook production, and as a result, increasingly dropped trappings of any religion at all. In addition to the aforementioned sources, see Jean H. Baker, *Affairs of Party: The Political Culture of Northern Democrats in the Mid-Nineteenth Century* (Ithaca: Cornell University Press, 1983), 28.

5. See F. Michael Perko, "Religious Education," in *Encyclopedia of American Religious Experience* ed. Charles H. Lippy and Peter W. Williams (New York: 1988), vol. 3), 1598, and Fraser, *Between Church and State.* On leadership, see David B. Tyack, "The Kingdom of God and the Common School," *Harvard Educational Review* 36:4 (1996): 447–69; Timothy L. Smith, "Protestant Schooling and American Nationality, 1800–1850," *The Journal of American History* 53:4 (March 1967): 679–95; David B. Tyack and Elisabeth Hansot, *Managers of Virtue: Public School Leadership in America, 1820–1980* (New York: Basic Books, 1982).

6. The claim that Supreme Court decisions in 1962 and 1963 "secularized" public schools utterly fails to consider this fact, equating symbolic gestures—a

moment of prayer and Bible reading without comment—to religious education. Mass, public education in New York was from its outset a secular civic undertaking, though it tolerated and often benefited from the efforts of churches and clergy.

7. As cited in Samuel S. Randall, *The Common School System of the State of New York* (Troy, N.Y.: Johnson and Davis, Steam Press Printers, 1851).

8. As cited in David B. Tyack, Thomas James, and Aaron Benavot, *Law and the Shaping of Public Education, 1785–1954* (Madison: University of Wisconsin Press, 1987), 23.

9. From Miller, "Sermon at the New Presbyterian Church," New York, July 4, 1795, 28–29, as cited in Alfred F. Young, *The Democratic Republicans of New York: The Origins, 1863–1797* (Chapel Hill: University of North Carolina Press, 1967), 524.

10. Donald R. Warren, *To Enforce Education: A History of the Founding Years of the United States Office of Education* (Detroit: Wayne State University Press, 1974), 25–30; Baker, *Affairs of Party*, 72-78. I intentionally borrowed this phrase from Mary Beth Norton, *Founding Mothers and Fathers: Gendered Power and the Forming of American Society* (New York : Alfred A. Knopf, 1996). For the role of women in educational theories of the early republic, see David Tyack and Elisabeth Hansot, *Learning Together: A History of Coeducation in American Public Schools* (New Haven: Yale University Press, 1990), chap. 2.

11. Thomas James, "Rights of Conscience and State School Systems in Nineteenth-Century America," in *Toward a Usuable Past: Liberty under State Constitutions,* ed. Paul Finkelman and Stephen Gotleib (Athens: University of Georgia Press, 1991), 117–47.

12. Brown, *The Strength of a People*, chap. 4.

13. Andrew S. Draper, *The New York Common School System* (Syracuse: C. W. Bardeen, 1903), 34–39.

14. Brown, *The Strength of a People*, 67, 103.

15. Tyack, James, and Benovot, *Law*, 31–34.

16. Gordon S. Wood, "Religion and the American Revolution," in *New Directions in American Religious History* ed. Harry S. Stout and D. G. Hart (New York: Oxford University Press, 1997), 173–74.

17. On Clinton, see E. Wilder Spaulding, *His Excellency George Clinton, Critic of the Constitution* (New York: Macmillan, 1938), 12. On Deism in New York, see Charles J. Mahoney, *The Relation of the State to Religious Education in Early New York, 1633–1825* (Washington, D.C.: Catholic University Press, 1941), 104–106.

18. As cited in Wood, "Religion," 174.

19. Ibid.

20. John Webb Pratt, *Religion, Politics, and Diversity: The Church-State Theme in New York History* (Ithaca: Cornell University Press, 1967).

21. Young, *The Democratic Republicans*, 518–20.

22. Peter S. Onuf, "State Politics and Republican Virtue: Religion, Education, and Morality in Early American Federalism," in *Toward a Usable Past: Liberty Under State Constitutions*, ed. Paul Finkelman and Stephen E. Gottlieb (Athens: University of Georgia Press, 1991), 91–116.

23. Nathan O. Hatch, *The Democratization of American Christianity* (New Haven: Yale University Press, 1989), 14.

24. See Wood, "Religion."

25. Pratt, *Religion, Politics, and Diversity*, 98–116; Young, *The Democratic Republicans*, 518–20.

26. While somewhat outdated, the idea of the covenanted community is sufficiently descriptive of the process I sketch here. See Page Smith, *As a City upon A Hill* (New York: Knopf, 1967), 64–67.

27. Nathaniel Prime, *A History of Long Island, from Its First Settlement by Europeans to the Year 1845, with Special Reference to Its Ecclesiastical Concerns* (New York: Robert Carter, 1845), 81. For a general discussion, see James Axtell, *The School upon a Hill: Education and Society in Colonial New England* (New Haven: Yale University Press, 1974), and Lawrence Cremin, *American Education: The Colonial Experience* (New York: Harper and Row, 1970), and *American Education: The National Experience* (New York: Harper and Row, 1980).

28. Charles J. Mahoney, *The Relation of the State to Religious Education in Early New York, 1633–1825* (Washington, D.C.: Catholic University Press, 1941), 92–93. The state legislature as quoted in ibid.

29. Onuf, "State Politics and Republican Virtue," 94.

32. Ibid., 102–15. For a brilliant account of the meaning of "the people" as a political construct, see Edmund S. Morgan, *Inventing the People: The Rise of Popular Sovereignty in England and America* (New York: W. W. Norton and Company, 1989). Notably, the legislature rebuffed an earlier (1785) scheme to put clergy on the board and make the Regents more powerful than it became in 1789.

31. In 1819, the sanctity of precolonial charters would be tested in the Supreme Court, in *Dartmouth College v. Woodward.*

32. Young argues that Republican interest in social reform in general and common schools in particular pushed Clinton as much as his own leadership pulled. See Young, *The Democratic Republicans*, 521.

33. Tyack, James, and Benavot, *Law*, 29–31.

34. Draper, *The New York Common School System*, 38; Randall, *The Common School System*, 5.

35. Milton M. Klein, *The Politics of Diversity: Essays in the History of Colonial New York* (Port Washington, N.Y.: Kennikat Press, 1974, 97-109), reprinted from *New York History* XLV (October, 1964): 291–303.

36. Mahoney, *The Relation of the State*, 89–91.

37. As cited in Daniel E. Wager, *Our County and Its People: A Descriptive Work on Oneida County, New York* (Boston: The Boston History Company, 1896), 79.

38. As cited in Randall, *The Common School System*, 6.

39. Mahoney, *The Relation of the State*, 94; Randall, *The Common School System*, 5–6.

40. As cited in Randall, *The Common School System*, 6–7.

41. Carl F. Kaestle, *Pillars of the Republic: Common Schools and American Society, 1780–1860* (New York: Hill and Wang, 1983), 26; John G. Richardson, "Settlement Patterns and the Governing Structures of Nineteenth-Century School Systems," *American Journal of Education* 92 (1984): 178–206; Elwood P. Cubberley, *Rural Life and Education: A Study of the Rural-School Problem As a Phase of the Rural-Life Problem* (New York: Houghton Mifflin, 1914, 83–85).

42. Pratt, *Religion, Politics, and Diversity*, 162.

43. Randall, *The Common School System*, 9.

44. Young, *The Democratic Republicans*, 526.

45. Randall, *The Common School System*, and Pratt, *Religion, Politics, and Diversity, 162*, offer varying explanations.

46. Several historians have shown that the use of the district system predated its formal legal sanction by state law. See Kaestle, *Pillars of the Republic*, 26; Richardson, "Settlement Patterns"; Cubberley, *Rural Life*, 83–85.

47. As cited in Randall, *The Common School System*, 9.

48. Ibid., 10.

49. *Report of the Committee* as cited in ibid., 11.

50. Ibid., 13–14.

51. Ibid., 10.

52. Emphasis in original. Ibid., 12–13.

53. Michael B. Katz, *Reconstructing American Education* (Cambridge: Harvard University Press, 1987), 25.

54. Even at the outset in the 1790s, appropriations to church schools caused controversy in the city. Eventually, the legislature decided to limit the schools that received funds under the 1795 act to one-sixth of the total. See Young, *The Democratic Republicans*, 526.

55. A. Emerson Palmer, *The New York Public School* (New York: Macmillan and Company, 1905), 48.

56. Carl F. Kaestle, *The Evolution of an Urban School System* (Cambridge: Harvard University Press, 1973); Diane Ravitch, *The Great School Wars* (New York: Basic Books, 1974), 6–19.

57. Ravitch, *School Wars*, 12–19.

58. Kaestle, *The Evolution*; Michael B. Katz, *The Irony of Early School Reform* (Cambridge: Harvard University Press, 1969).

59. Palmer, *The New York Public School*, 48. For the connection between class, reform, and religion in the antebellum period, see Paul E. Johnson, *A Shopkeeper's Millennium* (New York: Hill and Wang, 1978); Mary P. Ryan, *Cradle of the Middle Class* (New York: Cambridge University Press, 1981); Curtis D. Johnson, *Islands of Holiness: Rural Religion in Upstate New York, 1790–1860* (Ithaca: Cornell University Press, 1989).

60. Palmer, *The New York Public School*, 36.

61. Timothy L. Smith, "Protestant Schooling and American Nationality, 1800–1850," *Journal of American History* 53:4 (March 1967), 679–95, 683.

62. Ravitch, *School Wars*, 3–5.

63. Sean Wilentz, *Chants Democratic: New York City and the Rise of the American Working Class, 1788–1850* (New York: Oxford University Press, 1984), 77.

64. Edward Countryman. "The Rights of Mankind," in *The Empire State: A History of New York* ed. Milton M. Klein (Ithaca: Cornell University Press, 2001), 241, 245.

65. Ravitch, *School Wars*, 20–71.

66. The superintendent, John Spencer, was also the secretary of state, as cited in Ravitch, *School Wars*, 63.

67. As cited in Ravitch, *School Wars*, 71.

68. As cited in ibid., 64.

69. Timothy Smith and Charles Mahoney both do this, for example. See Smith, "Protestant Schooling," and Mahoney, *The Relation of the State.*

70. Barbara Shupe, Janet Steins, and Jyoti Pandit, eds. *New York State Population, 1790–1980: A Compilation of Federal Census Data* (New York: Neal-Schuman, 1987), ix. On the history of the Erie Canal, see Carol Sheriff, *The Artificial River: The Erie Canal and the Paradox of Progress* (New York: Hill and Wang, 1997).

71. Lee Benson *The Concept of Jacksonian Democracy; New York as a Test Case* (Princeton: Princeton University Press, 1961), 4.

72. Johnson, *Islands of Holiness.*

73. See Johnson, *Shopkeeper's Millennium*, and Mary Ryan, *Cradle of the Middle Class.*

74. Glenn C. Altschuler and Jan M. Saltzgaber, *Revivalism, Social Change, and Community in the Burned-Over District: The Trial of Rhoda Bement* (Ithaca: Cornell University Press, 1983), 27.

75. I quote Hatch's title here, which aptly describes his thesis.

76. Johnson, *Islands of Holiness*, 136.

77. Winthrop S. Hudson, *American Protestantism* (Chicago: University of Chicago Press, 1961), 96. Hudson argues that this minority "effectively penetrated the life of society" at the local level, but the assertion is sketchy for New York State during the early republic.

78. Richardson, "Settlement Patterns," 178–206.

79. James H. Hotchkin, *History of the Purchase and Settlement of Western New York* (New York: 1848), 378–79.

80. Johnson, *Islands of Holiness*, 8.

81. David B. Tyack, "Onward Christian Soldiers: Religion in the American Common School," in *History and Education*, ed. Paul Nash (New York: Random House, 1970): 212–55. Smith, "Protestant Schooling"; Kaestle, *Pillars*, 13–29.

82. Smith, "Protestant Schooling," 680; David B. Tyack, "The Kingdom of God and the Common School: Protestant Ministers and the Educational Awakening in the West," *Harvard Educational Review* 36 (Fall 1966).

83. Laurence Moore, *Selling God: American Religion in the Marketplace of Culture* (New York: American Philological Association, 1994), 66–89.

84. For an overview, see Lloyd Jorgensen, *The State and the Non-Public School* (Columbia: University of Missouri Press, 1987) 22–24. The "chicken soup" phrase is my own—an ironic reference to the book series popular at the time of this writing.

85. Curtis Johnson found that in Columbia County, for example, leading men did not join the revivalist fold until the eve of the Civil War, when the Second Great Awakening had sufficiently tamed the communitarian doctrine of local churches that sought to monitor and control individual behavior. See Johnson, *Islands of Holiness.*

86. Strangely, Mahoney uses this incident as evidence of the strength of Pan-Protestantism. To that end, he recounts the story in some detail in *The Relation of the State*, 111–12.

87. See county commissioner reports reprinted in New York State. *The Superintendent of Common Schools Annual Report,* 1843, especially pp. 667–69, 673. See also *Annual Report,* 1839, p. 40.

88. *Annual Report*, 1843, 668–69.

89. Fraser, *Between Church and State*, 23–40; Jorgensen, *The State and Non-Public School*, 37–41. *Annual Report*, 1844, 157–58.

90. Charles E. Bidwell, "The Moral Significance of the Common School: A Sociological Study of Local Patterns of School Control and Moral Education in Massachusetts and New York, 1837–1840," *History of Education Quarterly* (Fall 1966): 50–91.

91. For example, see the *Annual Report of the State Superintendent of the Common Schools of the State of New York* (1844), 673–74. Late-nineteenth-century observations can be found in later chapters of this book. See for example, Elizabeth

Blanchard Cook, *The Nation's Book in the Nation's Schools* (Chicago: The Chicago Women's Educational Union, 1898).

92. R. Laurence Moore, "Bible Reading and Nonsectarian Schooling: The Failure of Religious Instruction in Nineteenth Century Public Education," *The Journal of American History* 86:4 (March 2000).

93. Timothy Walch, *Parish School: American "Catholic Parochial Education from Colonial Times to the Present* (New York: Crossroads Press, 1996), 26. The claim is nearly universal among histories of the Catholic Church. For other examples, see Charles J. Mahoney, The Relation of the State and Arthur Jackson Hall, *Religious Education in the Public Schools of the State and City of New York: A Historical Study* (Ph.D. diss., University of Chicago Press, 1914).

94. *Annual Reports*, 1840, 103.

95. See Bidwell, "The Moral Significance," 50–91.

96. *Annual Report,* 1839, 40.

97. Ibid., 144.

98. *Annual Report*, 1845, 75.

Chapter Three

1. New York State Archives (NYSA): *Incoming Correspondence to the State Superintendent of Public Instruction*, series 04340-57, letter from B. T. Sheldon, Dutchess County, 12/8/1876.

2. Samuel Brown, *The Secularization of American Education* (New York: Teachers College, 1912) is an early example of the practice of assuming that changes in state law reflected educational realities. In more recent scholarship, historians have been more careful to concede the possible disconnection between state law and local practice, but nonetheless, they rarely venture beyond discussions of state policy and frenzied media coverage of religious controversy.

3. *Annual Report of the State Superintendent*, 1871, 5–15.

4. Some leaders called for greater centralization throughout the 1860s, and some city boards of education changed to boards of "public instruction" as a move in that direction (see *Annual Reports of Albany and New York City*, 1865–1870, and *Annual Report of the State Superintendent*, 1862, for example). Nevertheless, even these attempts failed to make significant headway against the deeply entrenched tradition of local control, which remained in place until Progressive reformers began their all-out assault on localism in the 1890s. See Morton Keller, *Affairs of State: Public Life in Late Nineteenth-Century America* (Cambridge: Harvard University Press, 1977); David B. Tyack, *The One Best System* (Cambridge: Harvard University Press, 1974).

5. *Annual Report of the State Superintendent*, 1866, 1–20.

6. The 1868 statistics are from the *Annual Report of the State Superintendent*, 1869, 102–105. A description of the creation of the office of the State Superintendent and relevant laws can be found in the *Annual Report of the State Superintendent*, 1904, 44.

7. *Annual Report of the State Superintendent*, 1871, 5–29. The statistics are difficult to make sense of but amount to $2.8 million in disbursements from the state for a total expense of $6.5 million.

8. The state census defined suburban as "towns lying adjacent to cities of 20,000 population and towns containing villages of 1,000 inhabitants." Districts in these places closely followed the district system, sometimes as Union Free Schools, when population density and transportation infrastructure allowed. See C. W. Seaton, Superintendent of the Census, *Census of the State of New York for 1875* (Albany: Weed, Parsons, and Co., 1877), xv.

9. *Annual Report of the State Superintendent*, 1873, 331; 1870, 57–58;

10. Judging by the letters and appeals to the state.

11. There is limited evidence that commissioners settled local disputes as an intermediate step to appeal, though a surviving commissioner's record book from the Saratoga Springs Archives suggests that these were exclusively boundary disputes. See *Annual Report of the State Superintendent*, 1883, 271. Commissioners did sometimes weigh in among appeals documents, though rarely outside of appeals concerning teacher qualifications and boundary disputes. By the turn of the century, this practice seems to have changed somewhat. A commissioner reported in 1903 that he had settled five religious disputes since taking office. See *Annual Report of the State Superintendent of Public Instruction*, 1903, 379.)

12. Report of the Commissioner of Jefferson County, in *Annual Report of the State Superintendent*, 1872, 252.

13. *Annual Report of the State Superintendent*, 1869, 213.

14. *Annual Report of the State Superintendent*, 1877, 328.

15. For the variety of city school governance patterns, see chapter 7. The annual reports of New York City, Brooklyn, and Rochester mention an appeals process explicitly. New York City could justly be considered independent of Albany, because the state legislature had a direct hand in the city government. The question of state versus city control of education arose in 1887 in *Edson v. Board of Education*, in which the city of Binghamton argued that its charter did not recognize the authority of the State Superintendent. The State Superintendent decided the appeal in favor of state authority. Ten years later, a showdown between the State Superintendent and the board of education of Watervliet tested this finding, affirming the state's power. See John Seiler Brubacher, *The Judicial Power of the New York State Commissioner of Education* (New York: Teachers College Publications, 1927), 76–77, for a discussion.

16. For a fuller discussion and sources, see chapter 7.

17. Brubacher, *The Judicial Power*, 76–77. As we shall see later, few residents of cities filed appeals to the State Superintendent.

18. "Report of the Second Commissioner District of Greene County," in the *Annual Report of the State Superintendent*, 1877, 330.

19. See *Incoming Correspondence to the State Superintendent of Public Instruction*, New York State Archives.

20. *Annual Report of the State Superintendent*, 1885, 411.

21. *Annual Report of the State Superintendent*, 1874, 57–58; 1876, 56–58.

22. *Annual Report of the State Superintendent*, 1885, 55–56.

23. New York (State). *Revised statutes of the state of New-York, relating to common schools, passed in the year 1827, being part of the title second of chapter fifteenth of part first; together with amendments thereto by subsequent acts; with the forms and regulations prepared by the superintendent of common schools, and also a variety of decisions in cases of appeal to him* (Albany: Crowell, Van Benthuysen, and Burt, 1836); Samuel Sidwell Randall, *A digest of the common school system of the state of New-York together with the forms, instructions, and decisions of the superintendent : An abstract of the various local provisions applicable to the several cities &c. : and a sketch of the origin, progress, and present condition of the system* (Albany: C. Van Benthuysen, 1844).

24. Emerson Keyes, *Laws of New York relating to common schools, with comments and instructions and a digest of decisions. Prepared under the supervision of Neil Gilmour, superintendent of public instruction* (Albany: Weed, Parsons, and Co., 1879).

25. *Annual Report of the State Superintendent*, 1887, 287.

26. *Annual Report of the State Superintendent*, 1888–1892.

27. Iowa had a similar process of appeals in the nineteenth century.

28. A brief history of the appeals can be found in Thomas E. Finegan, *Judicial Decisions of the State Superintendent of Common Schools* (1913), 1–2.

29. Finegan, *Judicial Decisions*, 1. By the early twentieth century, it came to resemble a formal court proceeding much more closely (see Brubacher, *The Judicial Power*, 1–5). Brubacher also notes that the Superintendent actually lost the power through a clerical error from 1849 to 1853, although it is quite probable that it was not an error at all but part of a political backlash against centralization (64).

30. Title XII, Section 1, Chapter 555, Laws of 1864.

31. A fairly complete record of appeals begins with decision dates of January 1868 and on. Before that, five survive from 1858 to 1865, and a handwritten list of appeals exists from 1842. In his annual report in 1875, the Superintendent reported that from 1855 to 1865, the average number of appeals per year was 105. From 1865 to 1875, it was 124 (p. 54.) The jump can be explained by the change in state law requiring all public schools to be free of charge. The 1867 law caused a sudden avalanche of appeals over boundary lines and tax rates, because suddenly both mattered much more than previously.

32. Title XII, Section 1, Chapter 555, General School Laws of the State of New York, 1864.

33. By the 1890s, personal appearances by litigants, in addition to their written documents, became more common as railroads connected remote counties to the state capital.

34. Brubacher. *The Judicial Power*, 27, notes that not until 1887 did the rules of procedure mention attorneys, suggesting that around that time, their use had become more common.

35. Legal costs appear to have been greater for districts that could afford an attorney's full services than for individuals, who appear to have used attorneys to write or advise a single letter of appeal, but who then handled correspondence and follow-up themselves.

36. Because the decisions do not survive, it is difficult to determine whether the use of an attorney correlated with success in an appeal. Further research on this question, if possible, would be interesting.

37. Appeal Case number 4584, decided 9/27/1897, as cited in Finegan, *Judicial Decisions*, 121–25.

38. Title XII, Section 1, Chapter 555, Laws of 1864.

39. A selection of decisions appears in several nineteenth-century digests, and finally in a comprehensive digest by Finegan, *Judicial Decisions*, in 1913. Fortunately, he had completed most of his manuscript before the capital fire. These digests reflect the biases of their publishers about what were considered significant decisions but nevertheless manage to list roughly 1,200 or one-tenth of the total. I rely on Finegan's decisions, which are often the only surviving record of the results of appeals, but do not offer any quantitative analysis of them—using the originals themselves instead.

40. James Crooker, *General School Laws of the State of New York, in Force July 1, 1893; Together with the Rules of Practice Governing Appeals to the Department of Public Instruction* (Albany: The Argus Company, Printers, 1893), 156.

41. Beginning in 1888, the state Office of Education published indexes of the appeals annually, including brief descriptions of their contents after 1892.

42. Population statistics are an average of county populations in 1870 and 1885. (As reported in the *Annual Reports of the Superintendent of Public Instruction of the State of New York* for the years 1870 and 1885, pages 73–75 and 39–41 respectively. Remarkable demographic changes in this period make any discussion of population over time difficult. Moreover, the township system of New York State, which functioned as a quasi-county system, makes differentiating between towns and villages far too complex here. A complex statistical analysis is a promising line of further research.

43. Arthur Conan Doyle, *The Complete Sherlock Holmes* (New York: Doubleday, 1930), 346–47.

44. On democratic localism, see Michael B. Katz, *Reconstructing American Education* (Cambridge: Harvard University Press, 1987).

45. Nevertheless, the lists correspond closely. In fact, Tyack, James, and Benavot found not only similar categories but similar ratios of types of legal dispute in judicial cases from West's Digest. See David Tyach, Thomas James, Aaron Benavot, *Law and the Shaping of Public Education* (Madison, University of Wisconsin Press, 1987) 70, appendix. This correspondence is not surprising, since appellants had to translate their practical concerns into a legal basis for appeal if they wanted to win.

46. For a full account of this issue, see chapter 5.

47. Not notably to academies, which remained under the Regents system and functioned more as normal schools than as common schools. The tale of the Bible Wars is told at its best in Ravitch, *The Great School Wars* (New York: Basic Books, 1974).

48. Finegan, *Judicial Decisions*, 527.

49. For a survey of significant decisions, see ibid., 524–532.

50. See chapter 4, "voting," for further discussion.

51. A random selection of appeals survives from 1856 to 1872, but the complete collection spans 1873 to 1879 and the first half of 1886. The letters are filed by county and year.

52. This number includes all letters from Albany through Livingston counties, alphabetically, plus New York City and a portion of Madison County.

53. Letter from L. B. Sackett, Poughkeepsie, Dutchess County, September 17, 1873.

54. Letter from George M. Russel, Chas'es Mills, St. Lawrence County, January 22, 1875.

55. *Annual Report of the State Superintendent*, 1871, 11.

56. See Table 6.1.

57. Letter from W. P. Todd, dated May 23, 1873, from Canisteo, Steuben County.

58. *Annual Report of the State Superintendent*, 1876, 72.

59. James H. Blodgett, *Report of the Population of the United States at the Eleventh Census: 1890. Part II. Educational Institutions* (Washington, D.C.: Government Printing Office, 1897).

60. *New York State Census for 1875*, 46–51; *Annual Report of the State Superintendent*, 1876, 71.

61. David P. Baker, "Schooling All of the Masses: Reconsidering the Origins of American Schooling in the Postbellum Era," *Sociology of Education* 72: 4 (1999): 197–216; Ravitch, *Great School Wars*, 405.

62. Nathan O. Hatch, *The Democratization of American Christianity* (New Haven: Yale University Press, 1989); Arthur M. Schlesinger Sr. "A Critical Period in American Religion, 1875–1900," in *Religion in American History: Interpretive Essays*

ed. John M. Mulder and John F. Wilson, (Englewood Cliffs, N.J.: Prentice-Hall, 1978) 302–14; Wintrop Hudson, *American Protestantism* (Chicago: University of Chicago Press, 1961).

63. Charles Glenn explores this line of reasoning for the antebellum period in *The Myth of the Common School* (Amherst: University of Massachusetts Press, 1988).

Part 2

1. Church calls for public money to support church schools made little impact on district schools and played a far greater role in urban schooling (see chapter 9).

Chapter 4

1. Thomas Bender, *Community and Social Change in America* (New Brunswick, N.J.: Rutgers University Press, 1977), 88.

2. *Annual Reports of the State Superintendent*, 1882, 1893.

3. *Annual Reports of the State Superintendent*, 1866, 15–17.

4. Barbara Finkelstein, *Teacher Behavior in Popular Primary Schools in the Nineteenth Century United States* (New York: Falmer Press, 1989).

5. Beginning in 1880, women could vote in district meetings and hold district office, though they were not eligible to vote in town, state, or national elections. The first record I found of a female trustee was in Mina, Chatauqua County, in 1880. The Superintendent mentioned that several women held district offices in his 1881 report (p. 26).

6. Ibid.

7. *Annual Reports of the State Superintendent*, 1871, 271.

8. Report of the First District of Jefferson County in *Annual Reports of the State Superintendent*, 1872, 249.

9. In appeal decision number 2830, a trustee in Portland, Chatauqua County, fired a teacher immediately on the charge that she was discriminating against Irish children in a predominantly native district (January 9, 1879).

10. Letters to the State Superintendent contain many references to such instances, and also to the purchase of globes and maps from similar agents. For an example, see *Annual Reports of the State Superintendent*, 1877, 329–30.

11. We know this from subsequent appeals from the fired teachers themselves. See appeal decision number 2952, filed 12/17/1879, and 2441, filed 12/18/1875. See chapter 6 for a further discussion of both cases.

12. Appeal decision number 2349, filed 5/12/1875, from Champlain, Clinton County.

13. The appeals documents are full of examples of this phenomenon. See also Wayne E. Fuller, *One-Room Schools of the Middle West* (Lawrence: University of Kansas Press, 1994).

14. Appeal decision number 2827, filed February 25, 1879.

15. Appeal decision number 2889, filed 7/31/79, from Binghamton; number 2980, filed 12/22/79, from Newfield, Tompkins County; number 3315, filed 1/12/84, from East Chester, Westchester County; number 3480, filed 9/17/85, from Hartsville and Canistro, Steuben County.

16. Appeal decision number 2892, filed 9/15/79, from Oswego, Oswego County; unnumbered appeal decision, filed 12/17/68, from Nelson Beardsley, Middletown, Deleware County; and others not recorded.

17. Charles Nordhoff, *The Communistic Societies of the United States* (New York: 1875), 256.

18. Church elders selected the teacher, just as they directed the employment of all members of the society, and the trustee gave formal assent to the arrangement.

19. For a more complete picture of the Shakers, see Henri Desroche, *The American Shakers: From Neo-Christianity to Presocialism* (Amherst: University of Massachusetts Press, 1971). The details of the Watervliet Shakers come from appeal number 3193, filed April 8, 1882.

20. C. W. Eaton, *Census of the State of New York for 1875* (Albany: Weed, Parsons and Co. Printers, 1877).

21. Ibid.

22. Hamlin Littell, *From State Church to Pluralism: A Protestant Interpretation of Religion in American History* (New York: Macmillan, 1971), 36.

23. Kevin J. Christiano, *Religious Diversity and Social Change: American Cities, 1890–1906* (New York: Cambridge University Press, 1987), 32–36.

24. No accurate contemporary account exists of the percent of Irish immigrants that was Protestant or Catholic, either as full members of churches or in a broader cultural sense, or the percent of Irish immigrants that had no religion at all, though Irish immigrants were increasingly Catholic, and devout, as the nineteenth century progressed. Roughly one-third of German immigrants were Catholic. See Charles R. Morris, *American Catholic* (New York: Times Books, 1997), 50–51; Kirby A. Miller, *Emigrants and Exiles: Ireland and the Irish Exodus to North America* (New York: Oxford University Press, 1985).

25. John Webb Pratt, *Religion, Politics, and Diversity: The Church-State Theme in New York History* (Ithaca: Cornell University Press, 1967), 201.

26. Christiano, *Religious Diversity*, 37.

27. Although it described urban immigration, John Bodnar's, *The Transplanted: A History of Immigration in Urban America* (Bloomington: University of Indiana Press, 1985), describes a process that appears to apply to rural migration as well.

28. On the concept of "covenanted" communities in settlement, see Page Smith, *As a City upon a Hill: The Town in American History* (New York: Knopf, 1966).

29. Unnumbered appeal from district five, Ossining, Westchester County, filed June 7, 1872, decided August 7, 1872.

30. To this end, I used Edward MacLysaught, *The Surnames of Ireland* (Dublin: Irish Academic Press, 1985).

31. Lloyd Jorgenson notes that ethnically centered districts were common in rural Wisconsin in this period. See *The Founding of Public Education in Wisconsin* (Madison: State Historical Society of Wisconsin, 1956), 145–50.

32. Letters dated 1/11/1873 from Huntington, Suffolk County, and 10/14/1874 from New Utrecht, King's County.

33. See "German in Public Schools: Its Direct and Tangible Value," pamphlet by E. Steiger. (Letter to the Superintendent, filed April 28, 1874).

34. See letter dated 10/23/1879 from Lawrenceville, Saint Lawrence County, by William Kingston; letter dated 12/12/1879 from Vienna, Oneida County, by E. H. Huniston; letter dated 11/17/1876 from Brockport, Monroe County, by David A. Wallace; letter dated 12/28/1857 from Parishville, Niagara County, by H. M. Daggett; letter dated 3/30/1873 from Massena, Saint Lawrence County, by George Minkler; letter dated 7/13/1874 from North Castle, Westchester County, by Casper Brower; latter dated 6/24/1874 from Crawford, Orange County, by Leandro Gillespie.

35. By homogeneous Protestant I mean espousing a Pan-Protestant ideology that had become increasingly common after the Civil War. Individuals identifying themselves as such often did so in opposition to immigrants, describing themselves as "Americans," "Protestants," or "Native born." See John Higham, *Strangers in the Land: Patterns in American Nativism* (New Brunswick: Rutgers University Press, 1998) for more on nativism.

36. Appeal decision number 2755, Granville, Washington County, filed October 7, 1878.

37. Appeal decision number 3073, Marselis, Onondaga County, filed November 30, 1880.

38. Ibid. German language instruction—as a separate course of study—commonly accompanied German migration and was common practice in Buffalo, New York, and other cities with sizeable German populations. (See *Annual Reports of the Board of Education of Buffalo, New York*, 1870–1890, *Annual Reports of the Board of Education of the City of New York*, 1870–1890). For a close analysis of the politics of German language instruction, see Selwyn Troen, *The Public and the Schools: Shaping the Saint Louis System, 1838–1920* (Columbia: University of Missouri Press, 1975).

39. Textbooks became relatively politically and religiously neutral after the Civil War, as states passed uniform textbook laws and professional educators broke the antebellum Yankee ministers' monopoly on textbook production. See David B. Tyack, "Monuments Between Covers: The Politics of Textbooks," *American Behavioral Scientist,*Vol. 42 No. 6 (March, 1999): 922–32; R. M. Elson, *Guardians of Tradition: American Schoolbooks of the Nineteenth Century* (Lincoln: University of Nebraska Press, 1964); John Westerhoff, *McGuffey and His Readers: Piety, Morality, and Education in 19th Century America* (Nashville: Abington Press, 1978); Dolores P. Sullivan, *William Holmes McGuffey: Schoolmaster to the Nation* (Rutherford, N.J.: Farleigh Dickenson University Press, 1994); Thomas J. Davis, Images of Intolerance: John Calvin in Nineteenth-Century History Textbooks," *Church History* 65: 2 (1996): 234.

40. Appeal decision number 2755, Granville, Washington County, filed October 7, 1878, emphasis in original.

41. See letter from Romulus Center, Seneca County, dated 9/15/73, and appeal decision number 2755, July 1878, from Granville, Washington County.

42. Women fell into the second category, according to the case law of the State Superintendent. See *Annual Report of the State Superintendent*, 1881, 26.

43. Lee Benson. *The Concept of Jacksonian Democracy* (Princeton: Princeton University Press, 1961), 165; John Webb Pratt, *Religion, Politics, and Diversity: The Church-State Theme in New York History* (Ithaca: Cornell University Press, 1967), 158–203; David B. Tyack and Elisabeth Hansot, *Managers of Virtue: Public School Leadership in America, 1820–1980* (New York: Basic Books, 1982), 74; Jerome Mushkat, *The Reconstruction of New York Democracy, 1861–1874* (Rutherford, N.J.: Farleigh Dickenson University Press, 1981), 20–21; Jean H. Baker, *Affairs of Party: The Political Culture of Northern Democrats in the Mid-Nineteenth Century* (Cornell University Press, 1983); Paul Kleppner, *The Third Electoral System: 1853–1892: Parties, Voters, and Political Cultures* (Chapel Hill: University of North Carolina Press, 1979), 97–142; "The Democratic Party and its public schools. Gov. Tildon favors appropriations for the support of Roman Catholic parochial schools" and "Politics and the school question. Attitudes of the Republican and Democratic parties in 1876," from *25 Pamphlets on Education*, Department of Special Collections, Milbank Memorial Library, Teachers College, Columbia University.

44. Pratt, *Religion, Politics, and Diversity*, 158–203.

45. James C. Mohr, "New York, the Depoliticization of Reform," in *Radical Republicans in the North: State Politics during Reconstruction*, ed. James C. Mohr (Baltimore: Johns Hopkins University Press, 1976), 66–81.

46. Unnumbered appeal, dated March 30, 1870, from misc. appeals documents in box 13. For another example, see letter dated 12/12/1879 from Vienna, Oneida County, by E. H. Huniston.

47. Appeal decision number 2878, filed 4/10/1879.

48. Appeal decision number 3040, filed December 28, 1880. See Nordhoff, *Communistic Societies*, 256, for number of statistics on various Shaker communities in New York State.

49. Appeal decision number 2822, filed February 15, 1879. See also appeal decision number 3353, filed 10/20/1883, from Westchester, Westchester County.

50. For example, see letter dated 10/19/74 from Malden, Ulster County, by G. A. Davidson; letter dated 10/19/1874 from Big Indian, Ulster County, by David Davis.

51. *Rochester Daily Union and Advertiser*, January 8, 1880.

52. Letter from William W. Clark, in appeal decision number 2913, filed November 12, 1879.

53. Letter from George Morehouse, in appeal decision number 2913, filed November 12, 1879.

54. *Rochester Daily Union and Advertiser*, January 8, 1880.

55. Letter from Reverend S. M. Dayton, in appeal decision number 2913, filed November 12, 1879.

56. Letter dated 6/24/1874 from Canisteo, Steuben County, by W. P. Todd, commissioner.

57. *Census of the State of New York for 1875*, 42.

58. *Rochester Daily Union and Advertiser*, January 8, 1880.

59. See, for example, letter dated February 25, 1873, from Lancaster, Erie County, by Frederick H. James.

60. James W. Sanders, *The Education of an Urban Minority: Catholics in Chicago, 1833–1965* (New York: Oxford University Press, 1977). The bishops of Rochester and Buffalo showed similar hostility. See chapter 8 for a full discussion. See also letter dated November 2, 1874, by Horace Brown, Adams, Jefferson County, in *Incoming Correspondence.*

61. James C. Mohr, *The Radical Republicans and Reform in New York during Reconstruction* (Ithaca: Cornell University Press, 1972), 153-201; Morton Keller, *Affairs of State: Public Life in Late Nineteenth Century America* (Cambridge: Harvard University Press, 1977), 134.

62. Tyack and Hansot, *Managers of Virtue*, 74–75.

63. This analysis applies more to towns than villages, where economic relations more closely resembled classes. The public school as a creature of the middle class became increasingly evident in the high school movement. See Michael B. Katz, *Reconstructing American Education* (Cambridge: Harvard University Press, 1987), William J. Reese, *The Origins of the American High School* (New Haven: Yale University Press, 1995); David F. Labaree, *How to Succeed in School without Really Learning: The Credentials Race in American Education* (New Haven: Yale University Press, 1997).

64. Letter dated 2/25/1874 from Lancaster, Erie County, by F. H. James; Appeal decision 2306, filed 10/30/74 from Southfield, Richmond County.

65. There are many examples of this phenomenon throughout the appeals and letters to the Superintendent. For example, see unnumbered appeal dated January 29, 1872, from Cornwall, Orange County.

66. See letter dated November 2, 1874, by Horace Brown.

67. Report of the second district of Washington County, *Annual Report of the State Superintendent*, 1873, 358.

68. *Census of the State of New York for 1875*, 168–69.

69. The legal issue was a number of illegal voters. Appeal decision number 2791, filed 11/4/1878.

70. Ibid.

Chapter 5

1. Appeal decision number 4419, published in *Annual Report of the State Superintendent*, 1896, 85–89.

2. I say approximately because records for 1867 and 1887 to 1892 are incomplete. Moreover, after 1899, the Superintendent no longer identified appeals over religious meetings as distinctive from "improper use of schoolhouse." While some of these are described in the annual reports, others are not.

3. Letter dated November 17, 1879, from Saugerties.

4. Appeal decision number 1381, filed December 14, 1867, by A. L. Halbert, district six Bolivar, Allegany County. Appeal 1501, filed June 17, 1868, by Jackson Canfield, Orange County, also noted that the district would never have agreed to pay $4,500 for their school "for school purposes alone."

5. Appeal Decision number 2362, filed February 27, 1875.

6. This affected a boundary dispute as well in Jefferson County. See appeal decision number 2333, filed 11/1874, from Henderson, Jefferson County. See also letter dated 2/3/1879 from State Bridge, Oneida County, by Butcher.

7. Appeal decision number 3410, filed 2/17/1885.

8. Appeal decision number 2820, filed 2/10/1879, from Freemont, Steuben County; appeal decision number 2304, filed 11/10/1874, from Wellsville, Allegany County; appeal decision number 2860, filed 3/24/1879; letter dated 5/21/1874, from Stissing, Dutchess County, by E. R. Beckwith; letter dated 8/2/1875, from Dover Plains, Dutchess County, by Horace Butts; letter dated 10/14/1874 from Wells Bridge, Otsego County, by Beardsley; and others.

9. There are no reliable statistics from this period. Winthrop Hudson, *American Protestantism* (Chicago: University of Chicago Press, 1961) estimated that membership rose to one-eighth of the population in 1850 and one-seventh by 1860.

10. Curtis D. Johnson, *Islands of Holiness* (Ithaca, Cornell University Press, 1989), 51; Glenn C. Altschuler and Jan M. Saltzgaber, *Revivalism, Social Conscience, and Community in the Burned-Over District: The Trial of Rhoda Bement* (Ithaca: Cornell University Press, 1983), 27, 33. See also decision number 3410, filed 2/17/1885, from Rodman, Jefferson County.

11. Nathan O. Hatch, *The Democratization of American Christianity* (New Haven: Yale University Press, 1989); Jon Butler, *Awash in a Sea of Faith: Christianizing the American People* (Cambridge: Harvard University Press, 1990), 257–88.

12. Nathan O. Hatch, "The Puzzle of American Methodism," *Church History*, 63 (1994): 175–89.

13. Paul E. Johnson, *A Shopkeeper's Millennium* (New York: Hill and Wang, 1978); Johnson, *Islands of Holiness*; Mary P. Ryan, *Cradle of the Middle Class: The Family in Oneida County, New York, 1790–1865* (New York: Cambridge University Press, 1981).

14. Curtis Johnson has generated a paradigm for understanding Protestantism that transcends the litergical/pietistic dichotomy, instead creating a grid along two axies, antiformal versus formal and evangelical versus nonevangelical. See *Islands of Holiness*, 101.

15. A. Gregory Schneider, *The Way of the Cross Leads Here: The Domestication of American Methodism* (Bloomington: University of Indiana Press, 1993), 170, 203–207.

16. Appeal decision number 2860, filed 3/24/1879 from Penfield, Monroe County.

17. Unnumbered decision, filed 1/21/1871, from district number six, Candor, Tioga County.

18. Appeal decision number 2304, filed November 5, 1874, from Wellsville, Allegany County.

19. C. W. Eaton, *Census of the State of New York for 1875* (Albany: Weed, Parsons, and Co., Printers, 1877), 275.

20. Appeal decision numbers 4061, 4419, 3410, and 4021.

21. At approximately 2,500 letters a year and a complaint rate of .4 percent. Also, appeals for several years are lost, but they averaged one a year. See Table 5.1.

22. Hatch, "The Puzzle of American Methodism," 175.

23. Subdivision 6 of section 47, article 6, title 7, of the consolidated school law of 1894 defines the trustees' powers. Section 52 of the same article says that the trustee may permit "the schoolhouse, when not in use for the district school, to be used by persons assembling therein for the purpose of giving and receiving instruction in any branch of learning or education or in the science or practice of music." The statutes in the consolidated school law of 1864 are identical. (See section 52, article 6, title 7, of the consolidated school law of 1864.)

24. As cited in John Seiler Brubacher, *The Judicial Power of the New York Commissioner of Education* (New York: Teachers College Publications, 1927), 131.

25. For examples of decisions in sequential order, see Thomas E. Finegan, *Judicial Decisions of the State Superintendent of Common Schools* (1913), 877–84.

26. Decision number 2860, filed 3/24/1879.

27. *Statistics of the United States (Including Mortality, Property, Etc.) in 1860.* (Washington, D.C.: Government Printing Office, 1866), 434; *Compendium of the 11th Census: 1890. Part Two* (Washington, D.C.: Government Printing Office, 1894), 265.

28. Appeal decision number 2304 from Wellsville, Allegany County, 11/5/1874.

29. See appeal filed 1/21/1871 from Candor, Tioga County; letter dated 4/28/1874 from Golden, Erie County.

30. Letter dated 3/12/1886 from Corning, Steuben County, by Mrs. L. E. Wood.

31. Letter dated 8/2/1875 from Dover Plains, Dutchess County.

32. Decision number 4061, decided 3/12/1892, from New Baltimore, Greene County.

33. For other examples, see appeal number 2304; letter dated 5/9/1874 from Beaver Kills, Sullivan County, by Abraham Barber; letter dated 10/19/1874 from Big Indian, Ulster County, by David Davis.

34. Appeal with no decision number, decided 8/22/1870.

35. Ibid.

36. Appeal decision number 1871, filed 12/15/1870. *Census of the State of New York for 1875*, 4, 271.

37. Appeal with no decision number, filed 8/28/1873, from Hardinsburg, Ulster County.

38. Appeal decision number 1871.

39. Wayne E. Fuller, *One-Room Schools of the Middle West* (Lawrence: University of Kansas Press, 1994), 45.

40. Letter dated 8/20/1879 from Portville, Cattaraugus County, by McBride, who transcribed the notice in his letter.

41. Letter dated 8/24/1874 from Granger, Allegany County; letter dated 10/25/1873 from Clinton, Dutchess County; appeal with no decision number, filed 8/28/1873, from Middletown, Deleware County, and Hardinsburg, Ulster County; appeal decision number 2304, filed 11/5/1874, from Wellsville, Allegany County.

42. Appeal decision number 4419, published in *Annual Report of the State Superintendent*, 1896, 85–89.

CHAPTER 6

1. See Herbert Kliebard, ed, *Religion and Education in America: A Documentary History* (Scranton: International Book Company, 1969), 1–11.

2. The Superintendent held that optional exercises outside school hours were acceptable. See John Seiler Brubacher, *Judicial Power of The New York State Commissioner of Education* (New York: Teachers College Publications, 1927), 118.

3. Paul A. Carter, *The Spiritual Crisis of the Gilded Age* (Dekalb: Northern Illinois Press, 1971), 23–42.

4. For a sampling of these images, see Morton Keller, *The Art and Politics of Thomas Nast* (New York: Oxford University Press, 1968).

5. McQuaid of Rochester and Ryan of Buffalo, as well as individual priests in New York and Brooklyn, used this approach in the 1870s, which I discuss in detail in chapter 9. Father Gleason of Brooklyn bullied Catholic parents from the pulpit, saying, "Don't send your children to the public schools. You are jeopardizing your salvation, you are acting ignorantly and sinfully when you do so." See sermon from October 26, 1873, as cited in the *Catholic Union*, Buffalo, November 6, 1873, p. 5.

6. Charles R. Morris, *American Catholic: The Saints and Sinners Who Built America's Most Powerful Church* (New York: Random House, 1997), 69–71.

7. See chapter 1 for a full discussion.

8. James W. Fraser, *Between Church and State* (New York: Saint Martin's Press, 1999), 64.

9. David Grimstead, *American Mobbing* (New York: Oxford University Press, 1998), 223–24; Paul Kleppner, *The Third Electoral System* (Chapel Hill: University of North Carolina Press, 1979), 220–30. There is an unresolved paradox in Jean Baker's excellent book, *Affairs of Party: The Political Culture of Northern Democrats in the Mid-Nineteenth Century* (Ithaca: Cornell University Press, 1983). On the one hand, she argues that political party leaders "shaped and articulated inchoate mass sentiments but did not create them" (p. 23), and on the other hand, she asserts, correctly, that common schools had a strong tradition of avoiding partisanship, sectionalism, and sectarianism in actual practice (p. 28).

10. The argument of majority rule in religious instruction works better in units of analysis larger than the district. I treat neither issue here.

11. Letters to the State Superintendent suggest a similar story, though the small sample size is not conclusive.

12. *Annual Report of the State Superintendent*, 1879, 217–19.

13. George M. Fredrickson, "The Coming of the Lord: The Northern Protestant Clergy and the Civil War Crisis," in *Religion and the American Civil War*, ed. Randall M. Miller, Harry S. Stout, and Charles Reagan Wilson (New York: Oxford University Press, 1998), 110–30; Randall Miller, "Catholic Religion, Irish

Identity, and the Civil War," in *Religion and the American Civil War*, 261–96; Bertram W. Korn, *American Jewry and the Civil War* (New York: Atheneum, 1970), 15–56.

14. Miller, "Catholic Religion," 276.

15. Phillip S. Paludan, "Overview," in Miller, *Religion and the American Civil War*, 25–30.

16. Ibid., 30.

17. Hasia Diner, *The Jewish People in America: A Time for Gathering, The Second Migration, 1820-1880* (Baltimore: Johns Hopkins University Press, 1992), 156–60. This was true even though many Irish Catholics resisted the war. See Miller, "Catholic Religion."

18. Ward M. McAfee, *Religion, Race, and Reconstruction* (Albany: State University of New York Press, 1998), 27–56.

19. James Gibbons, *Our Christian Heritage* (Baltimore: J. Murphy and Company, 1889), 489–95.

20. David B. Tyack and Elisabeth Hansot, *Managers of Virtue* (New York: Basic Books, 1982), 74–75.

21. As cited in ibid.

22. As cited in Fraser, *Between Church and State*, 59–60.

23. "The School Question," *The Catholic World* 11 (April 1870): 95–104.

24. Tyack and Hansot, *Managers of Virtue*, 78.

25. *Christian Free Schools. The Matter Discussed, by Rev. Bernard John McQuaid at Rochester New York.* Reported and reprinted by the *Rochester Union and Advertiser*, December 9, 1871.

26. "Pastoral Letter of the Rt. Reverend Bishop Ryan," *The Catholic Union*, December 4, 1873, p. 3.

27. William T. Harris, "Some General Principles of Religious Instruction in the Schools," *The Independent* XLII: 2179 (September 4, 1890): 1.

28. Reported in the *Troy Morning Whig*, June 4, 1875.

29. Beecher can be found in No. 16, from *25 Pamphlets on Education* (Department of Special Collections, Milbank Memorial Library, Teachers College, Columbia University).

30. Robert S. Michaelsen, *Piety and the Public School* (New York: MacMillan, 1970), 95–116. The Catholic Church softened its position on Bible reading in the 1890s, with most New York-based clergy reconciling themselves to the necessity of public schooling—even for Catholic children.

31. Samuel Brown, *The Secularization of American Education* (New York: Teachers College, 1912), 63.

32. *Religion and Public Education: Reports of the Committee on Religion and Public Education, Presented to the Synod of New York of the Presbyterian Church in the United States of America, at Its Annual Meetings in Auburn, 1887 and in Poughkeepsie, 1889*, 43.

33. As cited in Brown, *Secularization*, 115.

34. Not to academies, which remained under the Regents system and functioned more as normal schools than as common schools.

35. For a survey of significant decisions, see Thomas E. Finegan, *Judicial Decisions of the State Superintendent of Common Schools* (1913), 524–32.

36. While it is possible that isolated, homogeneous districts could have engaged in denominational religious instruction, such instances were probably quite rare.

37. Such arrangements were possible under the common school system, but only if not a single resident objected and the teacher and trustee managed to keep the practice quiet. I have seen no evidence of explicitly denominational instruction beyond varying the version of the Scripture or choice of songs or prayer in opening exercises. Textbooks increasingly excluded God and religion after the Civil War, both as professional educators supplanted Yankee ministers in the supply of texts and as demand increased for textbooks that would not incite religious controversy or insult Catholic school board members. See Ruth Miller Elson, *Guardians of Tradition: American Schoolbooks of the Nineteenth Century* (Lincoln: University of Nebraska Press, 1964), 53–62, and Bessie Louise Pierce, *Public Opinion and the Teaching of History in the United States* (New York: Alfred A. Knopf, 1926), chap. 1–2.

38. *Religion and Public Education: Reports of the Committee on Religion and Public Education, Presented to the Synod of New York of the Presbyterian Church in the United States of America, at Its Meetings in Auburn, 1887 and in Poughkeepsie, 188*, 30–32.

39. For example, letter dated 3/6/1874 from Cato, Cayuga County, by Daratt. In fact, all letters that mention the starting time for school say it was 9:00 A.M.

40. Appeal decision number 2847, filed 2/13/1879.

41. Appeal with no decision number, filed 6/20/1870.

42. Letter dated 12/16/1882 from Saugerfield, Oneida County, by George Russell.

43. For a full discussion, see chapter 4.

44. McAfee, *Religion, Race and Reconstruction*, 39.

45. Annual Report of the State Superintendent, 1891, xxxiv–xxxvi.

46. See Wayne Fuller's descriptions of Midwestern schools in this period in *One Room Schools of the Middle West* (Lawrence: University of Kansas Press, 1994).

47. *Annual Report of the State Superintendent of Public Instruction*, 1903, 359.

48. As one commissioner put it, "Without the power to keep order in school, and that too, *generally*, without a resort to the rod, nobody is fit to teach." See *Annual Report of the State Superintendent*, 1881, 391.

49. Herbert M. Kliebard, "Constructing the Concept of Curriculum on the Wisconsin Frontier: How School Restructuring Sustained a Pedagogical Revolution," *History of Education* 25: 2, (1996): 123–39. For an example of New York developments, see *Annual Report of the State Superintendent*, 1880, 207–08.

50. Ibid.

51. As quoted in *Annual Report of the State Superintendent*, 1885, 303, 1880, 227. See also *Annual Report*, 1883, 249; *Annual Report* 1882, 215, 276–77.

52. *Annual Report of the State Superintendent, 1902*, appendix.

53. Appeal decision number 3410, filed 2/17/1885.

54. *Annual Report of the State Superintendent*, 1871, 245.

55. Appeal decision number 3155, filed 5/3/1881.

56. See *Annual Report of the State Superintendent*, 1885, 55–57.

57. See chapter 4.

58. Miller, "Catholic Religion" 265.

59. Letter dated 3/16/1874.

60. As cited in *Annual Report of the State Superintendent*, 1885, 55.

61. David B. Tyack, "The Kingdom of God and the Common School" *Harvard Educational Review* 36:4 (1966): 447–69; Timothy L. Smith, "Protestant Schooling and American Nationality, 1800–1850," *Journal of American History* 53:4 (March 1967): 679–95.

62. *Our Country: Its Possible Future and Present Crisis* (New York, Baker & Taylor Co. for the American Home Missionary Society, 1891).

63. *Annual Report of the State Superintendent*, 1870, 302.

64. John Higham, *Strangers in the Land* (New Brunswick: Rutgers University Press, 1998), chap. 2–3.

65. *Annual Report of the State Superintendent*, 1872, 292–93.

66. *Annual Report of the State Superintendent*, 1886, 343.

67. Paul A. Carter, *The Spiritual Crisis of the Guilded Age* (Dekalb: Northern Illinois Press, 1971), 23–42.

68. Henry King Carroll, *The Religious Forces of the United States, Enumerated, Classified, and Described on the Basis of the Government Census of 1890* (New York: Christian Literature Company, 1893).

69. Carter, *The Spiritual Crisis*, ix.

70. *The Forum*, December, 1886.

71. Tyack and Hansot, *Managers of Virtue*, 72–73.

72. This is Winthrop Hudson's main idea in *American Protestantism*, (Chicago: University of Chicago Press, 1961).

73. Higham, *Strangers in the Land*, chapters 2–3.

74. August Drahms, *The Criminal: His Personnel and Environment* (New York: 1900), 81.

75. *Annual Report of the State Superintendent*, 1879, 217–19.

76. Charles R. Kniker, "New Attitudes and New Curricula: The Changing Role of the Bible in Protestant Education, 1880–1920," in *The Bible in American Education: From Source Book to Textbook*, ed. David L. Barr and Nicholas Piediscalzi (Philadelphia: Fortress Press, 1982), 121–42.

77. *Annual Report of the State Superintendent*, 1903, xiv.

78. *Religion and Public Education*, 32–35.

79. Ibid., 35.

80. Ibid.

81. Ibid., 9–10.

82. Elizabeth Blanchard Cook, *The Nation's Book in the Nation's Schools* (Chicago: Chicago Woman's Educational Union, 1898), 16, 31–33.

83. Ibid.

84. Robert Michaelsen explores this as the "civil view" of religious instruction in *Piety and the Public School*, 100.

85. *Annual Report of the State Superintendent*, 1903, 383, 368.

86. As reported in the *Catholic Union*, Buffalo, February 19, 1874, p. 4.

87. Letter dated 7/13/1876 from Fairport, Monroe County, by Father J. Thompson.

88. Unnumbered appeal, dated 6/20/1870, from West Hurley, Ulster County.

89. Unnumbered appeal, filed 9/12/1870.

90. Letter dated 1/27/1874 from Montezuma, Cayuga County, by Julia O'Neil.

91. Ibid.

92. Latter dated 3/16/1874 from Cato, Cayuga County, by Daratt, commissioner.

93. Appeal decision number 2913, filed 11/12/1879.

94. John B. Buescher, *The Other Side of Salvation: Spiritualism and the Nineteenth Century Religious Experience* (Boston: Skinner House Books, 2003); Arthur Conan Doyle, *The History of Spiritualism* (New York: George H. Doran Company, 1926).

95. Letter dated 3/20/1873 by J. M. Phinney.

96. *Outgoing Correspondence of the Department of Public Instruction*, letter dated 4/1/1873.

97. Unnumbered appeal, filed 8/23/1870.

98. Appeal decision number 3443, filed 9/5/1885.

99. Appeal decision number 2847, filed 2/13/1879, from Arcade, Wyoming County.

100. Ibid.

101. Michaelsen, *Piety and the Public School*, 100.

102. *Annual Report of the State Superintendent*, 1885, 55–57.

103. Letter dated 4/14/1886; *Outgoing Correspondence*, dated 4/15/1886, from A. Draper.

104. Letter dated 12/20/1872.

105. See chapter 3.

106. Of the forty-seven cases of teachers challenging their annulled certificates in appeals from 1867 to 1886, none concerned religion as an explicit issue. The only example Finegan mentioned in 1912 came from an 1830 decision, which determined, "A teacher should not be questioned by the inspectors as to his religious opinions: but a person who openly derides all religion should not be employed as a teacher." See Finegan, *Judicial Decisions*, 1036.

107. Letter dated 3/16/1874 from Mentz, Cayuga County, by Daratt.

108. Letter dated 2/21/1874 from Tarrytown, Westchester County, by Casper Brower.

109. Appeal decision number 3443.

110. Appeal decision number 2886, filed 7/9/1879, from Dansville, Steuben County.

111. Ibid.

112. Ibid.

113. The first major case was *McCollum v. Board of Education of Champaign County*. See Vashti Cromwell McCollum, *One Woman's Fight* (Garden City: Doubleday, 1951).

114. Appeal decision number 2952, filed 12/17/1879.

115. Ibid. All documents in the appeal agree that this was Shults's purpose. Shults claimed that he did not have any conscientious objection to exercises per se, except for the strain they placed on district goodwill.

116. Ibid.

117. Ibid.

118. Decision number 2441, filed 12/18/1875.

119. Ibid. Technically, Bradman's appeal was brought on his behalf by another resident, S. S.Kling.

120. Ibid.

121. Letter filed 2/1/1876 from New Bremen, Lewis County.

PART 3

1. John W. Meyer and Brian Rowan, "Institutionalized Organizations: Formal Structure As Myth and Ceremony," *American Journal of Sociology* 83 (1977): 340–63.

CHAPTER 7

1. Auburn. *Annual Report of the Board of Education of the City of Auburn*, 1878, 20.

2. *Annual Report of the State Department of Education*, 1905, 45.

3. New York State. *Census of the State of New York for 1875*, 14–28.

4. Barbara Finkelstein, *Teacher Behavior in Popular Primary Schools the Nineteenth Century United States* (New York: Falmer Press, 1989); Diane Ravitch, *The Great School Wars* (New York: Basic Books, 1974), 100-106. Central high schools could exert pressure on all of the schools of a city to adopt a specific curriculum, for example, even without any formal regulations by a central board of education. See David F. Labaree, *The Making of an American High School: The Credentials Market and the Central High School of Philadelphia, 1838–1939* (New Haven: Yale University Press, 1988).

5. Although the original act made no mention of schooling, the legislature approved an educational plan a few months later.

6. Edward Smith, *A History of the Schools of Syracuse from Its Earliest Settlement to January 1, 1893* (Syracuse: C. W. Bardeen, 1893), 42–48.

7. Syracuse. *Annual Report of the Board of Education of the City of Syracuse*,1868, 1; 1889, 1; 1894, 1.

8. Quote from Syracuse. *Annual Report of the State Superintendent*, 1868, 108.

9. Brooklyn. *Annual Report of the Superintendent of Public Schools of the City of Brooklyn*, 1872, "Tabular Statements of the Public Schools, Evening Schools, and Orphan Asylums," 1–5.

10. See *Manuals of the Board of Education of the City of New York*, 1864–1876.

11. Personal communication from Alvina Tyropolis, Records Management Officer, Yonkers Public Schools, dated June 28, 2001, in possession of author; see also *Annual Reports of the Board of Education of the City of Yonkers*, 1881–1900.

12. *Annual Report of the State Superintendent of Public Instruction*, 1891, 415.

13. *Annual Report of the State Superintendent of Public Instruction*, 1905, 46.

14. See, for example, the annual reports of the Rochester and Syracuse boards of education.

15. David B. Tyack, *The One Best System* (Cambridge: Harvard University Press, 1974), 78–80.

16. Lockport appears to have been an exception to this generalization, as may have been the case with other small cities with few schools. See *Minutes of the Lockport Board of Education*, 1880–1890.

17. Theodore L. Reller, *The Development of the City Superintendency of Schools in the United States* (Piladelphia: Author, 1935), 101.

18. *The Catholic Union*, Buffalo, March 30, 1873, p. 4.

19. *Proceedings of the Common Council of the City of Buffalo* (Buffalo: Joseph Warren and Co., 1868–1900), 1885, 841; Buffalo. *Annual Report, Superintendent of Education*: 1886–87: 42–43; Gordon H. Higgins, *The District of Buffalo, New York and Its Schools from Settlement to Present Reconstruction* (Ph.D. diss., University of Buffalo School of Education, 1953), 99; Reller, *The Development of the City Superintendency of Schools in the United States* 8; Higgins, *A District of Buffalo*, 99.

20. Buffalo. *Annual Report of the Superintendent of Public Schools*, 1864, 28, 31.

21. *Proceedings of the Rochester Board of Education*, 3/31/1892. As we can see from Table 6.2, Rochester did reform its board of education, paring it down from twenty to five members by 1904.

22. Rochester. *Annual Report of the Superintendent of Schools*, 1858, 9–12.

23. Tyack, *One Best System*, 129–46.

24. See, for example, Harold Coffin Syrett, *The City of Brooklyn, 1865–1898: A Political History* (New York: Columbia University Press, 1944), 116.

25. Albany. *Annual Report of the Board of Public Instruction of the City of Albany*, 1866.

26. New York City. *Manual of the Board of Public Instruction of the City of New York*, 1871–72, 1873; Ravitch, *The Great School Wars*, 87–99.

27. Troy. *Manual of the Board of Education of the City of Troy*, 1873.

28. Elmira. *Annual Report of the Board of Education of the City of Elmira*, 1873, 1.

29. Ravitch, *The Great School Wars*, 97.

30. *Proceedings of the Brooklyn Board of Education*, 3/2/1869.

31. Brooklyn. *Educational Review* 8 (October 1894): 308–309.

32. Utica. *Annual Report of the Board of Education of the City of Utica*, 1889, 15; Ibid., 1890–95.

33. Paul Kleppner, *The Cross of Culture: A Social Analysis of Midwestern Politics* (New York: Free Press, 1970); Richard Jensen, *The Winning of the Midwest: Social and Political Conflict, 1888–1896* (Chicago: University of Chicago Press, 1971); Gerald Suttles, *The Social Order of the Slum: Ethnicity and Territory in the Inner City* (Chicago: University of Chicago Press, 1968); Morton Keller, *Affairs of State* (Cambridge: Harvard University Press, 1977).

34. For an overview of scholarly interpretations on the democratic functions of political machines, see Robert Barrows, "Urbanizing America," 106–107, and Ballard

C. Campbell, "Public Policy and State Government," in *The Guilded Age: Essays on the Origins of Modern America* ed. Charles W. Calhoun (Wilmington, Del.: Scholarly Press, 1996). Note that Republicans and native Protestants proved their own propensity to graft as well as Democrats and Catholics, particularly during the Grant administration.

35. Laurence Admiral Glascoe, *Ethnicity and Social Structure: Irish, German, and Native Born of Buffalo, New York 1850–1860* (Ph.D. diss., State University of New York at Buffalo, 1973), as cited in Maxine S. Seller, *Ethnic Communities and Education in Buffalo, New York: Politics, Power, and Group Identity 1838–1979* (Buffalo: State University of New York at Buffalo, 1979), 10–12.

36. The *Proceedings of the Common Council of the City of Buffalo*, 1873 and 1874, give limited evidence for this event, but a thoughtful account can be found in Seller, *Ethnic Communities and Education*, 18.

37. James C. Mohr, "New York: The Depoliticization of Reform," in *Radical Republicans in the North: State Politics During Reconstruction*, ed. James C. Mohr (Baltimore: Johns Hopkins Press. 1976), 68-79; Jerome Mushkat, *The Reconstruction of New York Democracy, 1861–1874* (Rutherford, N.J.: Farleigh Dickenson University Press, 1981), 20; David B. Tyack and Elisabeth Hansot, *Managers of Virtue: Public School Leadership in America, 1820–1980* (New York: Basic Books, 1982), 72-83; Keller, *Affairs of State*, 122-42.

38. Tyack, *One Best System*, 88.

39. See Rochester. *Proceedings of the Board of Education of the City of Rochester* and *Annual Reports of the Board of Education of the City of Rochester*, and Elmira. *Proceedings of the Board of Education of the City of Elmira.*

40. Brooklyn, *Daily Eagle*, July 9, 1873.

41. Seller, *Ethnic Communities*, 13.

42. *Proceedings*, 8/17/1875. Poughkeepsie is discussed at length in chapter 8.

43. On the ethnoreligious geography of cities, see Ralph Janis, *Church and City in Transition: The Social Composition of Religious Groups in Detroit, 1880–1940* (New York: Garland, 1990); Stuart M. Blumin, *The Emergence of the Middle Class: Social Experience in the American City, 1760–1900* (New York: Cambridge University Press, 1989).

44. Blumin *The Emergence*; Seller, *Ethnic Communities*, 9–10.

45. Robert Barrows, "Urbanizing America," in *The Guilded Age*, 91–110, 98–99.

46. Howard Ralph Weisz, *Irish-American and Italian-American Educational Views and Activities 1870–1900, a Comparison* (New York: Arno Press, 1976), 81; Ravitch, *The Great School Wars*, 108.

47. The annual reports of the boards of education and superintendents of New York City, Brooklyn, and Buffalo all list separate colored schools in the 1870s.

48. Buffalo. *Annual Report of the Superintendent of Education of the City of Buffalo*, 1874, 130, 146–47. Note, once again, that many ethnically Irish children of

the 1870s and 1880s had parents who had been born in the United States and were thus counted as "American born."

49. The board listed colored children separate from American ones. I have left the categories separate.

50. Finkelstein, *Governing the Young*; Ravitch, *The Great School Wars*, 100–106. Central high schools could exert pressure on all of the schools of a city to adopt a specific curriculum, for example, even without any formal regulations by a central board of education. See Labaree, *The Making of an American High School.*

51. See the annual reports or board proceedings of Elmira, Buffalo, Rochester, New York City, and Lockport.

52. See, for example, Helen Todd, "Why Children Work, the Children's Answer," *McClure's Magazine* 40 (April 1913): 68–79.

53. Finkelstein found it common for teachers to act as "interpreters of culture," that is, taking time to explain terminology or portions of text to the class as a whole. See Finkelstein, *Governing the Young*, 25.

54. "Italian Children Make Good Americans," *Buffalo Times*, November 24, 1902, from *Schools Scrapbook Collection*, Buffalo Public Library.

55. David W. Galenson, "Ethnic Differences in Neighborhood Effects on the School Attendance of Boys in Early Chicago," *History of Education Quarterly* 38:1 (Spring 1998): 17–35. See also James W. Sanders, *The Education of an Urban Minority: Catholics in Chicago, 1833–1965* (New York: Oxford University Press, 1977). On Boston's and Massachusetts's insensitivity to Catholics, see Lloyd Jorgenson, *The State and the Non-Public School* (Columbia: University of Missouri Press, 1987) chap. 8.

56. Carleton Mabee, *Black Education in New York State, From Colonial Times to Present* (Syracuse: Syracuse University Press, 1979) 193–212.

57. Weisz, *Irish-American and Italian-American Educational Views and Activities 1870-1900, a Comparison*, 78–80.

58. *State Census for 1875*, 47; Weisz, *Irish-American*, 78.

59. Albany. *Annual Report of the Board of Education of the City of Albany*, 1885, 143–44.

60. Brooklyn. *Proceedings of the Board of Education*, 4/7/1881.

61. Ibid., 4/12/1881, 4/16/2001, 4/20/1881, 8/2/1881.

62. Lockport. *Minutes of the Lockport Board of Education*, 2/1/1880.

63. Ibid., 1880–1885, 5/29/1885.

64. Tyack, *One Best System*, part 4; Tyack, "School Governance in the United States: Historical Puzzles and Anomalies," in *Decentralization and School Improvement: Can We Fulfill the Promise?* ed. Jane Hannaway and Martin Carnoy, (San Francisco: Josey-Bass, 1993),1–32; On progressive educational penal reform, see

Benjamin Justice, "'A College of Morals': Educational Reform at San Quentin Prison, 1880–1920," *History of Education Quarterly* 40: 3 (Fall 2000): 279–301.

65. Ravitch, *The Great School Wars*, 144–58; Tyack, *One Best System*, 133.

66. New York State. *First Annual Report of the Education Department of the State of New York*: (Albany: New York State Education Department, 1905), 46–47.

CHAPTER 8

1. Lloyd Jorgenson, *The State and the Non-Public School* (Columbia: University of Missouri Press, 1987), 74–98; Ravitch, *The Great School Wars* (New York: Basic Books, 1974), 67–76; Arthur Jackson Hall, *Religious Education in the Public Schools of the State and City of New York, A Historical Study* (Ph.D. diss, University of Chicago, 1914), 80-87.

2. Edward Smith, *A History of the Schools of Syracuse From its Earliest Settlement to January 1, 1893* (Syracuse: C. W. Barden 1893), 48–49; Syracuse. *Annual Report of the Board of Education of the City of Syracuse*, 1868, 109.

3. New York City. *Manual of the Board of Education, 1866*, 36–37. Brooklyn. *Proceedings of the Board of Education of the City of Brooklyn*, 5/7/1867.

4. Lockport. *Rules and Regulations of the Board of Education and Public Schools of the City of Lockport, New York. Adopted June 23, 1885*, 14.

5. For example, Troy and Rochester.

6. Brooklyn. *Proceedings of the Board of Education of the City of Brooklyn*, 5/7/1867. Syracuse. *Annual Report of the Board of Education of the City of Syracuse*, 1868, 109, and others.

7. Jamestown. *Annual Report of the Board of Education of the City of Jamestown*, 1890, 24.

8. "Board of Education," *Rochester Union and Advertiser*, 6/18/1875; Brooklyn. *Proceedings*, 5/7/1867; Rochester. *Proceedings of the Rochester Board of Education*, 9/6/1875; *Annual Report of the State Superintendent*, 1903, 358.

9. State Superintendent Weaver, in his decision on the Long Island City case, 1872. As cited in Thomas E. Finegan, *Judicial Decisions of the State Superintendent of Common Schools* (1913), 530.

10. Timothy L. Smith, "Protestant Schooling and American Nationality, 1800–1850," *The Journal of American History*, 53: 4 (March 1967), 679–95.

11. *The Catholic Union*, November 18, 1874, p. 5; December 2, 1874, p. 8; December 9, 1874, p. 9; December 16, 1874, p. 4; S. V. Ryan, "'A Plea for Christian Schools': Lecture by Rt. Rev. S. V. Ryan, D. D., Bishop of Buffalo, Delivered at St. James Hall, Thursday Evening, February 25, 1875." Printed in full in *The Catholic Union*, Buffalo, March 3, 1875, pp. 4–8; Bernard McQuaid, *Christian Free Schools. The Matter Discussed. Part Two. A Lecture Delivered at Corinthian Hall, Rochester,*

New York, on May 16, 1872, 19 (bound in *12 Pamphlets on Education*, Special Collections Department, Milbank Library, Teachers College); Jorgenson, *The State and the Non-Public School* 118–19.

12. Paradoxically, Pope Pius rejected the notion of religious liberty in his infamous syllabus of errors in 1864, even as Catholics in America demanded it.

13. *The Bible in the Public Schools: The Opinion and the Decision of the Supreme Court of Ohio in the Case of John D. Minor versus the Board of Education, City of Cincinnati. Extracted from Volume 23, Ohio State Reports* (Cincinnati: Robert Clarke and Company, 1873) (bound in *12 Pamphlets on Education*, Special Collections Department, Milbank Library, Teachers College); F. Michael Perko, *A Time to Favor Zion: A Case Study of Religion As a Force in American Educational Development, 1830–1870* (Ph.D. diss., Stanford University, 1981).

14. See *Proceedings of the Buffalo Common Council, Proceedings of the Rochester Board of Education, Proceedings of the Brooklyn Board of Education, and Proceedings of the Elmira Board of Education, Syracuse Board of Education*, 1867–1871. Nor did the village of Saratoga Springs (see minutes of the Saratoga Springs Board of Education, City of Saratoga Springs Archives).

15. Appeal of the Trustees of Ward One against the Board of Education, Reply of the Board of Education.

16. *Census of the State of New York for 1875*, 28.

17. Unnumbered appeal, filed 2/7/1872, entitled *Board of Trustees of Ward One vs. Board of Education of Long Island City.*

18. *Trustees vs. L.I. City Board of Education*, statement of William Sieberg. The board also fired an Irish teacher, P. J. O'Grady, who appealed to the State Superintendent of Public Instruction. See unnumbered appeal, filed 8/11/1871.

19. "Reply of the Board of Education" from unnumbered appeal, filed 2/7/1872.

20. Unnumbered appeal, filed 2/7/1872.

21. No. 429 of the Acts of the Plenary Council of Baltimore. P. CIII, 1868 edition, as cited in appeals documents.

22. See all three appeals cases from Long Island City, 1872.

23. Appeal of the Trustees, testimony of Sieberg.

24. Appeal of the Trustees, reply of the board.

25. Appeal of the Trustees.

26. Testimony of Sieberg.

27. Unnumbered appeal from Long Island City by Edward McBennett, dated 1/ 31/1872.

28. Point number 38 in Appeal by the Trustees.

29. Finegan, *Judicial Decisions*, 524-32.

30. Ibid., 530–31.

31. Finegan noted no such case as of 1913, the year of his publication.

32. Eugene Lawrence, "Hunter's Point—Compulsory Education," *Harper's Weekly*, December 23, 1871.

33. Eugene Lawrence, "The Bible at Hunter's Point," *Harper's Weekly*, January 6, 1872; "The Bible in the Schools," June 29, 1872; "Romish Ingratitude," July 13, 1872; "Hunter's Point—Romish Politics," August 17, 1872; Thomas Nast, "Romish Ingratitude," July 13, 1872; "Romish Politics—Anything to Beat Grant,"August 17, 1872.

34. Thomas Nast, "Romish Politics—Anything to Beat Grant," *Harper's Weekly*, August 17, 1872.

35. Auburn. *Annual Report of the Board of Education of the City of Auburn*, 1877, 33–34.

36. Emphasis in original. "Popular Education versus Sectarianism," *Hours at Home* 11:1, (May 1870). Bound in 25 *Pamphlets on Education* at the Special Collections Branch of the Milbank Library, Teachers College.

37. Timothy Walch, *Parish School: American Catholic Parochial Education From Colonial Times to the Present* (New York: Crossroad Publishing Co.,1996), 37.

38. Waclaw Kruszka, *A History of the Poles in America to 1908*, ed. James S. Pula (Washington, D.C.: Catholic University of America, 1993), 110.

39. McQuaid, *Christian Free Schools*, 10.

40. McQuaid, *Christian Free Schools*; Howard Ralph Weisz, *Irish-American and Italian-American Educational Views and Activities 1870–1900, a Comparison* (New York: Arno Press, 1976), xii.

41. Weisz, *Irish-American and Italian-American Educational Views*, 54–56, as quoted on p. 56.

42. David P. Baker, "The Politics of American School Expansion, 1870–1930," in *The Political Construction of Education: The State, School Expansion, and Economic Change*, ed. Bruce Fuller and Richard Rubinson (New York: Praeger, 1992), 189–206.

43. Auburn. *Annual Report of the Board of Education of the City of Auburn*, 1880, 29.

44. McQuaid, *Christian Free Schools.*

45. David Baker, "Schooling All of the Masses Reconsidering the Origins of American Schooling in the Postbellum Era," *Sociology of Education* 72:4 (1999): 197–216. Baker estimates that percentage as Catholic enrollment/Catholic + public enrollment. Adding in the many private, non-Catholic schools in the city would no doubt push that 12 percent down significantly. Using Ravitch's figures, estimated Catholic enrollment/all school enrollments in New York City was 8 percent in 1870, 11 percent in 1880, 16 percent in 1890, and 17 percent in 1900.

46. *Annual Report of the State Superintendent*, 1882, 38-41 (see Ravitch, *The Great School Wars*, 405–406).

47. Baker, "Schooling All of the Masses," 197–216; Ravitch, *The Great School Wars*, 405.

48. See comments of superintendent in Rochester. *Proceedings of the Board of Education*, 9/6/2875; comments of principal of School Two, Long Island City, in unnumbered appeal, by Edward McBennett dates 1/31/1872; "Report of the Superintendent of Dunkirk," in *Annual Report of the State Superintendent*, 1903, 358.

49. Elizabeth Blanchard Cook, *The Nation's Book In the Nation's Schools* (Chicago: The Chicago Women's Educational Union, 1898), appendix.

50. As a child I attended a number of Pan-Christian worship ceremonies at Catholic and Protestant churches, usually under the auspices of the Boy Scouts of America. When Catholic priests led the prayer, they stopped at the end of the Catholic (short) version. When Protestant ministers led the prayer, they plowed through to the end of the Protestant (long) version. In both situations, the congregation behaved in the same fashion: some stopping short and some going long, and in all cases without comment from the leadership.

51. 7/27/1889, 50.

52. See also Timothy Walch, *Parish School: American Catholic Parochial Education from Colonial Times to the Present* (New York: Crossroad, 1996), 57–62.

53. Weisz, *Irish-American and Italian-American Educational Views*, 51–78.

54. Maxine Seller, *Ethnic Communities and Education in Buffalo New York: Politics, Power and Group Identity, 1838–1979* (Buffalo: State University of New York Press at Buffalo, 1979), 51.

55. Ibid., 77.

56. Brooklyn. *Proceedings of the Board of Education*, 4/5/1887, 6/7/1887.

57. Selma Berrol, "The Open City: Jews, Jobs, and Schools in New York City, 1880–1915," in *Educating an Urban People: The New York City Experience*, ed. Diane Ravitch and Ronald K. Goodenow (New York: Teachers College Press, 1981), 101–15, 105.

58. Commissioner Michaels of Rochester cited a recent appeal to the board of education of Albany by a leading rabbi there.

59. McQuaid, *Christian Free Schools*, 19.

60. Rochester. *Proceedings of the Board of Education of the City of Rochester*, 1872–1875.

61. See *Troy Daily Press*, 1874–1875, *Troy Morning Whig*, 1874–1875, *Saint Lawrence Republican* and *Ogdensburg Weekly Journal*, 1866–1877, *Albany Argus* 1873–1875; for an example of the religious press, see Buffalo, *The Catholic Union*, which kept up a steady barrage of articles on religion in public schools throughout the 1870s.

62. *Albany Argus*, July 9, 1875, p. 4.

63. *Troy Daily Press*, vol. VII, 1874–1875; board meetings were on the first Tuesday of each month and reported on in Wednesday's paper. The final meeting was on June 1, 1875.

64. Troy. *Manual of the Board of Education*, 1873.

65. The committee's action was reported in the *New York Times*, "The Bible to be Banished from the Troy Public Schools," May 30, 1875, p. 2 col. 6.

66. Ibid., Wednesday, June 2, 1875.

67. *Troy Daily Press*, June 2, 1875.

68. Ibid., June 5, 1875.

69. "Shall the State Conduct Religious Exercises in State Schools?," *Rochester Daily Union and Advertiser*, June 7, 1875.

70. "Board of Education," *Rochester Union and Advertiser*, June 18, 1875; Rochester. *Proceedings of the Board of Education*, 6/7/1875, 6/21/1875.

71. "Board of Education," *Rochester Union and Advertiser*, June 18, 1875; Rochester. *Proceedings of the Board of Education*, 6/7/1875, 6/21/1875.

72. "Religious Exercises of Every Nature Prohibited in the Rochester Public Schools," *Rochester Union and Advertiser*, June 8, 1875; "The Prohibition of Religious Exercises in the Public Schools," *Rochester Union and Advertiser*, June 16, 1875.

73. According to the *Catholic Union* of Buffalo, July 15, 1875, p. 1.

74. Edward Michael Connors, *Church-State Relationships in Education in the State of New York* (Washington, D.C.: Catholic University of America Press, 1951), 78.

75. "Board of Education," *Rochester Union and Advertiser*, June 18, 1875; Rochester. *Proceedings of the Board of Education*, 6/21/1875.

76. Ibid.

77. Rochester. *Proceedings of the Board of Education*, 9/6/1875.

78. Ibid. His statements also were published in the *Annual Report of the Board of Education* for that year.

79. Ibid.

80. *Proceedings*, 2/7/1876, 2/5/1877. The measure passed with the exception that the asylums be allowed to close on religious holidays not observed by the public schools.

81. *Proceedings*, 3/31/1879. On the New Rochelle decision, see Yonkers. *The Statesman*. June 5, 1879; Yonkers. *The Yonkers Gazette*. June 14, 1879.

82. *Manual of the Board of Education*, 1877.

83. I could find no record in the *New York Times*.

84. *Annual Report of the State Superintendent*, 1885, 55.

85. Ibid.

86. *Religion and Public Education*, 27–30, 30.

87. On the WCTU as a social protest movement, see Jonathan Zimmerman, *Distilling Democracy: Alcohol Education in America's Public Schools, 1880–1925* (Lawrence: University Press of Kansas, 1999).

88. *Religion and Public Education*, 8–11.

89. Ibid., 42–61, 51.

90. *Annual Report of the State Superintendent*, 1903, xxv.

91. *Annual Report of the State Superintendent*, 1903, xiii–xxvii.

92. *Annual Report of the State Superintendent*, 1903, appendix A, pp. 353–85.

93. Cook, The Nation's Book.

94. *Religion and Public Education*, 11–12; John Webb Pratt, *Religion, Politics and Diversity: The Church-State Theme in New York History* (Ithaca: Cornell University Press, 1967), 225-–56; as quoted in ibid., 252.

95. *Annual Report of the State Superintendent of Public Instruction*, 1903, 379.

96. Ibid., xiii.

97. Ibid., xxv.

98. Ibid., xxxvii.

99. Benjamin Justice, "Released Time for Week-day Religious Instruction," *Encyclopedia of New York State* (Syracuse: Syracuse University Press, forthcoming). The New York State Supreme Court, the Court of Appeals, and the United States Supreme Court all upheld a White Plains released-time program in *Zorach v. Clauson* (1952). See also chap. 6, Jonathan Zimmerman, *Whose America: Culture Wars in the Public Schools* (Cambridge: Harvard University Press, 2002).

Chapter 9

1. Successful plans included Corning, Elmira, Poughkeepsie, Ogdensburg, Troy, and Utica. By small city, I mean all of those excluding the largest five: Albany, Brooklyn, Buffalo, New York City, and Rochester.

2. Richard J. Gabel, *Public Funds for Church and Private Schools* (Washington, D.C.: Catholic University of America Press, 1937), 348–72.

3. Ibid., 588–90.

4. John Webb Pratt, *Religion Politics and Diversity: The Church-State Theme in New York History* (Ithaca: Cornell University Press, 1967), 219–23.

5. Edward Michael Conners, *Church-State Relationships in Education in New York* (Washington, D.C.: Catholic University of America Press, 1951), 94.

6. Lloyd Jorgenson, *The State and the Non-Public School* (Columbia University of Missouri Press, 1987), 113-–14; Pratt, *Religion, Politics and Diversity*, 196–97, 197;

7. Pratt, *Religion, Politics and Diversity*, 198.

8. State Council of Political Reform. *Political Reform*. Document 4. (Albany: 1870), 6 (Special Collections, Milbank Library, Teacher's College at Columbia University).

9. Connors, *Church-State Relationships*, 95.

10. Pratt, *Religion, Politics and Diversity*, 199, 219–221.

11. State Council, *Political Reform*, 8–10.

12. This observation hardly needs substantiation, but complaints to this effect can be found regularly in the proceedings of the Brooklyn, Rochester, and Elmira school boards, the Buffalo Common Council, the minutes of the Lockport Board of Education, and even in the minutes of the village of Saratoga Springs.

13. *Proceedings of the Board of Education of the City of Brooklyn*, 9/4/1877.

14. *Proceedings of the Board of Education of the City of Brooklyn*, 4/3/1877, 5/17/1887. See also Buffalo. *Annual Report of the Superintendent of Public Education*, 1873, 10-12; Syracuse. *Annual Report of the Superintendent of Public Instruction*, 1868, 24, 50.

15. *Proceedings of the Board of Education of the City of Elmira*, July 9, 1877.

16. *Proceedings of the Board of Education of the City of Brooklyn*, 9/4/1877.

17. This practice was ubiquitous. Rochester, Buffalo, Brooklyn, Poughkeepsie, and Elmira all mention renting church spaces in the 1870s in their *Proceedings* and *Annual Reports* of the 1870s, 1880s, and 1890s from Episcopal, Methodist, Lutheran, Dutch Reformed, Baptist, Congregational, and Roman Catholic churches.

18. See the Saint Raphael's case of 1886, discussed later in this chapter.

19. Marie Patrice Gallagher, *The History of Catholic Elementary Education in the Diocese of Buffalo, 1847–1944* (Washington, D.C.: Catholic University of America Press, 1945), 52–53. Appeal decision number 4642, as cited in Thomas E. Finegan, *Judicial Decisions of the State Superintendent of Common Schools* (1913), 568.

20. Gallagher, *The History*, 32; Daniel E. Wager, *Our County and Its People: A Descriptive Work on Oneida County, New York* (Boston: Boston History Company, 1896), 351; personal communication from Sister Mary Christine Taylor (author of *A History of Catholicism in the North Country* [Camden, N.Y.: A. M. Farnsworth Sons, 1972]), dated August 7, 2001; Finegan, *Judicial Decisions*, 538–54.

21. Michael Horigan, *Elmira: Death Camp of the North* (Mechanicsburg, Penn.: Stackpole Books, 2002).

22. *New York State Census for 1875*, 9.

23. Elmira. *Annual Report of the Board of Education*, 1890, 17.

24. Gallagher, *The History*, 32.

25. *Annual Report*, 1873, 21.

26. *Proceedings*, 6/21/1875.

27. See, for example, Ibid., 6/5/1875.

28. See *Proceedings*, March–June 1875.

29. Ibid.

30. Elmira. *Proceedings*, 9/20/1875.

31. Ibid., 6/19/1876.

32. Appeal decision number 4722, as cited in Finegan, 565.

33. Connors, *Church-State Relationships*, 110.

34. Appeal decision number 4722, as cited in Finegan, *Judicial Decisions*, 565; Connors *Church-State Relationships*, 110–13.

35. Patrick McSweeny, "The School Question," *Catholic World* 43, 256 (July 1886): 508–509.

36. McSweeny, "Christian Public Schools," *Catholic World* 44: 264 (March 1887): 796. Connors *Church-State Relationships*, (113) found that the daily schedule changed from 4 p.m. to 3 p.m. sometime between 1875 and 1887.

37. McSweeny, "The School Question," 509.

38. Connors, *Church-State Relationships*, 113–14.

39. Patrick McSweeny, "Is There 'No Reason for a Compromise?'" *Catholic World* 47: 282 (September 1888): 798.

40. Connors, *Church-State Relationships*, 114.

41. Corning, Elmira.

42. See, for example, *The Catholic Union*, January 6, 1875, p. 4.

43. See chapter 1.

44. March 26, 1874, p. 3.

45. S.V. Ryan, " 'A Plea for Christian Schools': Lecture by Rt. Rev. S. V. Ryan, D. D., Bishop of Buffalo, Delivered at St. James Hall, Thursday Evening, February 25, 1875." Printed in full in *The Catholic Union*, Buffalo, March 3, 1875, p. 6.

46. *The Catholic Union*, November 18, 1874, p. 5; December 2, 1874, p. 8; December 9, 1874, p. 9; December 16, 1874, p. 4; Ryan, "A Plea for Christian Schools," pp. 4–8.

47. Ryan, "A Plea for Christian Schools," p. 6.

48. Buffalo. *Annual Report of the Superintendent*, 1867, 79. Rochester and New York City also offered German. Brooklyn conspicuously did not.

49. Selwyn Troen, *The Public and the Schools: The Shaping of the Saint Louis System, 1838–1920* (Columbia: University of Missouri Press, 1975).

50. Buffalo. *Proceedings of the Common Council of the City of Buffalo*, 1874: 177–78.

51. Ibid.

52. Ibid.

53. Ibid., 204–205.

54. *Proceedings of the Common Council*, 1874, 235.

55. *The Catholic Union*, March 26, 1874, pp. 3–4.

56. *The Catholic Union*, November 18, 1874, p. 5; December 2, 1874, p. 8; December 9, 1874, p. 9; December 16, 1874, p. 4.

57. *The Catholic Union*, December 2, 1874, p. 5.

58. *The Catholic Union*, February 10, 1875, p. 8.

59. Ryan, "A Plea for Christian Schools," pp. 4–8; *The Catholic Union*, March 18, 1875, p. 4.

60. Ryan, "A Plea for Christian Schools," pp. 4-8.

61. *The Catholic Union*, Buffalo, March 3, 1875, p. 1.

62. *The Catholic Union*, April 15, 1875, p. 1.

63. *The Catholic Union*, April 1, 1875, p. 4; *Proceedings of the Buffalo Common Council*, (March 29) 1875, 202–203.

64. *Proceedings of the Buffalo Common Council*, 1875 (March 29), 202-203.

65. Michael B. Katz, *Reconstructing American Education* (Cambridge: Harvard University Press, 1987), chap. 3.

66. Following Buffalo's experience, Catholics in New York City filed a similar petition for support of parochial schools along the lines of the Poughkeepsie plan and were also denied. See *The Catholic Union*, April 8, 1875, p. 5.

67. As cited in *The Catholic Union*, April 15, 1875, p. 1.

68. *The Catholic Union*, September 12, 1875, p. 5.

69. *Albany Argus*, April 1, 1875. In fact, the majority committee had recommended that all such exercises, left to the discretion of teachers, should be stopped, but the board then took no further action. See *Proceedings of the Common Council*, 1875, (March 29), 202-203.

70. *The Catholic Union*, November 11, 1875, p. 4.

71. (See generally Yonkers. *Yonkers Gazette*, April-June, 1879; Yonkers. *The Statesman*, April-June, 1879.) Letter dated 2/11/1879 by Keyes, from Yonkers, Westchester County; Reply of Superintendent dated 2/12/1879; *Yonkers Gazette*, May 3, 1879; *The Statesman*, Oct. 31, 1878, April 17, 1879, May 1, 1879.

72. *Yonkers Gazette*. May 24, 1879, June 7, 1879; *The Statesman*, June 5, 1879.

73. Letter (and clippings) dated 6/17/1879 by Ellis; Reply of Superintendent dated 6/23/1879; *Yonkers Gazette*, June 14, 1879; *The Statesman*, June 12, 1879; Yonkers. *Annual Report of the Yonkers Board of Education*, 1881–1882, 9–10.

74. *Annual Report of the State Superintendent*, 1876, 58.

75. Pratt, *Religion, Politics, and Diversity*, 218–221.

76. *Annual Report of the State Superintendent*, 1874, 55-56; 1872, 210; 1870, 171.

77. Finegan, *Judicial Decisions*, 537.

78. *Annual Report of the State Superintendent of Public Instruction*, 1904, 121–22.

79. Finegan, *Judicial Decisions*, 537.

80. Ibid., 538.

81. Ibid.

82 Pratt, *Religion, Politics, and Diversity*, 225–40. For a discussion of the rhetoric at the national level, see Jorgensen, *The State and the Non-Public School*, chap. 6–7. On inter-Catholic arguments over the school question, see Robert D. Cross, *The Emergence of Liberal Catholicism in America* (Cambridge: Harvard University Press, 1958), and Daniel Flavian Reilly, *The School Controversy* (Washington, D.C.: Cathoic University Press, 1943). A good sampling of the view-points on the question can be found in "The Education of the People: A Symposium," *The Independent* 42 (September 4, 1890): 1–13.

83. As cited in Pratt, *Religion, Politics, and Diversity*, 252. For the best account of the school question at the convention to date, see chap. 9.

84. Finegan, *Judicial Decisions*, 538-54, 552.

85. Ibid., 554–60.

86. Ibid.

87. Ibid., 121–26.

88. Ibid.

89. Ibid., 560–74; also see James A. Burns, *The Growth and Development of the Catholic School System in the United States* (New York: Benziger Brothers, 1912), 268.

90. Pratt, 263–64; also see Burns, *Growth and Development*, 267–68.

91. According to an e-mail correspondence with Sister Mary Christine Taylor of Ogdensburg (in the possession of the author), Ogdensburg began an arrangement in 1893 with a Catholic academy.

92. Connors, *Church-State Relationships*, 140–41; Pratt, *Religion, Politics, and Diversity*, 264.–65.

93. Pratt demonstrates, for example, that the issue barely made a dent in the proceedings of the state constitutional convention of 1915.

94. Finegan, *Judicial Decisions*, 585–88.

95. Burns, *Growth and Development*, 258.

96. *The Catholic Union*, Buffalo, December 19, 1872, p. 4.

97. See chapter 6 for a deeper discussion.

Chapter 10

1. Gordon Wood, "Rambunctious American Democracy," *The New York Review of Books*, vol. XLIX, no. 8 (May 9, 2002): 20–23.

2. R. Laurence Moore, "Bible Reading and Nonsectarian Schooling: The Failure of Religious Instruction in Nineteenth Century Public Education," *Journal of American History* 86:4 (March 2000): 1; Cortland principal cited in *Annual Report of the State Superintendent of Public Instruction*, 1903, 354.

3. Charles L. Glenn, *The Myth of the Common School* (Amherst: University of Massachusetts Press, 1988).

4. *Annual Report of the State Superintendent of Public Instruction*, 1903, 383.

5. Ibid., 363.

6. Ibid., 385, 361.

7. Stephen Macedo, *Diversity and Distrust* (Cambridge: Harvard University Press, 2000), 63–67. The single best source for post-bellum enrollments remains James H. Blodgett, *Report of the Population of the United States at the Eleventh Census: 1890. Part II. Educational Institutions* (Washington, D.C.: Government Printing Office, 1897). He notes, for example, that some of the parochial schools reported by churches as regular schools in their yearbooks were, in fact, after-school programs.

8. Faye Crosby and other scholars of late-twentieth-century discrimination have noted, for example, that "One cannot and must not rely on disadvantaged people to be their own advocates" (Faye Crosby, "The Denial of Personal Discrimination," *American Behavioral Scientist* 27 (1984): 371–86, 381. As I have suggested throughout this book, however, to impose such a view upon the history of religious minorities in the post-bellum era would ignore important sources of power for such groups.

9. Lawrence J. McCaffrey, *The Irish Catholic Diaspora in America* (Washington, D.C.: Catholic University Press, 1997), 116, 116–37.

10. See, for example, I. W. Hart, ed., *Proceedings of the Constitutional Convention of Idaho, 1889* (Caldwell, Idaho: Caxton Printers, 1912), 679-729, 1436-1449, 2070-2073. The proposed state constitutions before the House Committee on Territories show an interesting progression from 1872, with no mention of "sectarian schools," to 1882, when money to sectarian schools is prohibited, to 1893, when no money to sectarian schools is mentioned as a "usual provision" to be expected in a state constitution. See Lloyd Jorgenson, The State and the Non-Public School (Columbia: University of Missoui Press, 1987), 140–44.

11. Ibid. These were Alabama (1875), California (1879), Delaware (1897), Florida (1887), Illinois (1870), Kentucky (1891), Louisiana (1879), Minnesota (1877), Mississippi (1890), Missouri (1875), Nebraska (1875), Nevada (1880), New Hampshire (1877), New York (1894), Pennsylvania (1874), South Carolina (1894), and Texas (1876). Some states, such as Rhode Island, had constitutional proscriptions preceding the Civil War.

12. David Tyack," Onward Christian Soldiers: Religion in the American Common School," in *History and Education*, ed. Paul Nash (New York: Random House, 1970), 212–55, 235-–36; Steven K. Green, "The Blaine Amendment Reconsidered." *American Journal of Legal History*, vol 36 (1992): 38–69.

13. Samuel Windsor Brown, *The Secularization of American Education*, (New York: Teachers College, 1912), 103–19. The states were Colorado (1876), North Dakota (1889), South Dakota (1889), Montana (1889), Washington (1889), Idaho (1890), Wyoming (1890), and Utah (1896).

14. Ward McAfee argues that Colorado's constitutional provision was required for its entry into the Union in 1876 by the Republican Congress, but subsequent decades are beyond the scope of his book (*Religion, Race, and Reconstruction: The Public School in the Politics of the 1870s* [Albany: State University of New York Press, 1998]) 220.

15. Pam Belluck, "Board for Kansas Deletes Evolution from Curriculum," *New York Times*, national desk, August 12, 1999; James Glanz, "Darwin vs. Design: Evolutionists' New Battle," *New York Times*, national desk, April 8, 2001.

16. M. Raymund McLaughlan, *Religious Education and the State: Democracy Finds a Way*. (Washington, D.C.: Catholic University Press, 1967).

Bibliography of Primary Works Cited

As I scoured New York State by phone and computer in search of archival materials, I came to wish for comprehensive lists, by location, of the materials that interested me. Thus I have organized this primary source bibliography by location rather than alphabetically in the hope that it will better serve historians in the field. Readers should note that the Special Collections Department of the Milbank Library at Teachers College and Cubberley Library at Stanford University both have large, and often redundant, collections. For New York State sources, Milbank is the stronger, including boxes of uncatalogued annual reports from cities and villages throughout the state and bound volumes of pamphlets addressing the school question. I also should note for potential researchers the important distinction between annual reports by boards of education and superintendents and the minutes/proceedings of the meetings of boards of education. Not surprisingly, the latter are much more revealing. In cases where minutes or proceedings no longer exist or are difficult to access, historians may find them reproduced in local newspapers. Boards met once or twice a month, on the same days, and newspapers reported on them predictably. Some libraries, such as Lockport, Buffalo, Saratoga Springs, and Rochester, have local history scrapbooks and public school papers from the late nineteenth century, though (in keeping with the thesis of this book) such documents rarely address religion per se.

Buffalo Public Library, Local History Section

Buffalo. *Annual Reports of the Superintendent of Education.*

Buffalo. *Proceedings of the Common Council of the City of Buffalo*. Buffalo: Joseph Warren and Co., 1868–1900.

"Italian Children Make Good Americans." *Buffalo Times*, November 24, 1902, from Local History, Schools Scrapbook Collection.

Cubberley Education Library, Stanford University

Albany. *Annual Report of the Board of Public Instruction of the City of Albany.*

Auburn. *Annual Report of the Board of Education of the City of Auburn.*

Brooklyn. *Annual Report of the Superintendent of Public Schools of the City of Brooklyn.*

Brooklyn. *Proceedings of the Board of Education of the City of Brooklyn.*

Crooker, James. *General School Laws of the State of New York, in Force July 1, 1893; Together with the Rules of Practice Governing Appeals to the Department of Public Instruction.* Albany: The Argus Company, Printers, 1893.

Elmira. *Annual Report of the Board of Education of the City of Elmira.*

Thomas E. Finegan. *Judicial Decisions of the State Superintendent of Common Schools*, 1913.

General School Laws of the State of New York, 1864.

Gloversville. *Annual Report of the Board of Education of the City of Gloversville.*

Ithaca. *Annual Report of the Board of Education of the City of Ithaca.*

Jamestown. *Annual Report of the Board of Education of the City of Jamestown.*

Emerson Keyes. *Laws of New York Relating to Common Schools, with Comments and Instructions and a Digest of Decisions. Prepared under the Supervision of Neil Gilmour, Superintendent of Public Instruction.* Albany: Weed, Parsons & Co., 1879.

New York (City). *Manual of the Board of Education of the City of New York.*

New York (City). *Journal of the Board of Public Instruction* (and other titles).

New York (State). *Annual Report of the State Superintendent of Public Instruction.* Albany: Weed and Parsons.

New York (State). *Consolidated School Law of 1894.*

New York (State). *First Annual Report of the Education Department of the State of New York.* Albany: New York State Education Department, 1905.

New York (State). *Revised statutes of the state of New York, relating to common schools, passed in the year 1827, being part of the title second of chapter fifteenth of part first; together with amendments thereto by subsequent acts; with the forms and regulations prepared by the superintendent of common schools, and also a variety of decisions in cases of appeal to him.* Albany: Crowell, Van Benthuysen and Burt, 1836.

Oswego. *Annual Report of the Board of Education of the City of Oswego.*

Poughkeepsie. *Annual Report of the Board of Education of the City of Poughkeepsie.*

Randall, Samuel Sidwell. *A digest of the common school system of the state of New-York together with the forms, instructions, and decisions of the superintendent: an abstract of the various local provisions applicable to the several cities &c.: and a sketch of the origin, progress, and present condition of the system.* Albany: C. Van Benthuysen, 1844.

Syracuse. *Annual Report of the Superintendent of Public Education of the City of Syracuse.*
Troy. *Manual of the Board of Education of the City of Troy.*
Utica. *Annual Report of the Board of Education of the City of Utica.*
Yonkers. *Annual Report of the Board of Education of the City of Yonkers.*

Department of Special Collections, Milbank Memorial Library, Teachers College, Columbia University

The Bible in the Public Schools: The Opinion and the Decision of the Supreme Court of Ohio in the Case of John D. Minor versus the Board of Education, City of Cincinnati. Extracted from Volume 23, Ohio State Reports. Cincinnati: Robert Clarke and Company, 1873, from *12 Pamphlets on Education.*

"The Democratic Party and Its Public Schools. Gov. Tildon Favors Appropriations for the Support of Roman Catholic Parochial Schools" and "Politics and the School Question. Attitudes of the Republican and Democratic Parties in 1876," from *25 Pamphlets on Education.*

Elmira. *Proceedings of the Board of Education of the City of Elmira.*

McQuaid, Bernard. *Christian Free Schools: The Matter Discussed. Part Two. A Lecture Delivered at Corinthian Hall, Rochester, New York, on May 16, 1872, 19*, from *12 Pamphlets on Education.*

"Popular Education versus Sectarianism." *Hours at Home*, vol. 11, no. 1, May 1870, from *25 Pamphlets on Education.*

State Council of Political Reform. *Political Reform*. Document 4. Albany: 1870 pub. unknown, 6.

Lockport Board of Education

Lockport. *Minutes of the Lockport Board of Education.*

Microfilm

Authored Articles Cited

Harris, William T. "Some General Principles of Religious Instruction in the Schools." *The Independent*, September 4, 1890, Vol. XLII, No. 2179, p. 1.

McQuaid, Rev. Bernard. John. *Christian Free Schools: The Matter Discussed*, by Rev. Bernard John McQuaid at Rochester, New York. Reported and reprinted by the *Rochester Union and Advertiser*, December 9, 1871.

McSweeny, Patrick. "Christian Public Schools." *Catholic World* 44:264 (March 1887): 796.

McSweeny, Patrick. "Is There 'No Reason for a Compromise?'" *Catholic World* 47:282 (September, 1888): 798.

McSweeny, Patrick. "The School Question." *Catholic World* 43:256 (July 1886): 508–509.

Ryan, S.V. "Pastoral Letter of the Rt. Reverend Bishop Ryan." *The Catholic Union*, December 4, 1873, p. 3.

Ryan, S.V. "'A Plea for Christian Schools': Lecture by Rt. Rev. S. V. Ryan, D. D. , Bishop of Buffalo, Delivered at St. James Hall, Thursday Evening, February 25, 1875." Printed in full in *The Catholic Union*, Buffalo, Wednesday, March 3, 1875, pp. 4–8.

Newspapers and Journals

Albany Argus
The Catholic Union
Catholic World
Daily Eagle
Dutchess Farmer
Educational Review
The Forum
The Independent
New York Times
North American Review
Rochester Daily Union and Advertiser
Saint Lawrence Republican and Ogdensburg Weekly Journal
Troy Daily Press
Troy Morning Whig
Utica Morning Herald

New York State Archives

Appeals Case Files of the State Superintendent of Public Instruction, series B0496-78, B0496-78A.

"German in Public Schools: Its Direct and Tangible Value," pamphlet by E. Steiger. (Letter to the Superintendent, filed April 28, 1874, from series 04340–57.)

Incoming Correspondence to the State Superintendent of Public Instruction, series 04340–57.

Outgoing Correspondence of the State Superintendent of Public Instruction, series A2000–78, A2000–78A.

Rochester Public Library, Local History Section

Rochester. *Annual Reports of the Superintendent of Schools.*

Rochester. *Proceedings of the Rochester Board of Education.*

Saratoga Springs Historical Archives

Saratoga Springs. *Minutes of the Saratoga Springs Board of Education.*

Saratoga Springs. *Record Book of the Saratoga County Commissioner.*

Miscellaneous School Records

Stanford University Library System/Inter-Library Loan

Blodgett, James H. *Report of the Population of the United States at the Eleventh Census.* 1890. Part II. Educational Institutions. Washington, D.C.: Government Printing Office, 1897.

Carroll, Henry King. *The Religious Forces of the United States, Enumerated, Classified, and Described on the Basis of the Government Census of 1890.* New York: Christian Literature Company, 1893.

Compendium of the 11th Census: 1890. Part Two. Washington, D.C.: Government Printing Office, 1894, 265.

Cook, Elizabeth Blanchard. *The Nation's Book in the Nation's Schools.* Chicago: The Chicago Women's Educational Union, 1898.

Drahms, August, *The Criminal: His Personnel and Environment.* New York: Macmillan, 1900.

Eaton, C. W. Superintendent of the Census. *Census of the State of New York for 1875.* Albany: Weed, Parsons and Co., 1877.

Gibbons, James. *Our Christian Heritage.* Baltimore: J. Murphy and Company, 1889.

Hart, I. W. ed. *Proceedings of the Constitutional Convention of Idaho, 1889.* Caldwell, Idaho: Caxton Printers, 1912.

Religion and Public Education: Reports of the Committee on Religion and Public Education, Presented to the Synod of New York of the Presbyterian Church in the United States of America, at Its Meetings in Auburn, 1887 and in Poughkeepsie, 1889.

Statistics of the United States (Including Mortality, Property, Etc.) in 1860. Washington, D.C.: Government Printing Office, 1866.

Strong, Josiah. *Our Country: Its Possible Future and Present Crisis.* New York: Baker & Taylor Co. for the American Home Missionary Society, 1891.

Todd, Helen. "Why Children Work, the Children's Answer." *McClure's Magazine* 40 (April 1913): 68–79.

Index